Advanced C Pr

The Peter Norton Prog

Who This Book Is For

Intermediate to advanced C programmers who want to extend their programming expertise to Advanced C and add new performance to their programs.

What's Inside

- An abundance of practical ready-to-run programs that show the best ways to handle the keyboard, files and disks, graphics and the screen, the mouse, and more

- Expert tips on writing Advanced C programs, for more speed and power programming

- A learn-by-doing approach to programming that shows code in action in a direct, highly readable style

About the Peter Norton Microcomputer Libraries from Brady

All of the volumes in the Peter Norton Libraries, written in collaboration with Peter Norton Computing, provide clear, in-depth discussions of the latest developments in computer hardware, operating systems, and programming. Fully tested and rigorously reviewed by the experts at Peter Norton Computing, these libraries deserve a special place on your bookshelf. These libraries are comprised of two series:

The Peter Norton Hardware Library gives you an insider's grasp of your computer and the way it works. Included are such best-selling classics as *Inside the IBM PC*, *Inside the Apple Macintosh*, and *The Hard Disk Companion*.

The Peter Norton Programming Library focuses on creating programs that work right away and offers the best tips and techniques in the industry. It includes *Advanced BASIC*, *C Programming*, *C++ Programming*, *QBasic Programming*, *Advanced DOS*, and more.

Advanced C Programming

Steve Oualline
The Peter Norton Computing Group

Brady Publishing

New York   London   Toronto   Sydney   Singapore   Tokyo

Brady Publishing

A Divison of Simon & Schuster, Inc.
15 Columbus Circle
New York, NY 10023

Manufactured in the United States of America
10 9 8 7 6 5 4 3 2 1

Library of Congress Cataloging-in-Publication Data

Oualline, Steve.
       Advanced C / Steve Oualline [and] Peter Norton Computing.
              p.   cm.
       1. C (Computer program language)   I. Peter Norton Computing
Corporation.   II.   Title.
       QA76.73.C15083   1992   91-48026
                                                                         CIP

ISBN 0-13-663188-6

Pages produced by Micro Text Productions using Ventura Publisher. Pages
electronically imposed using ImpoStrip. Cover generated using Quark Express.

Contents

Chapter 3

User-Friendly Programming 41

Chapter 4

8086 Details 45

Chapter 5

Modular Programming and Libraries 67

Chapter 6

Simple Interrupts and TSR Programming 105

Preface

This book is designed for programmers who know C and want to use it to create useful programs. Advanced concepts such as interrupt systems, real-time programing, parsing and TSR programs are described using real programs. The focus of the book is to show how to use advanced programing techniques to solve real program problems.

These programs show you how to get the maximum use out of DOS or when DOS isn't enough, to go directly to the hardware. The architecture of the 8086 is discussed in detail so you can make full use of the processor. This book will take you into some of C's darker corners so that you can fully utilize the language.

All of the programs presented here are complete with source code. You can learn a great deal by not only reading about them, but running them, taking them apart and putting them back together. The programs all come with MAKEFILEs for easy compilation.

We decided to use Borland's Turbo C as the C dialect for this book. It is the most robust and reliable compiler we've encountered. Users of Microsoft C can benefit from this book, but should be aware that some of the advanced library routines, especially the graphics library, are different.

Organization

Chapter 1 reviews the C language and extensively discusses good programming style.

Chapter 2 reviews some of the advanced features of C.

Chapter 3 describes how to create a user friendly program.

Chapter 4 describes in detail how the 8086 is organized and how C and the 8086 work together.

Chapter 5 discusses modular programing in the context of creating a extended string library.

Chapter 6 gives you a very detailed description of how interrupts work. This leads up to the creation of a "Hello World" TSR program.

Chapter 7 shows how you can directly access the hardware from C. Two versions of a terminal emulator (interrupt and noninterrupt) are presented.

Chapter 8 introduces event drive program with a game of "mouse and cat."

Chapter 9 adds graphics and animation so we can create a simple breakout game.

Chapter 10 leaves the world of games to get down to business. A simple menu system is described which can be used to create many interactive applications.

Chapter 11 presents you with a program to automatically generate menu templates for use by the menu system.

Chapter 12 demonstrates the power of recursion by creating a program to scan the disk for duplicate files.

Chapter 13 discusses the art of parsing using a simple calculator like program.

Chapter 14 puts together TSRs and interrupt programming to create a "mimic" program that clones the screen image from one system to another.

It is hoped that the programs presented here will form the core of a set of tools and techniques that will enable you to become a master C programmer. The information presented here should help you create well crafted programs that are both useful and profitable.

Basic C Review

Introduction

In this chapter, we'll quickly review the C programming language with emphasis on programming techniques and style. The mechanics of programming are generally simple, but mechanics alone are not enough to enable you to construct great programs.

Painting is very easy if you know the mechanics: put paint on brush, put brush on canvas, stroke, repeat until done. But painting the Mona Lisa requires much more than just how to wave a brush. This chapter will help you develop a style and technique so that you can create programming masterpieces.

Have you ever read a book that you really enjoyed? Have you ever been forced to read a manual that was so poorly written you hated it? What's the difference between the two? Style. Your C program should be a joy to read. Good style means that your programs are well designed in addition to being easy to maintain and upgrade.

Comments

The comment is the most neglected statement in the C language. The syntax is quite simple: anything between "/*" and "*/" is a comment and is ignored

1

by the compiler. But what should we put in the comments? Everything. Comments contain information on what the program is supposed to do, how it does it, the program's limitations and even a revision history.

In short, they should explain the program completely to the programmer.

The beginning of the program should contain a set of heading comments. These are usually boxed to make them stand out and separate them from the code.

TIP

If your editor has a macro facility you can create a macro to quickly draw the top and bottom of your comments. Turbo C's editor has no macros, but there is a way to easily construct boxed comments. First create a file named "C" containing:

```
/*********************************************************
 *******************************************************/
```

Then every time you want to start a boxed comment use the file read command (^KRC) to insert this file into your program. Notice that the length of our comment line (57 characters) was chosen for easy editing. The last character is one past a tab stop.

This comment block serves as a sort of title page and introduction to the program. The following is a list of what might go into the heading comments. Not all sections will apply, and you should put in only what is useful.

Name

This is the title of your program. This line should contain the short name required by DOS (8 characters or less) and a more descriptive name. For example:

```
/*********************************************************
 * calc -- a general purpose decimal calculator         *
 *******************************************************/
```

Purpose

This is a one or two paragraph description of the program. It serves much the same function as an abstract does in a technical paper. By reading it, the programmer can get an idea of what the program does and decide if this program is useful to him.

Copyright

If you want to copyright your code, put a statement like "Copyright 1992 by Acme Programming" here.

Some code is not copyrighted, but is instead protected by trade secret laws. You might want to put a message like: "This code is an unpublished work of the Acme Programming company and is protected by license and trade secret laws" here. The exact wording of this section should be determined by an attorney.

Author

You've worked pretty hard on your program. Take credit for it by signing your work. This also gives any maintenance programmers an idea who wrote the program so that he can ask you for help and information when a bug appears.

Usage

Murphy's law of documentation states: 90% of the time the documentation will be lost. Out of the remaining 10%, 9% of it will be the wrong revision and totally useless. The 1% of the time you have the document and the correct revision of the document it will be written in Japanese.

To avoid the problem of lost documentation, write a short reference into the program.

Restrictions

If your program is limited, what are it's limitations? For example:

```
/*************************************************************
 * Restrictions -- This program is a quick and dirty        *
 *      hack designed to be used by an expert.  It does     *
 *      not do extensive input checking and typing the      *
 *      wrong command may result in strange behavior        *
 *************************************************************/
```

Algorithms

If the program uses any special techniques or fancy algorithms, list them here. If possible, point to references that describe them. (See below.)

References

Sometimes a programmer will copy pieces of code or algorithms from another source (as long as you don't break the copyright laws). This section should list the original source of any works copied into your program. That way, if some-

thing breaks, the maintenance programmer can look up
the original algorithm to see what it was originally designed
to do.

Revision history   This is a list of revisions made to the program. It includes
the name of the person who changed the program, when
the change was made and what was done. In some cases a
version number is included here as well.

This list should serve as just the starting point for developing your own heading style. In some cases, more information may be needed. For example, in a
school environment, you may need to put in the class name, assignment
number, and your student I.D. A government job may require a contract
number.

Heading comments can easily be a page or two long. They serve as an introduction to your program.

Simple Variable Declarations

In C all variables must be declared. The form of a simple variable declaration
is:

```
type        name;           /* comment */
```

Type is a basic C variable type (**int, float, char**, etc.).

Name is the variable name. Names begin with a letter or underscore (_) and
contain any number of letters, digits or underscores. They are case sensitive.
For example, "total," "TOTAL" and "Total" are three different variables. In
actual practice you should give your variables different names and not depend
on case differences.

Names should be descriptive. Short names should be avoided. For example: q
is a bad variable name while quantity_on_hand is a good one. It is possible,
but rare to have a variable name that is too long. For example:
quantity_on_hand_for_this_week_excluding_weekends is too
long. Although very descriptive, the amount of typing required to use this
variable name makes it impractical.

TIP	A good variable name can be constructed by putting together two or three words separated by underscore (_).

By convention, variable names are all lowercase (e.g., `total_entries`) with underscores or upper/lowercase (`TotalEntries`). All lowercase has an advantage over upper/lowercase, because it can be put through most spell checkers to check for typos.

Names should be significantly different from each other. For example, the names `total` and `totals` are a poor choice of variable names because they are easily confused. A better choice is `todays_total` and `year_total`.

The comment following a variable declaration describes the variable in detail. By always commenting on your variable declarations you are creating a mini-dictionary, defining the terms (variables) you are using inside your program.

Units are extremely important and should be included whenever possible. For example, say a piece of rope is 5 long. Is that 5 inches, 5 yards, 5 miles, 5 centimeters or 5 light years? It makes a big difference.

The following are some examples of good variable declarations:

```
int total_entries; /* number of account entries in table */
float area;        /* area of current figure in square inches */
int verbose;       /* When nonzero output extra information */
```

Basic Data Types and Quantifiers

C provides the following basic data types:

char	character or single byte integers
int	integer or whole numbers
float	floating point or real number
double	double precision floating point

Character constants are written using single quotes ('): `'a'`, `'b'`, `'x'`. Keep in mind that single quotes denote a character, double quotes (`"`) are used for strings.

Integer constants are specified as a series of digits with no decimal point. Example: 1, 99, -6133.

Floating point constants contain a decimal point (.): 0.23, 12.45, 996.0. C does not require a digit in front of the decimal point, .23 is the same as 0.23. However, by putting a leading 0 in front of a number you make it clearer. Similarly, 996. is the same as 996.0, but good programming practice dictates the use of the second form. A floating point zero should be written as 0.0.

Floating point numbers can be written in the exponential form: *dd.ddE+dd*. For example: 12.34E+5 is the same as 12.34×10^5.

Types of Integers The qualifiers **long, short, signed,** and **unsigned** can be used to modify an integer declaration. By default, all integers are signed. In Turbo C, the range of an integer is -32768 (-2^{15}) to 32767 ($2^{15}-1$). An unsigned integer sacrifices negative numbers in exchange for more than twice as many positive values. The range of an unsigned integer is 0 to 65535 ($2^{16}-1$).

If there is no qualifier, C will choose a precision that works best for the computer you are working on. The qualifier **short** is used to indicate that less than the default precision is needed. The qualifier **long** indicates that extra precision is needed. If no qualifier is used, the C compiler chooses the integer size that works best on the target machine. Long integer constants have an L following the number. For example: 123 is an integer, 123L is a long integer. Actually, an uppercase or lowercase l may be used. Uppercase is preferred since the lowercase l can easily be confused with the number one (1). For example: 1211L is more readable than 12111. Table 1-1 lists the precision of the various flavors of integers using Turbo C.

Type	Size (bytes)	Size (bits)	Range		
short	2	16	-32768	to	32767
unsigned short	2	16	0	to	65535
int	2	16	−32768	to	32767
unsigned int	2	16	0	to	65535
long	4	32	−2147483648	to	2147483647
unsigned long	4	32	0	to	4294967295

Table 1-1. Integers Using Turbo C

Types of Characters   Character variables can be used as very short integers. They can be either signed or unsigned. The default is compiler dependent; Turbo C character variables default to signed.[1] The ranges of character variables are listed in Table 1-2.

Type	Size (bytes)	Size (bits)	Range		
signed char	1	8	-128	to	128
unsigned char	1	8	0	to	256

Table 1-2. Ranges of Character Variables

Types of Floating Point   There are three flavors of floating point numbers: **float**, **double**, and **long double**. Single precision floating numbers are declared with **float**. Double precision provides twice the precision and range. Some compilers, including Turbo C, provide for extended precision or long double. The ranges and accuracy of floating point numbers is detailed in Table 1-3.

Type	Size (bytes)	Size (bits)	Range			Precision
float	4	32	$-3.4E+38$	to	$3.4E+38$	6 digits
double	8	64	$-1.7E+308$	to	$1.7E+308$	15 digits
long double	10	80	$-1.1E+4932$	to	$1.1E+4932$	17 digits

Table 1-3. Ranges and Accuracy of Floating Point Numbers

Simple Expression and Assignment Statement

The general form of the assignment statement is:

```
variable = expression;
```

Variable is any valid variable name previously declared. *Expression* is any C expression. C recognizes the following simple operators listed in Table 1-4.

---

1   Turbo C has a command line option to choose which type of character (**signed** versus **unsigned**) is the default.

Operators	Description
Arithmetic	
+	Addition
–	Subtraction
*	Multiplication
/	Division
%	Modulus
Bitwise	
&	Bitwise *And*
|	Bitwise *Or*
^	Bitwise *exclusive Or*
~	Complement or bitwise inverse
<<	Shift left
>>	Shift right
Logical	
&&	Logical *And*
||	Logical *Or*
!	Logical *Not*
<	Less Than
>	Greater Than
<=	Less Than or equals
>=	Greater Than or equals
==	Equals
!=	Not equals

Table 1-4. C Operators

There are 15 precedence rules in C. (&& comes before || but after <<, etc.) In actual practice it is much easier to remember two:

- multiply and divide come before addition and subtraction,
- put parentheses around everything else.

Shorthand Operators

The increment operator (++) can be used to increment a variable. For example:

```
total = total + 1;
    /* is equivalent to */
total++;
```

The increment operator should only be used in a statement by itself. C allows you to use it inside other expressions. For example:

```
counter = total++;          /* legal, but don't do it */
```

is legal, but is considered poor programming practice because it contains a side effect. A side effect is an operation that happens in addition to the main operation. In this case the main effect is the assignment, the side effect is the incrementing of total. Even when straightforward programming methods are used, programs can be difficult to understand. Side effects merely add to the confusion and should be avoided. This should be written as:

```
counter = total;
total++;
```

An important point needs to be made here. Just because C allows you to do something, doesn't mean that it's a good idea. As shown in Listing 1-1, using increment on anything other than a line by itself is generally a bad idea. Consider the following code:

```
/************************************************************
 * square -- demonstrate a problem when ++ is used       *
 *        inside another statement                       *
 ************************************************************/
#include <stdio.h>
#define sqr(x) ((x) * (x))      /* define macro to square
number */
main() {
    int y = 1;                     /* start y out low */
    (void)printf("1 squared is %d\n", sqr(y++));
    return (0);
}
```

What is the value of 1 squared? According to this program it is 2. Why? Because the macro sqr(y++) expands to ((y++) * (y++)), causing y to be incremented twice. The extra, hidden increment of y is the source of the problem.

There are other, more complex ways of causing trouble using increment as a side effect, but you will avoid them all if you always put increment statements on lines by themselves.

The decrement operator (--) operates in a similar fashion but decreases the value of the variable, rather than increasing it.

Other Shorthand Operators

Suppose you want to add 2 to a variable. You could use the statement:

```
x = x + 2;
```

However, C supplies you with a shortcut: the **add to** operator (+=). The previous statement can be written as:

```
x += 2;
```

Similar shorthand operators exist for other operations and are summarized in Table 1-5.

Operation	Shorthand
x = x + y;	x += y;
x = x - y;	x -= y;
x = x * y;	x *= y;
x = x / y;	x /= y;
x = x % y;	x %= y;
x = x & y;	x &= y;
x = x l y;	x l= y;
x = x ^ y;	x ^= y;
x = x << y;	x <<= y;
x = x >> y;	x >>= y;

Table 1-5. Shorthand operators

?: Operator

The general form of the conditional operator is:

```
(condition) ? expression1 : expression2
```

If the condition is true, the result of this operation is *expression1*. Otherwise, *expression2* is used. For example, suppose we want to assign to the variable `amount_owed` the number of dollars that a person owes. However, if the amount is negative, we want to tell him that he owes nothing. We would use the statement:

```
amount_owed = (amount > 0) ? amount : 0;
```

TIP Use the conditional operator cautiously. It can easily make your code confusing. Whenever possible consider using **if** statements.

If statement

The general form of the **if** statement is:

```
if (expression)
    statement;
```

If the value of the expression is nonzero, the statement will be executed. Examples follow:

```
if (total == 0)
    (void)printf("No data to process\n");
if (error != 0)
    (void)printf("%d errors found\n", errors);
```

It is possible to write the last example as:

```
if (error)
    (void)printf("%d errors found\n", errors);
```

however, this is considered poor programming practice. You should always explicitly write any conditional expressions and not rely on the fact that "`if (error)`" is the same as "`if (error != 0)`".

Poor Programming Practice   You can put an assignment statement inside the expression for an **if**. The following is legal C code:

```
if ((total = first_half + second_half) > 100)
    (void)printf("Large mode enabled\n");
```

However, this violates the KISS (Keep it simple, stupid) rule. C is complex enough just using one statement to perform one operation. When you combine two operations in one statement (an **if** and an assignment) you are asking for trouble. A far better way of coding is:

```
total = first_half + second_half;
if (total > 100)
    (void)printf("Large mode enabled\n");
```

The general form of the **if/else** statement is:

```
if (expression)
    statement1;
else
    statement2;
```

If the expression is true (nonzero) the first statement is executed. If it is false (zero), the second is executed. For example:

```
if (errors == 0)
    (void)printf("No errors found\n");
else
    (void)printf("%d errors found\n", errors);
```

The **if/else** syntax is ambiguous. Consider the following code fragment (maybe incorrectly indented):

```
if (a != 0)
    if (b != 0)
        (void)printf("Statement1");
else
    (void)printf("Statement2");
```

Which **if** does the **else** go with?

1. It goes with the first one, so the code is equivalent to:

```
if (a != 0) {
    if (b != 0)
        (void)printf("Statement1");
} else
    (void)printf("Statement2");
```

2. It goes with the second **if** and the code is equivalent to:

```
if (a != 0) {
    if (b != 0)
        (void)printf("Statement1");
    else
        (void)printf("Statement2");
}
```

3. If you don't write code like this, you don't have to worry about this question.

The correct answer is 3. If you don't write silly code you don't have to answer silly questions. (For the purist, **else** goes with the nearest **if**, so answer 2 is correct.)

While Loop

The **while** loop allows for the repetitive execution of a section of code. The general form of a **while** statement is:

```
while (expression)
        statement;
```

The **while** statement will execute the code in "statement" as long as the expression is true (nonzero). When the expression becomes false, the **while** statement exits.

Break/Continue

The **break** statement will exit a loop such as a while statement. For example, the following will exit when the last element processed is zero.

```
while (1) {
        /* loop forever or until break */
        process_element(current_element);

        if (current_element == 0)
            break;
    next_element();
}
```

The **continue** statement causes the loop to begin again from the beginning.

```
while (more_data) {

    name = get_name();
    owed = get_amount_owed();

    /* Don't worry about those people who owe nothing */
    if (owed <= 0)
        continue;

    (void)printf("%s owes %d dollars\n", name, owed);
}
```

For Statement

The **for** statement is an extremely flexible form of a looping statement. It should not be confused with the limited for statements of other languages such as Pascal and BASIC. The general form of a **for** statement is:

```
for (initial_statement; expression; iteration_statement)
    statement;
```

The *initial_statement* is used to initialize a loop variable or perform any other initialization. This controls how many times the loop is executed. As long as the expression is true (nonzero), the loop will continue to execute. When the expression becomes false, the loop exits. The *iteration statement* is executed at the end of each loop.

Suppose we want to sum the first ten elements of an array. We can construct the following code fragment:

```
sum = 0;
for (current_element = 0; current_element < 10;
    current_element++)
        sum += elements[current_element];
```

Note that the element index will go from zero to nine. Unlike most programming languages C uses zero-based indexing, so the ten elements of our array are numbers zero–nine.

Another way of expressing what the **for** statement does is:

```
initial_statement;
while (expression) {
```

```
    statement;
    iteration_statement;
}
```

Switch Statement

The **switch** statement is a shorthand alternative to a series of nested **if** statements. The general form of the **switch** statement is:

```
switch (expression)
    case constant1:
        statement;
        statement;
        break;
    case constant2:
        statement;
        /* Fall Through */
    default:
        statement;
        break;
}
```

NOTE Each case clause ends with either a **break** statement or the comment /* Fall Through */. The comment indicates that the fall through is intentional and not the result of a forgotten **break**. The **default** case can appear anywhere. You should always specify a default even if you want to ignore all out-of-range expressions. The statement:

```
default:
    /* do nothing */
    break;
```

clearly indicates that the program is to ignore defaults. If the default is left out, it is impossible to tell whether or not the programmer accidentally or intentionally omitted it.

Do/While

The syntax of the **do/while** loop is similar to the **while** loop.

```
do {
    statement;
} while (expression);
```

The loop will execute until the expression becomes false. This is similar to the **while** statement:

```
while (1) {
    statement;
    if (expression)
        break;
}
```

In fact, **do/while** is infrequently used since the **while** loop can easily be made to perform the same functions.

Summary

You've now got the basic building blocks needed to construct a C program. What's better, you've learned *how* to use them so that your programs are clear and easy to understand. In later chapters we will build on these tools to constructively handle more complex data and to use C to create useful programs.

Functions, Structures and Arrays

Introduction

So far, we have reviewed just simple statements. In this chapter we'll go over how to group them into functions and modules to create more complex programs, and we will cover complex data types. We will also discuss the C pre-processor: a useful, but very tricky utility. Finally, we conclude with a section on the various I/O systems available.

Functions

The function is the basic building block of all C programs. It serves to enclose executable instructions into neat little packages. Functions can be thought of as sections in a manual or chapters in a book.

Functions should begin with a comment block explaining what they do and how. A standard comment block looks like:

```
/*************************************************************
 * exists -- checks to see if a file exists                  *
 *                                                           *
 * Parameters                                                *
 *      name -- the name of the file to check                *
 *                                                           *
 * Returns                                                   *
 *      1 -- file exists                                     *
 *      0 -- no such file                                    *
 *************************************************************/
```

The first line contains the name of the function and a short explanation of what it does. Next we have a section that describes each of the parameters. This is followed by an outlining paragraph explaining what is returned by the function. If the function requires more basic explanation, additional comments should be included here.

Two pages of comments for a half page function is not unheard of. We once wrote a function designed to transform a bitmapped image from simple raster format into a complex, convoluted format required by an inkjet printer. The comments were written first and included two graphics made out of text characters. They went through two revisions before the first line of code was written. Because the design had been thought out and documented beforehand, when it came to writing the code, *WE* were able to get it right the first time.

The comment block is followed by the function header. Its format is:

```
type function_name(parameter_list)
```

The *type* specifies the value of the data returned by the function. If the function does not return a value, the type **void** is used.

NOTE   Always specify the type of a function. If you leave it out, it will default to **int**; however, other people will not be able to tell if it's supposed to be an integer function or if you left the type out.

The *function_name* is the actual name of the function.

The *parameter_list* specifies the names of the parameters used to pass information to the function. The format of a parameter list is:

```
(type name, type name, type name......)
```

Where *type* is the type of the parameter and *name* is its name.

Suppose we wanted to create a function to tell if a file exists. The function declaration would be:

```
int exists(char *name)
```

This type of function declaration is referred to as the ANSI (American National Standards Institute) standard declaration because it is a feature of the C language added by the ANSI committee. Older C compilers use a different syntax:

```
type function_name(name1, name2,...)
type name1;
type name2;
```

This older style is accepted by Turbo C and you will find it in many old C programs; however, this style of coding is more error prone than the ANSI style and should be avoided. When possible you should convert your programs from the older style to ANSI format.

A single basic block follows the function declaration. This is the body of the function. The format of a basic block is

```
{
    variable-declarations
    executable statement
}
```

So the full version of our exists function is:

```
/***********************************************************
 * exists -- checks to see if a file exists                *
 *                                                         *
 * Parameters                                              *
 *      name -- the name of the file to check              *
 *                                                         *
 * Returns                                                 *
 *      1 -- file exists                                   *
 *      0 -- no such file                                  *
 ***********************************************************/
int exists(char *name)
```

```
{
    if (access(name, 0))
        return (1);       /* File exists */

    /* No such file */
    return (0);
}
```

Return Statement

The **return** statement is used by a function to pass a value to the outside world. The general form of the return statement is:

```
return (expression);
```

All functions, except for **void** functions, should use the **return** statement. The following function computes the area of a square:

```
/***********************************************************
 * rectangle -- compute the area of a rectangle            *
 *                                                         *
 * Parameters                                              *
 *      length -- length of the rectangle                  *
 *      width -- width of the rectangle                    *
 *                                                         *
 * Returns                                                 *
 *      area of the rectangle                              *
 *                                                         *
 * Note: A very simple example of a function               *
 ***********************************************************/
int rectangle(int length, int width)
{
    int area;    /* Area of the rectangle */

    area = length * width;

    return (area);
}
```

Local and Global Variables

Variables have two attributes: *scope* and *class*. Scope is the area of the program where the variable is recognized. Variables declared outside of any function are *global.* That is, their scope is the entire program. They can be accessed by anyone. Variables declared at the beginning of a block are *local,* and can only be used inside the block.

Class is permanent or temporary. Permanent variables are created when a program loads, are initialized at load time, and reside in the DATA segment of the program. Temporary variables are created when the program enters the block where they are declared. They are initialized whenever the block is entered and disappear when the program leaves the block. Space for temporary variables is taken from the stack as needed. When the program leaves the block, this space is returned to the stack.

All global variables are permanent. Local variables are permanent if they have been declared **static**. It is unfortunate, but C overloads the qualifier **static**. This word has two meanings. If used on a global variable or function, it indicates that the variable or function can only be used by the functions inside that file (it affects scope). If used on a local variable, it indicates a permanent variable.

Listing 2-1 shows the difference between permanent and temporary variables.

Listing 2-1.

```
/*
 * Demonstrate the difference between permanent and
 * temporary variables
 */
main()
{
    int index;   /* Loop index */

    for (index = 0; index < 5; index++) {
            static int permanent = 0;/* A permanent variable */
            int temporary = 0;       /* A temporary variable */

            (void)printf("Permanent %d Temporary %d\n",
                    permanent, temporary);
            permanent++;
            temporary++;
    }
    return (0);
}
```

We have defined a variable named `permanent` as a permanent variable (nothing like using obvious names). The variable `temporary` is of course a temporary variable. The permanent variable is initialized once; the temporary variable is initialized at the beginning of the block, in this case, the beginning of the **for** loop. Both variables are incremented at the end of the loop, and at the end of the block the loop starts over, and the temporary variable is initialized again. This makes the increment at the bottom of the loop completely useless. As we can see, the value of the permanent variable changes (since it is initialized only once), while the temporary variable remains the same. The output of Listing 2-1 is:

```
Permanent 0 Temporary 0
Permanent 1 Temporary 0
Permanent 2 Temporary 0
Permanent 3 Temporary 0
Permanent 4 Temporary 0
```

There is one more qualifier we need to discuss: **extern**. It is used to tell C that a variable is defined in another (or the same) module. Because the variable is defined elsewhere, an **extern** has no initialization part. The initialization is reserved for the real declaration. Table 2-1 shows the scope and class of various variables:

Qualifier	*Meaning*
none, outside block	Global, permanent variable, initialized once
none, inside block	Local, temporary variable, initialized at start of block
static, outside block	Global to this file only, permanent variable, initialized once
static, inside block	Local, permanent variable, initialized once
extern, inside block	Defined as global, permanent variable elsewhere, initialized elsewhere once
extern, outside block	Defined as global, permanent variable elsewhere, initialized elsewhere once

Table 2-1. Scope and Class of Various Variable Types

It is possible in C to have hidden variables. For example, if you declare the variable `index` globally, then later define a local version of `index`, the local variable will hide the global declaration. Listing 2-2 demonstrates a hidden declaration.

Listing 2-2.

<table>
<tr><td>Scope
of
index</td><td>

```
int index;                    /* Current item we are working */
/*...........*/

int count_items(void)
{
```
</td></tr>
<tr><td>Index
hidden</td><td>

```
    int index;                /* Index into item list */
    /* Global "index" is now hidden */
}
main()
{
    /* ..... */
    return (0);
}
```
</td></tr>
</table>

It is not considered good programming practice to use hidden variables. After all, which `index` are you talking about: the global one or the one in `count_items`? We want to make things as simple as possible and it doesn't help when we use the same names for two things.

Arrays

Arrays are used to store groups of similar data. The general form of an array declaration is:

```
type name[number-of-elements];                    /* comment */
```

The *type* is a C data type (**char**, **int**, etc.). This is followed by the variable *name*. The parameter *number-of-elements* determines how big the array is. For example, the following declares an array of three integers.

```
int data[3];              /* Place for three numbers */
```

The three elements of this array are numbered 0,1, and 2. As we said earlier, C uses *zero*-based counting. You might think, since the dimension of `data` is three, that `data[3]` would be valid, but you'd be wrong.

Multi-dimension arrays can be created by tacking on additional dimensions enclosed in square brackets. For example, the following defines a two-dimensional array (also called a matrix).

```
int    table[30][20];                    /* Transformation table */
```

Note that each dimension requires its own set of square brackets. For example, to get the value of the last element, we would use the statement:

```
value = table[29][19];
```

Typedef

The **typedef** statement allows the programmer to define new types. The **typedef** statement is very similar to a normal C data declaration, except that it begins with the word **typedef** and the name of the new type is placed where the variable name normally goes. To define a new type whole_number, a new kind of **int**, you would use the statement:

```
typedef  int   whole_number;
```

At first glance it might seem that you could do the same thing with **#define** statements, and you could for simple types. But **typedef** allows you to create complex data types. For example:

```
typedef   int  bunch[20];   /* Define a bunch of things */
```

This can then be used as:

```
bunch  data_group;       /* A group of data */
void init_data(void)
{
    int   index;       /* index into the group */

    for (index = 0; index < 20; index++)
        data_group[index] = index;
}
```

Enum

Suppose you want to define a variable to hold the days of the weeks. You could use **#define** statements:

```
#define SUNDAY   0
#define MONDAY   1
#define TUESDAY  2
#define WEDNESDAY  3
#define THURSDAY   4
```

```
#define FRIDAY   5
#define SATURDAY   6
```

Although this works, it is somewhat tedious. Through the use of the **enum** statement, C will do the definitions for you. For example:

```
enum week_days {SUNDAY, MONDAY, TUESDAY, THURSDAY,
    FRIDAY, SATURDAY};
```

The general form of an **enum** statement is:

```
enum type-name {element1, element2, ....} variable-name;
```

The *type-name* defines the name of this **enum** list. The *variable-name* is the name of a variable to be declared by this statement. You can omit *type-name* and the variable will be declared with an anonymous type. The *variable-name* can be omitted. In this case the **enum** is good for later declarations using the *type-name*.

Structures

Arrays are used to store a group of elements that have exactly the same types. If you want to store data with different types, you need a structure. The general form of a structure definition is:

```
/* Comment describing structure */
struct structure-name {
    type name; /* Comment */
    type name; /* Comment */
    type name; /* Comment */
} variable-name;
```

The structure name may be omitted, in which case the variable is said to have an *anonymous* structure type. If the variable name is omitted, then only a structure type is defined. In extreme cases, both the variable name and structure name may be omitted, and you have a syntactically correct, but totally useless piece of code.

In an array, each element is numbered. A structure uses fields instead of elements. Each field has its own type and name. To reference the field names we use the notation:

```
variable.field
```

For example, the following structure is used to define a typical mailing label.

```
struct mail {
    char name[30];          /* Name is the form last, first */
    char address[30];       /* Street address */
    char city[20];          /* City where he lives */
    char state[3];          /* Two character state abbreviation */
    unsigned long int zip;  /* Zip code */
};
struct mail current;      /* Current name we are adding to list
*/

/*...... */

    (void)strcpy(current.name, "Smith, John");
    (void)strcpy(current.address, "1024 Hopper Place");
    (void)strcpy(current.city, "Los Angeles");
    (void)strcpy(current.state, "CA");
    current.zip = 92999L;
```

Structures may be initialized when they are declared. The initializers are enclosed in curly brackets. For example, the previous declaration could be written as:

```
struct mail current = {
    "Smith, John",              /* Name */
    "1024 Hopper Place",        /* Address */
    "Los Angeles",              /* City */
    "CA",                       /* CA */
    929999L                     /* Zip */
};
```

In order to better synchronize the initializers with the fields, we have included comments with the field name that is initialized by each item.

Unions

In a structure each element is stored separately. You might think of a structure as a box divided up into individual compartments, each with its own label. In a union, all elements are stored in the same space. A union is like a box that can hold one thing, but has many labels pasted on the front.

One example of a union is:

```
union convert {
    long    integer;    /* A random integer */
    float   floating;   /* A random floating point number */
} convert;
```

Storing an integer into the field `integer` will destroy any value in `floating` since they use the same space. Similarly storing something in `floating` will destroy `integer`.

A union can be very useful in separating a 16-bit integer into two 8-bit values.

```
union split {
    /* 16 bit integer as two halfwords */
    struct bytes {
        unsigned char _low;
        unsigned char _high;
    } bytes;
    /* full 16 bit word */
    int full;
} split;
```

Now we can access the variable split as a 16-bit value (`split.full`) or as two bytes (`split.bytes._high` and `split.bytes._low`). Access to the bytes is cumbersome, so typically **#defines** are used to make it simpler and easier:

```
#define high bytes._high        /* Shorthand for high byte */
#define low bytes._low          /* Shorthand for low byte */
```

Bit Fields

Normally in a structure integers take up 16 bits. If less than 16 bits are needed you can specify the number of bits for each field. For example, the following packed structure takes up only one byte (8 bits). Fields for 7 bits are defined. A structure must end on a byte boundary, so the compiler will add an invisible pad bit to bump the number to 8.

```
struct person {
    unsigned int age:6;         /* Allow ages from 0-64 */
    int sex:1;                  /* 1 for male, 0 for female */
};
```

> Assuming age goes from 0-64 can be dangerous. There are people who are 65 and older. One state agency used to store a person's age as two digits. An old lady who was 99 became 00 on her next birthday. That wasn't too bad, but when she reached 107 they sent a truant officer out to her house to find out why she wasn't in the first grade.

The code to access the data in bit fields is large and cumbersome. Unless you are storing large amounts of data and really need to save space, you are probably better off using a normal, unpacked structure.

Pre-Processor

The pre-processor is a specialized text editor or macro processor that is run on your programs before the main compile begins. It gives you a great deal of flexibility in writing your programs. It also can give you a great deal of headaches.

Because it is a separate pass, the pre-processor has its own syntax and grammar. Most importantly, the pre-processor does not understand C syntax. This results in many problems because all the common sense you learned as a C programmer does not work for the pre-processor. This section describes the pre-processor directives as well as some suggestions for avoiding problems and surprises.

Simple #define Directive

The **#define** directive allows the program to define a simple replacement macro. The general form of the simple **#define** is:

```
#define NAME string
```

NOTE   By convention most constant names are all uppercase.

This tells C that every time it sees the string NAME to replace it with string. This is very similar to the global search and replace function in the Turbo C editor.

Normally this is used to define simple constants. For example:

```
#define ARRAY_MAX 30
int array[ARRAY_MAX]; /* Define a place to put the data */
void init_array(void)
{
 int index;          /* index into the array */

      for (index = 0; index < ARRAY_MAX; index++)
          array[index] = index;
}
```

But you must use this feature carefully. The following constant definition is a trap:

```
#define LENGTH 3 + 5                /* First part + Second Part */
```

This definition works just fine for simple statements such as:

```
size = LENGTH;
```

but totally fails when used as:

```
double_size = LENGTH * 2;
```

At first glance you would expect `double_size` to be set to 16. After LENGTH is 8 and twice 8 is 16. But the pre-processor is just a dumb text editor. LENGTH is not 8, it's 3 + 5. And "3 + 5 * 2" is 13, not 16.

For this reason, you should *always* surround any expressions in a **#define** statement with parentheses. If we had defined LENGTH as:

```
#define LENGTH (3 + 5)
```

our problem with double_size would not have happened.

TIP Put parentheses around all **#define** constants that are more than a single number.

Macros can be used to define more than just constants. For example:

```
#define FOR_ALL for (index = 0; index < SIZE; index++)
```

This allows you to write code like:

```
FOR_ALL
    array[index] = 0;
```

NOTE   Using **#define** to redefine the C syntax should be minimized. Although convenient, our FOR_ALL macro somewhat obscures C's syntax, making our program more difficult to understand and debug.

Macros can be properly used to define commonly used statements such as:

```
#define GET_LINE (void)fgets(line, sizeof(line), stdin);
```

Care should be taken when defining a macro that takes up more than one statement. For example:

```
#define ABORT (void)printf("Aborting");exit(1);
```

It is easy to think of ABORT as a single statement. After all it's a single word. But this is dangerous. The following program will always exit, even when the value is in range:

```
void check_range(int value)
{
    if (value > MAX_VALUE)
    ABORT
}
```

Here the macro ABORT hides the fact that there are two statements present. After macro substitution, this function looks like:

```
void check_range(int value)
{
    if (value > 30)
        (void)printf("Aborting");exit(1);
}
```

Properly indented this is:

```
void check_range(int value)
{
    if (value > 30)
        (void)printf("Aborting");
    exit(1);
}
```

From the previous example, it's easy to see why this function always exits. In order to avoid problems like this you should always enclose multi-statement macros in {}. We should have written ABORT as

```
#define ABORT {(void)printf("Aborting");exit(1);}
```

This way if ABORT is put inside an **if**, it will still work.

TIP   Always enclose multi-statement macros in curly braces ({}).

Parameterized Macros

So far, we have discussed simple replacement macros, but C allows parameterized macros. For example, the following macro gives the programmer a quick way of getting the square of a number:

```
#define SQR(number) (number * number)
```

This can be used as:

```
size = SQR(5);
```

The pre-processor will expand this macro as:

```
size = (5 * 5);
```

But the following will NOT work:

```
size = SQR(length + width);
```

because this expands to:

```
size = (length + width * length + width);
```

which is not the same as:

```
size = ((length + width) * (length + width));
```

To avoid this type of problem, you should always put parentheses around each parameter in the macro definition. Properly written, our SQR macro is:

```
#define SQR(number) ((number) * (number))
```

| TIP | Always put parentheses () around the parameters in a parameterized macro. |

There is one other surprise lurking in our SQR macro. Consider the following:

```
value = 1;
square = SQR(value++);
(void)printf("Value is %d\n", value);
```

You might remember from Chapter 1 that we told you to always put ++ and --
on lines by themselves. We violated this rule in this code fragment and it's
going to cause trouble. If value starts at one and the next line contains a
single ++ then value will become two. Wrong.

If we expand our SQR macro we get:

```
square = ((value++) * (value++);
```

As we can see from this, we really increment value twice. Because of this, and
the other problems that occur when you use ++ inside another statement, you
should always put ++ and – on lines by themselves. Properly written, this code
is:

```
value = 1;
square = SQR(value);
value++;
(void)printf("Value is %d\n", value);
```

#ifdef / #endif Directives

Suppose you want to add debugging statements to your code for development,
but want them taken out of the production version. You could put in the
statement and then comment them out. For example:

```
/*---Begin Commented out section ------------
    (void)printf("Search key %d\n", key);
    /* Dump the entire list */
    dump_list(start);
---- End commented out section */
```

There is a problem with this example, however. First of all, you must add the
comments for every section of your code you want to get rid of. Also, you

might notice that in this example, we have a comment within a comment. This is not allowed in C; our commented out section would end prematurely. A better way of controlling what code is included in the program is through conditional compilation. When the pre-processor sees the statement:

```
#ifdef SYMBOL
```

It will compile the next section of code *only* if the symbol is defined. The section ends with the statement:

```
#endif /* SYMBOL */
```

Our previous example should be written as:

```
#ifdef DEBUG
    (void)printf("Search key %d\n", key);
    /* Dump the entire list */
    dump_list(start);
#endif /* DEBUG */
```

When we want to debug our program we put the statement:

```
#define DEBUG
```

at the beginning. When we want the production version (without debugging), we use the statement:

```
#undef DEBUG
```

Strictly speaking, the #undef DEBUG is not needed; however, it does serve to indicate that DEBUG is in conditional compilation.

It is also possible to define a symbol from the command line. The tcc switch -Dsymbol will define symbol. A similar switch, -Usymbol, will cause the symbol to become undefined. These definitions will be overridden by any **#define** or **#undef** directives in the source. Suppose we wanted to control whether or not we got the debug or production version of our program at compile time. If we used the command:

```
tcc -ml -eprog -DDEBUG prog.c
```

we would get the debug version. To get the production version we would need the command:

```
tcc -ml -eprog -UDEBUG prog.c
```

Sometimes we have a section of code that we want to remove temporarily for some reason. Rather than comment this out, you should use conditional compilation:

```
#ifdef UNDEF
    print_table();
    finish_entries();
#endif UNDEF
```

Of course, this works only if the symbol UNDEF is never defined. Any programmer who defines this symbol should be shot.

There are two companion directives: **#else** and **#ifndef**. The statement:

```
#ifndef DEBUG
```

will cause the code to be compiled if the symbol DEBUG is *not* defined. The else clause is used to define an alternate set of statements. For example:

```
#ifdef DEBUG
    (void)printf("Debugging version\n");
#else /* DEBUG */
    (void)printf("Production version\n");
#endif /* DEBUG */
```

#include Files

The **#include** directive tells the pre-processor to take the contents of another file and place them in your program. Include files are also known as header files, because most include directives and come at the head of the program.

The general form of an include directive is:

```
#include <file.h>        /* Standard system include */
#include "file.h"        /* Local include file */
```

Header files are extremely useful for modular programming, as we will see in Chapter 5, Modular Programming and Libraries. Things like common data structures, prototypes, constants, and external variable declarations are put in these include files.

If the header file name is enclosed in double quotes (") then the file is local and C expects to find the file in the current directory. If the file name is enclosed in angle brackets (<>), then it is a standard system file, which is found in the Turbo C directory `\tc\include` (on the drive where you installed Turbo C).

System include files are used for defining the data structures and prototypes for functions in the standard libraries. For example, the line:

```
#include <stdlib.h>
```

will bring in the prototypes for most of the standard C functions. If you use the standard I/O package, you will need to put the line:

```
#include <stdio.h>
```

in your program.

Problems occur when the same file is included more than once. Of course, you won't put something like:

```
#include "defs.h"
#include "defs.h"
```

in your program, but suppose you need to include two files: `module_a.h` and `module_b.h`. They both need the definitions in `defs.h` so they both include this file. So when you put:

```
#include "module_a.h"
#include "module_b.h"
```

in your program, you wind up including `defs.h` twice.

The following diagrams show what happens when we include the file `defs.h` twice.

The first time this file is included, the symbol _DEFS_H_ is not defined, so we include all the code inside the file. This includes a statement defining the symbol _DEFS_H_ so that when we include the file again, the **#ifndef** kicks in and because the symbol *is* defined, the entire contents of the file are **#ifndef**ed out:

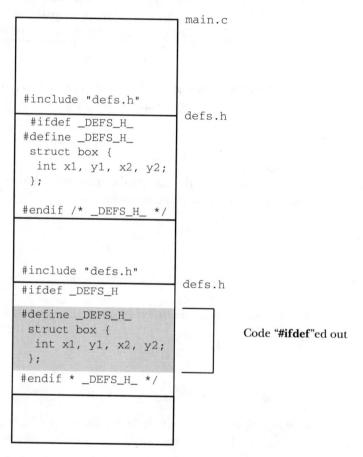

```
                                          main.c




#include "defs.h"
                                          defs.h
 #ifdef _DEFS_H_
#define _DEFS_H_
 struct box {
  int x1, y1, x2, y2;
 };

#endif /* _DEFS_H_ */



#include "defs.h"
                                          defs.h
#ifdef _DEFS_H

#define _DEFS_H_                           Code "#ifdef"ed out
 struct box {
  int x1, y1, x2, y2;
 };
#endif * _DEFS_H_ */
```

There is a way of getting around the problem of double includes. At the beginning of the file *defs.h* we put

```
#ifndef _DEFS_H_
#define _DEFS_H_
```

and at the end of the file we put in

```
#endif /* _DEFS_H_ */
```

Advanced #if Usage

In addition to the simple **#ifdef** and **#ifndef** directives, C supports a more general **#if** directive. The general form of this directive is:

```
#if expressions
```

If the expression evaluates to true (nonzero), then the next section of code will be compiled. All simple arithmetic and logical operators may be used. For example:

```
#if MAX_ENTRIES < MAX_SORT
#define SMALL_SORT
#endif
```

The operator **defined** can be used to test if a symbol is defined. For example:

```
#if defined(DEBUG)
```

is the same as

```
#ifdef DEBUG
```

#elif

The **#elif** directive is shorthand for "else if". It can be used to create a set of nested conditionals.

For example, the following code goes through the symbols PROC_TABLE, NAME_TABLE and ID_TABLE in order and defines TABLE_SIZE so that it is the same as the first of the three symbols found:

```
#if defined(PROC_TABLE)
#define TABLE_SIZE PROC_TABLE
#elif defined(NAME_TABLE)
#define TABLE_SIZE NAME_TABLE
#elif defined(ID_TABLE)
#define TABLE_SIZE ID_TABLE
#endif
```

#error Directive

The **#error** directive will abort the compilation of your program and print an error message. This is useful when we want to check our constant definitions for consistency. For example:

```
#if (NAME_TABLE > MAX_TABLE) || (ID_TABLE > MAX_TABLE)
#error MAX_TABLE too small. Make it bigger and recompile
#endif
```

Special Pre-defined Symbols

Turbo C has pre-defined a number of special symbols. Some of these are ANSI standard and some are special to Turbo C.

The ANSI standard symbols are:

__LINE__   Current line number of the input file.
__FILE__   Current file name (in double quotes).
__DATE__   Date of compilation (in double quotes).
__TIME__   Time of compilation (in double quotes).
__STDC__   Defined if this is an ANSI standard C compiler. For Turbo C
            you must specify the compile time switch -A to define this symbol.

The symbols __LINE__ and __FILE__ are useful in printing error messages:

For example:

```
switch (flag) {
    case 0:
        do_zero();
        break;
    case 1:
        do_one();
        break;
    default:
        (void)fprintf(stderr,
            "Internal error: Bad flag in file %s line %d\n",
            __FILE__, __LINE__);
        break;
}
```

The symbols __TIM__ and __DATE__ are useful in version control. For example:

```
(void)printf("Super Calculator\n");
(void)printf("Version %s created at %s\n",
        __DATE__, __TIME__);
```

The symbol local to Turbo C are:

__TURBOC__ Always defined to be the current version number of the Turbo C compiler. Version 1.0 is 0x0100, 1.2 is 0x0102, and so on.

__PASCAL__ Defined if Pascal calling sequences are used (enabled by the -p on the command line). This is useful if you are mixing Pascal and C programs, a process far too complex to be covered in this book.

__MSDOS__ Always defined.

__CDECL__ Defined if C calling sequences are used (no -p option during the compile).

__TINY__ Tiny memory model used. (Memory models are discussed in Chapter 4, 8086 Details.)

__SMALL__ Small memory model used.

__MEDIUM__ Medium memory model used.

__COMPACT__ Compact memory model used.

__LARGE__ Large memory model used.

__HUGE__ Huge memory model used.

#pragma Directive

ANSI standard C provides a compiler dependent escape clause so that the program can give special commands to the compiler. The **#pragma** directive is used for Turbo C specific commands. (Other compilers define other **#pragma** commands.)

If you are using in-line assembly code, you must put the line

```
#pragma inline
```

at the beginning of your program. (There is a compile time switch -B that does the same thing, but it is better to put the command in your program.)

Secondly, you can selectively enable and disable warning messages. The general form of the #pragma warn directive is:

```
#pragma warn +xxx
#pragma warn -xxx
#pragma warn .xxx
```

The plus sign (+) turns on a warning, the minus (-) turns it off and the dot (.) sets it to the value specified by the command line.

For example, suppose we are defining a dummy function that will be filled in later. Because it is a dummy it has no body. This means that it will not use its parameters, which will normally generate a warning. But we can selectively turn off the warning with the following code:

```
#pragma warn -wpar      /* Turn off parameter warnings */
void dummy(int start, int stop)
{
    /* To be filled in */
}
#pragma warn .wpar      /* Restore state of parameter warning */
```

Summary

We now have the raw material at our disposal to create a program. In the next chapter we will start using it to create programs, first by learning how to construct well-defined modules and, later on, how to construct fun and useful programs, all using the foundation that we have laid here.

User-Friendly Programming

Computers by their nature are unfriendly. As one person put it "This blasted machine keeps doing what I tell it, not what I want it to do." You have a duty as a programmer to make your programs as easy to use as possible.

What makes a program user-friendly? It's friendly if it is easy to use. This means making the user interface simple and intuitive. In a text editor, the user expects the Up Arrow key to move the cursor up and the Down Arrow to move the cursor down. Think about how difficult it would be if the Up Arrow moved the cursor left and the Down Arrow deleted the current line.

When you ask the user questions, make it clear what you are asking. For example, the prompt:

```
File?
```

is very unfriendly. What type of file is wanted? Is it an input file, an output file or something else? A better prompt is:

```
Name of file to edit?
```

Consistency is very important when designing software. One database known for its poor user interface required the user to type a one-character response to most menus. Some required you to type in a character (entering return would select the default). Others required you to type the character and return. As a result the users were confused. Often they would type a character and nothing would immediately happen. The database was extremely slow and sometimes took up to 30 seconds before it would display the next menu. The user would see nothing happen so he would think that it was a menu needing a return, and would hit the key. When the database finally got around to displaying the next menu, there would be a carriage return sitting in the input buffer, so it would assume that the user wanted the default and continue. Forcing the user to put a return after every entry would have provided him with a far better and more consistent interface. Confusion would have been avoided.

Confusion can also be caused by terse and obscure error messages. One of the most unhelpful error messages we have seen was:

```
JOB KILLED BY IEH240I.
```

We looked up this error in the Messages and Codes manual, only to discover that this book contained all the error messages except the IEH series, which was listed in the FORTRAN manual. This new manual provided me with the explanation of the code:

```
IEH240I Job killed by fatal error.
```

This was not helpful, because we knew it was a fatal error the moment it killed our job. It turns out that there was another error code hidden earlier in the listing that disclosed the true error.

Error messages should be clear and, if possible, help the user get around the problem. For example:

```
Error: Disk write protected. Insert new disk and hit return.
```

You should be aware that most people don't program computers and don't think like computer programmers. The meaning of messages should be clear. For example, consider the message:

```
FXT Table full.
```

The user doesn't know if this is an error message, a warning, or an information line. A more descriptive message is:

```
Error: FXT Table full.
Execute a pack command to reclaim FXT space.
```

This is clearly identified as an error, by the word "Error:" at the beginning of the line. Also, the user is given some help in correcting the problem.

Most PC computers have a self-test that executes on start-up. One had a very interesting, but unhelpful, error message:

```
Keyboard missing.
Press F1 to continue.
```

If the keyboard is missing, where do we press F1?

Even when you very carefully design all your messages to be as clear and easy to understand as possible, there will still be people who misinterpret them.

One user was working on a memo, saved it and was rather angry when he found that it had disappeared. He called in a programmer to try to find out what had happened.

"Maybe your disk was full," said the programmer.

"Oh no," replied the user. "I checked and it said 'Disk Space OK.'"

The programmer tried the fellow's disk and sure enough there was the message:

```
Disk space: OK
```

After deleting a few files, the message read:

```
Disk space: 15K
```

It turned out that 0K meant that there were zero kilobytes free. The user had interpreted the error message in a way completely unanticipated by the programmer.

User-friendly means helping the user when he does something wrong. If the user makes a mistake he should be gently pointed in the right direction. Help should be readily available. This does not mean that the user should be bombarded by a page of help text each time he makes a mistake. A simple message like:

```
Unrecognized command: next For help type "help"
```

is sufficient.

Some programs allow the user to do dangerous things. For example, formatting a disk will erase all the files. Before the user is allowed to do something that will wipe out three months of work, he should be warned and asked if he wants to continue. For example:

```
Warning: This will erase all files on disk A:
Do you want to continue?
```

Finally the user interface should not get in the way of the expert user. Menus are fine for the novice user, but there should be some shortcut for the expert. The Macintosh is widely regarded as very user-friendly for the novice user, but it is a nightmare for the experts.

Opening a file on a Macintosh is as simple as point and click. Fine for someone who is just starting on computers, but consider the touch typist. For them, typing in a file name is a quick and simple process. Moving your hand from the keyboard to the mouse, looking at the screen, locating the file, pointing to it, clicking and moving your hand back to the keyboard is slow.

One of the best user interfaces we have seen used pull-down menus for the novice, but every menu item had listed beside it a keyboard sequence that performed the same operation. After using the menus a few times, the user would start to remember the key sequences and begin to use them, thus greatly speeding up his work.

Throughout this book we will concentrate on making our programs as simple and as user-friendly as possible. When programming you should always keep the user in mind. After all, he's the one paying you for the program.

8086 Details

Introduction

Ideally, a high-level language like C should hide all the details of the underlying processor. Unfortunately, to make full use of the PC, you must understand the design of the 8086 architecture and memory organization. This chapter takes you inside the 8086 and DOS. It also describes special C constructs you can use to make full use of your system.

Background

When engineers were designing the 8086 and DOS, they made the following assumptions:

- Memory would remain expensive.

- Most programs would continue to be written in assembly language for speed and compactness.

- Most applications would not take more than 64K of memory. (That's not a typo, its really 64K, not 640K.)

- No one would want (our could ever afford) more than 640K of memory.

Unfortunately all of the assumptions were false. The price of memory plummeted. When the PC first came out, people bought a 32K PC and upgraded it to 64K. Now, it is next to impossible to find a system with less than 640K.

As memory size grew, so did the size of applications. The applications quickly became too large and complex for assembly language, so programmers turned to high-level languages like C and Pascal to solve their problems.

The Structure of the 8086

High-level languages adapt to the 8086 with great difficulty. The instruction set is highly specialized and not uniform. Every register has its own set of instructions which work differently for it, making automatic register allocation difficult. Also, we will see how the memory is organized into a series of 64K segments, making the use of pointers difficult. Although great for small assembly programs, the 8086 is a compiler designer's nightmare.

Almost all documentation describing the DOS system calls assumes that you know the basic structure of the 8086. The interface between DOS and the application program was designed to be easy for assembly programmers. (As contrasted to UNIX where the interface is designed for C programmers.) In order to make full use of DOS you must first understand the general structure of the 8086 as shown in Figure 4-1.

The registers are used to hold the results of the current calculation. For example, most calculators have one main register that holds the current calculation and is used for display. The 8086 has several registers. The AX, BX, CX, and DX registers hold 16 bits. These can be used as full 16-bit registers or two 8-bit registers. For example, AX is 16 bits; AH is the upper half of AX and AL the lower half.

The four registers SD, DI, BP, and SP can only be used as 16-bit registers. These are special purpose registers used for things like string moves, array accesses and stack operations.

The Arithmetic Logic Unit (ALU) does all the calculations. These include all the normal arithmetic operations (add, subtract, multiply, etc.), as well as logical operations such as equals, not equals, less than, etc.

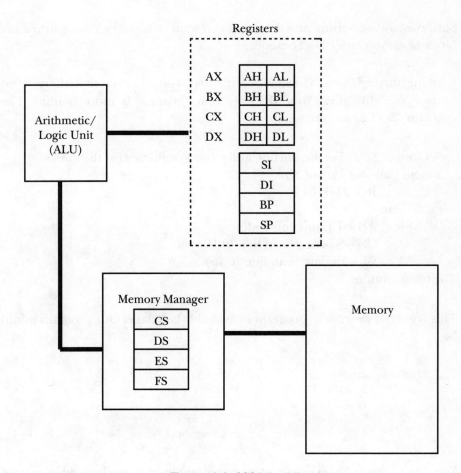

Figure 4-1. 8086 Architecture

As we will see later, the 8086 uses a segmented memory architecture. The memory manager holds the segment register (CS, DS, ES, SS) and uses them to translate a segment/offset type memory address into a real memory access.

Normally, when you program in a high-level language you don't need to know anything about the underlying structure of the machine. In particular, the C compiler determines which registers are used and how.

The problem is that DOS was written with assembly language programmers in mind. C hides many of the system calls through the use of library routines. However, if you want to make full use of DOS you will have to learn a little about assembly language programming.

Suppose you are writing an editor and you want to turn the cursor into a big block when you enter insert mode.

Looking through your C reference manual, you discover that there is no "cursor_size" function. Your DOS reference manual is more helpful. The entry for "Set Cursor Size Reads":

Set Cursor Size - Set the starting and ending scanlines for the cursor
System Call - Set Cursor Size
> INT 21H/01

called with
> AH – 1 (Function code)
> CH – Starting Scan line (0-15)
> CL – Ending Scan line (0-15)

returns Nothing.

This is great if we want to program in assembly language. Our program would be:

```
; Assembly code              ;/* C equivalent */
    MOV    AH,Offset 1       ; AH = 1;
    MOV    CH,Offset 0       ; CH = 0;
    MOV    CL,Offset 15      ; CL = 15;
    INT    10H               ; system_call_type_10();
```

You don't have to be an expert at assembly language to see how this program works.

In C, our code is not so straightforward. Turbo C provides us with a function int86 so that we can call the system directly.

The description of the function is:

```
include <dos.h>
int int86(int intno;union REGS *inregs;union REGS *outregs)
```

where
> intno　– the interrupt number
> inregs　– general purpose registers before interrupt
> outregs – general purpose registers after interrupt

it returns the value of the AX registers.

The union REGS is defined in the header file <dos.h>. It is used to store all the general purpose registers. Because each register can be treated as two 8-bit values or one 16-bit value, it is a union.

```
union  REGS    {
      /* Registers as 16-bit values */
      struct WORDREGS {
          unsigned int ax, bx, cx, dx, si, di, cflag, flags;
      } x;
      /* Registers as 8-bit values */
      struct BYTEREGS {
          unsigned char al, ah, bl, bh, cl, ch, dl, dh;
      } h;
};
```

We want registers AH=1, CH=0, CL=15. Translating this into C we get:

```
{
      union REGS in_regs;     /* Registers for an INT 10 call */
      union REGS out_regs;    /* Registers for an INT 21 call */

      regs.h.ah = 1;      /* Change cursor size function */
      regs.h.ch = start;
      regs.h.cl = end;
      (void)int86(0x10, &in_regs, &out_regs);
```

A full listing of a utility to set the cursor to any size is presented at the end of this chapter. This simple example shows how we can make full use of DOS from C. (Note: Documentation for the system call states that the parameters should be the first and last scan line. In actual practice we've found that some systems limit the set of legal cursor shapes and generate strange results for some values.)

Turbo C also provides us with a way of directly accessing the register through the use of special pseudo-variables. They provide a more straightforward, but tricky, way of performing DOS system calls. For example, our cursor setting function can be written as:

```
{
      _AH = 1;      /* Change cursor size function */
      _CH = start;
      _CL = end;
      geninterrupt(0x10);
```

It takes more than system calls to make effective use of the computer. We also need to know how to use memory. In order to do that, we need a full understanding of how the memory on an 8086 functions.

8086 Memory Usage

At the time the 8086 was designed, 64K was considered a large amount of memory. After all, memory was very expensive. The 8086 goes to great lengths to conserve memory for programs that use less than 64K.

The 8086 uses a segmented memory architecture. (Almost all advanced microprocessors such as the Motorola 68000 use linear memory addressing.) That means that every memory address consists of two parts: a segment and offset, typically written as SEGMENT:OFFSET. For example, 3000:0056. In this case the segment is 3000 (HEX) and the offset is 0056 (HEX). The actual memory address is computed by

```
SEGMENT * 16 + OFFSET = address
```

Example:

```
0x3000 * 0x10 + 0x0056 = 0x300056
```

The 8086 divides the memory into three segments. The code segment contains the program's instructions. It is pointed to by the CS segment register. The data segment contains all the static and global variables. The DS registers point to this section of memory. Finally there is the stack segment pointed to by the SS segment. These segment registers can point to different sections of memory, or they can all point to the same section.

Figure 4-2 shows a memory map for two sample programs. The first is rather large, containing 64K of code, 64K of data, and 64K of stack. It was designed to use a different memory segment for each type of data. The segment registers CS, DS, and SS all point to different areas of memory. The second program is much smaller. In fact the whole program, Code, Data, and Stack all fit within one 64K segment. In this case, all three segment registers point to the same segment, a combination segment.

There is one additional segment register, ES the extra segment registers. This is used to allow access to data outside the range of the three main segments.

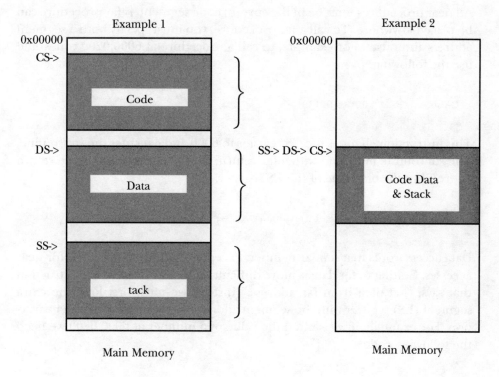

Figure 4-2. *Examples of Program Memory Usage*

Near and Far Pointers

Because of its segmented architecture, the 8086 has two types of memory addresses, near and far.

The CS register always points to the current code segment. A near procedure must be within the current code segment. The near procedure call instruction requires only a 16-bit address as its argument. For example, if the CS register contains 2000, the following code will call the procedure at 2000:0100:

```
CALL    NEAR 0100H    ;Call procedure at CS:0100
```

At the end of this procedure, a return instruction is executed. Since this is a near procedure, a near return is executed:

```
RET     NEAR          ;Perform a near return
```

All near procedures must be in the current code segment. A far procedure can be placed anywhere. To call a far procedure, you must specify both a segment address and offset. For example, to call a procedure at 6000:0200 you would use the following:

```
CALL    FAR 6000H:0200H
```

This instruction changes the CS register to 6000 and executes the subroutine. The subroutine must end with a far return. This restores not only the return address but the old value of the CS register.

```
RET FAR             ;Return from a far call.
```

Data access works in a similar manner, except the register DS is used for near accesses. Getting to far data is more difficult, however. There is no instruction that says, "get data from far address." Instead we must first load the extra segment (ES) register with the segment address and then do the move instruction. For example, if we wanted the value of a number at 6000:0800 we need the following code:

```
MOV  AX,Offset 6000H    ;AX=6000
MOV  ES,AX              ;ES=AX=6000
MOV  AX,ES:0800H        ;AX=Contents of ES:0800
```

NOTE   It would be easier to load ES with 6000 directly, but that's not allowed. The construct ES:0800H tells the processor to use the ES register as the segment register for this operation instead of the default DS register.

As you can see the mix of near and far data can make programming difficult.

Ideal C Memory Model

The C view of memory divide the memory up into five areas: code and constants (TEXT), initialized data (DATA), uninitialized data (BSS), temporary variables (STACK), and the heap.

Code contains the instructions for the program as well as any constants used by the program. For historical reasons, this is referred to as the TEXT segment. The data in this segment never changes and on UNIX systems the entire segment is marked read-only.

The DATA segment contains all the initialized permanent variables. This consists of all initialized global and **static** variables.

The BSS (block storage segment) contains all the global and **static** variables that haven't been initialized. Initialized data are separated from uninitialized data because the program is loaded. When loading initialized data, you must tell the system, "I want space for 20 initialized variables and their values are 183, 333, 98213, ..." Loading uninitialized data is much simpler, "I want 400 bytes of uninitialized space."

Temporary data are stored in the STACK segment. To understand a stack, think of a man doing his taxes. He starts out with a clean desk (empty stack). He gets his 1040 form out and starts filling in the blanks until he reaches LINE 49: "Enter total deductions from LINE 32 of Form 1040-DE, Itemized Deductions." Well, he hasn't done Form 1040-DE so he gets it out, puts it on the top of his desk and begins working, until he reaches LINE 6: "Enter adjusted medical expenses from LINE 8 of worksheet 1040-MW." Cursing, he gets out the form and begins working on it.

By now, you may have realized that he has a stack of papers three pages high. When he finishes with 1040-MW he will take it off the stack and continue working on 1040-DE. After that is finished, he will return to Form 1040.

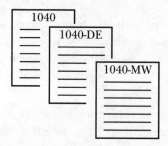

C works much the same way. When a function is called, space for temporary variables is allocated on the stack. This is called pushing a stack frame onto the stack. When the function is finished the stack frame is removed; this is called a pop.

Let's see how this works with a real example. Listing 4-1 contains a simple `main` function which calls two functions `b` and `c`.

Listing 4-1.

```
void a(void)
{}
void b(void)
{
     a();
}
void c(void)
{}
main()
{
     b();
     c();
}
```

When the program begins only main is active, so stack only has allocated space for main's temporary variables. When main calls b a new stack frame is pushed onto the stack and space is allocated for b's temporary variables. Another frame is pushed on top of the first two when b calls a. Each successive call creates a new stack frame. These frames are destroyed and given back to the free pool when the function returns. When a returns a frame is popped, and so on.

Figure 4-3 illustrates stack usage during the execution of this program.

Notice that the stack starts out at the high addresses and grows toward the low addresses. So the stack grows downward. Most memory diagrams are written with the lower addresses at the top of the figure, so it is important to remember which end is up. In the case of the stack "down" is ↑.

When malloc is called it gets data from a section of memory called the heap. The heap can grow as needed. If malloc needs more memory, it will get it from DOS. The heap grows "upwards" (↓ in our memory maps).

C Memory Models for the 8086

Unfortunately, the 8086 is not the ideal machine for C. Far from it. Taking the ideal C memory model and mapping into the segment architecture of the 8086 is an arduous task. If you are only going to write simple or straightforward programs, then you don't need to get near the hardware or worry about which memory model to use. Just use the "huge" memory model and

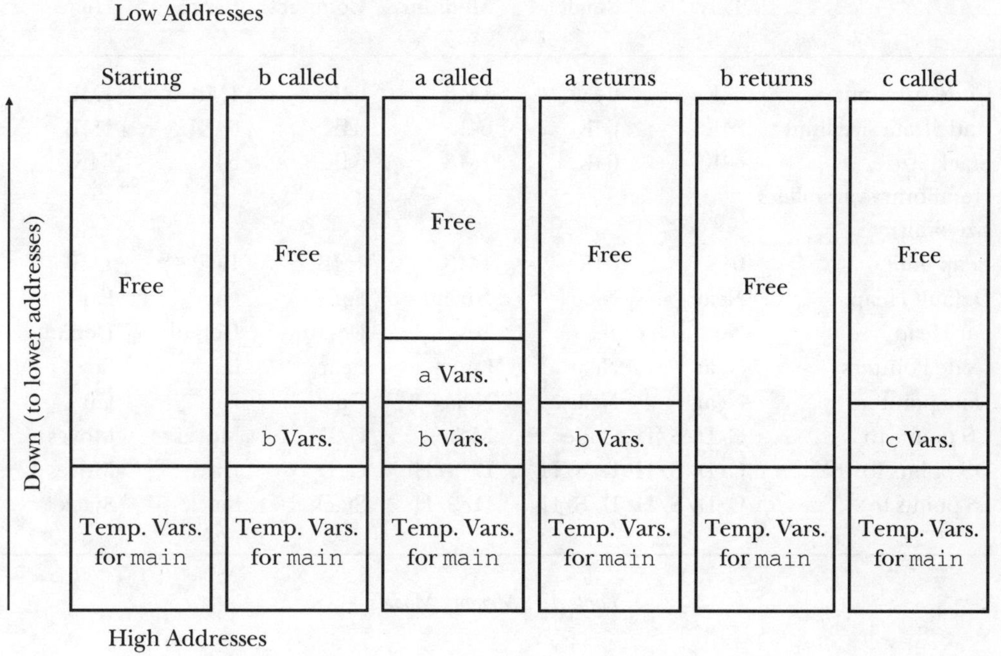

Low Addresses

Starting	b called	a called	a returns	b returns	c called

Down (to lower addresses)

		Free			
Free	Free		Free		Free
		a Vars.		Free	
	b Vars.	b Vars.	b Vars.		c Vars.
Temp. Vars. for `main`	Temp. Vars. for `main`	Temp. Vars. for `main`	Temp. Vars. for `main`	Temp. Vars. for `main`	Temp. Vars. for `main`

High Addresses

Figure 4-3. *Stack Usage.*

skip this section. If you are writing highly optimized tricky programs like TRS utilities, you will need to know all about the various memory models.

Different memory models would not be needed if all programs were the same size. For example, if all programs were less than 64K long, then C could stick everything into one segment and only use near pointers. Similarly, if all programs were very big, then C could use far pointers for everything. (It could anyway, but this would be inefficient.)

But in the real world some programs are big, some are small, and many are in between. Turbo C can use six different memory mapping methods. These are called the memory models and have been given the very names, "Tiny", "Small", "Medium", "Compact", "Large", and "Huge".

The features of each model are summarized in Table 4-1.

	Tiny	Small	Medium	Compact	Large	Huge
Code size limit	64K	64K	1MB	64K	1MB	1MB
static Data size limit	64K	64K	64K	64K	64K	1MB
Stack Size (temporary variables size limit)	64K	64K	1MB	64K	64K	64K
heap limit	64K	64K	1MB	1MB	1MB	1MB
Default Heap	Near	Near	Near	Far	Far	Far
Far Heap	No	Yes	Yes	Default	Default	Default
Code Pointers	Near	Near	far	near	far	far
Data pointers	Near	Near	Near	Far	Far	Far
CS points to	C/D/S/H	Code	Moves	C/D	Moves	Moves
DS points to	C/D/S/H	D/S/H	D/S/H	C/D	Data	Moves
SS points to	C/D/S/H	D/S/H	D/S/H	Stack	Stack	Stack

Table 4-1. Memory Models

C/D/S/H means that the segment register points to a single segment containing Code, static Data, Stack, and Heap

D/S/H indicates that static Data, Stack, and Heap are contained in a common segment.

C/D represents a single segment containing both code and static data.

Other limitations:

Model	Special Limitation
Tiny	Code+Data+Stack+Heap combined must be less than 64K
Small	Data+Stack+Heap combined must be less than 64K
Compact	Code+Data combined must be less than 64K

NOTE In some memory models, Turbo C has split the heap into two parts, the near heap and the far heap. In the Small model and Medium models, all data pointers default to near. So a call to `malloc` will return a near pointer (pointing into the near heap). A call to the far version of this routine (`farmalloc`) will return a far pointer (pointing to the far heap). In all other memory models only one type of heap is available.

Memory Model Details

Tiny   All data and code are stuck in one segment. The segment registers CS, DS, and SS all point to the same segment. This is the smallest possible model. Near pointers are used for everything. By using the `tcc` command line option `-lt` you can create a .COM program file instead of a .EXE one. The .COM files load much faster than .EXE files.

         This is ideal for small TRS utilities that will permanently remain in memory. Since the amount of memory is limited, we want to lock up as little as possible. Only very small programs can use this model.

Small   Data and code are in separate segments. The stack and heap are lumped with the data. This model allows you 64K for code and 64K for all types of data. Most simple to medium programs can easily use this model.

         Near pointers are used throughout; however, if you require large amounts of data from the heap, a far heap is available. To access any data in this heap, you need to explicitly declare your pointers **far**.

Medium   This model is designed for the program with lots of code and little data. The code is broken into multiple segments. There is a limit of 64K of code per file; however, multiple files may be linked together to create a program with much more than 64K total code.

         Data, Stack, and Heap combined must be less than 64K long. The far heap is available.

This model is good for a program that has a great deal of code operating on a small amount of data. A good example would be a graphics program where you can perform many complex operations on the picture, but the picture data are relatively small (<64K).

Compact

Code size must be less than 64K, but Stack, Data, and the Heap all have their own segments. This means that the Stack and Data each can grow up to 64K. There is no far heap in this model since the default heap is **far**.

In this model near pointers are used for code and far pointers for data. This model is used for simple programs that operate on large amounts of data. An example might be a simple text editor where the command set is small, but the edit buffer is as big as possible.

Large

This model is similar to compact, except that the code size uses far pointers and can exceed 64K. Most big programs require this model.

Huge

This is the largest memory model available. Far pointers are used for both code and data. Both the CS and the DS registers move as needed. You are still limited to 64K of stack space, so allocating a large number of temporary variables is discouraged.

This model is useful for programs that use a large amount of both code and data. An example might be a graphics shading program that must process a large amount of image data thought a complex algorithm in order to render an image.

In most cases where speed and program size are *not* critical, this is a good model to use because it frees you from the restrictions placed on you by other models.

Figure 4-4 illustrates the memory layout for the various models. Unlike the memory maps presented in the Turbo C Users' Guide, these are drawn to scale so that you can see the relative sizes of each mode.

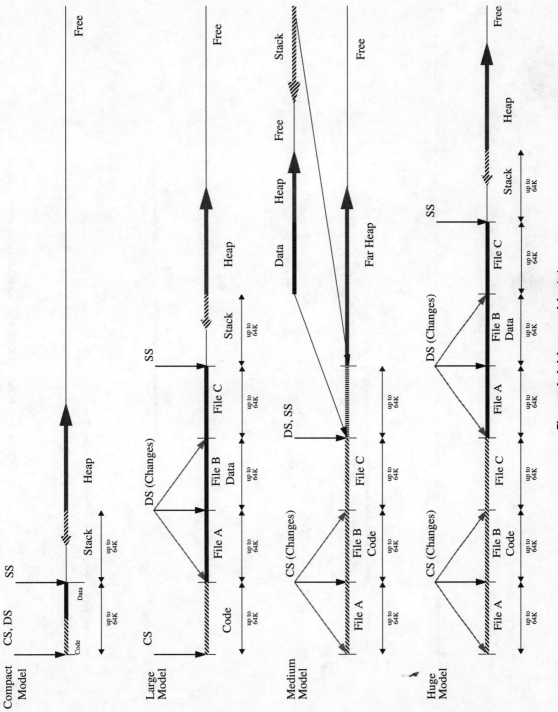

Figure 4-4. Memory Models

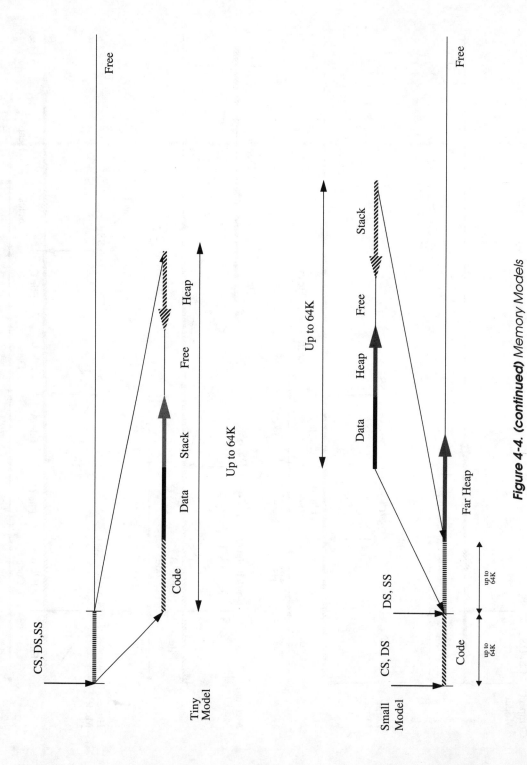

Figure 4-4. (continued) Memory Models

Mixed Mode Programs

It is possible to mix both near and far data and code in a single program. Turbo C added the keywords **near** and **far** to the standard language. By using them you can override the default set by the memory model. In general, you should avoid mixed mode programming. It adds a great deal of confusion to your code for very little gain.

Controlling the Size of Your Program

Now we've seen how memory is laid out for the various memory models, but how do we control the amount of memory used by the program? The size of CODE and DATA segments is determined by the compiler. The stack size defaults to 4K and the heap size defaults to as big as possible. The following list shows how the heap size is determined for each of the memory models:

Model	Default Heap Size
Tiny	64K–Code Size–Data Size–Stack Size
Small	64K–Data Size–Code Size
Medium	64K–Data Size–Code Size
Compact	Can grow to use all free memory
Large	Can grow to use all free memory
Huge	Can grow to use all free memory

C provides a variable: _stklen which you can use to change the size of the default stack. The following shows how to allocate a 64K (the biggest allowed) stack.

```
#include <dos.h> /* Get DOS dependent variables */
/* Assign stack size the biggest possible */
unsigned int _stklen = 0xFFFF;
```

NOTE This only works on the Compact, Large, and Huge models. In the other models the stack shares the segment with other things, so it can't take all the space in the segment.

The variable _heaplen is used to specify the size of the heap. This only works for the near heap found in the tiny, small, and compact memory models. In the other memory models, the heap can grow to use all of DOS's available memory.

In practice, for the smaller memory models, C allocates a single space with the stack at one end and the heap at the other. The heap grows up and the stack grows down. What's between them is unused. If they ever collide, your program will crash. In this case, the heap will overwrite variables on the stack or the stack will overwrite variables on the heap. Either way, bad data will be generated that can cause your program to behave very strangely.

Register Variables

Turbo C has special pseudo-variables set up so that you can access the variables directly. Since these are the 8086 registers that Turbo C uses for its calculations, they may change at any moment. However, as we will see in later chapters, they can be very useful in very special circumstances.

Register	Purpose
_AX	General purpose 16-bit register used for almost any arithmetic calculations
_AH	Top half of _AX
_AL	Bottom half of _AL
_BX	General purpose 16-bit register, also used in calculations
_BH	Top half of _BX
_BL	Bottom half of _BL
_CX	General purpose 16-bit register, also used in calculations

_CH	Top half of _CX
_CL	Bottom half of _CL
_DX	General purpose 16-bit register, also used in calculations
_DH	Top half of _DX
_DL	Bottom half of _DL
_SP	Stack pointer, the stack contains temporary data.

Be very careful with this register as changing it will cause C to "lose" all temporary data and function return addresses.

As we will see, TSR type programs must set up their own stack, a very tricky operation which does involve changing _SP.

_BP	Base pointer used to point to current stack frame. Do not change this or you will "lose" all your temporary variables.
_DI	Destination pointer. Originally designed as a general string pointer, it is one of the two registers allocated by the **register** directive for general purpose data.
_SI	Source pointer. Cousin of _DI
_CS	Code segment. Changing this register causes execution to begin at another location. *Do not change under any circumstances.*
_DS	Data segment. Points to the permanent data. By changing this register, you can use more than 64K of data, but you have to access it without the help of C. It is far better to use one of the larger data models and let C worry about the _DS register.
_SS	Stack segment. Points to temporary storage. Normally you should not change this register; however, TSR programs

need to set up their own stack, so they must change this register.

_ES   Extra segment. Used whenever you **dereference** a far pointer.

Summary

As you can see, the 8086 is a strange and complex beast. Taming it can be difficult. In the programs that follow we will show you how to make full use of your knowledge of this machine to write highly efficient and effective programs.

Listing 4-2. "cursor.c"

```
/*************************************************************
 * cursor -- change shape of cursor                         *
 *                                                          *
 * Usage                                                    *
 *      cursor <start> <end>                                *
 *                                                          *
 * Where                                                    *
 *      start -- first scanline for cursor (0-15)           *
 *      end -- last scanline for cursor (0-15)              *
 *                                                          *
 * WARNING: No limit checking is done on the input          *
 *      so bogus values will generate bogus cursors         *
 *************************************************************/
#include <dos.h>
#include <stdlib.h>
#include <stdio.h>

 /* DOS function code for changing cursor size */
#define CHANGE_SIZE 1
/* Interrupt function call for bios */
#define INT_BIOS        0x10

main(int argc, char *argv[])
{
    int start;          /* First scanline of cursor */
    int end;            /* Last scanline of cursor */

    void usage(void);   /* Tell how to use this */

    /* Change cursor size */
```
continued

Listing 4-2 continued.

```
        void change_cursor(int start, int end);

        if (argc != 3)
            usage();

        start = atoi(argv[1]);
        end = atoi(argv[2]);

        change_cursor(start, end);
        return (0);
}
/**********************************************************
 * change_cursor -- change size of cursor                 *
 *                                                         *
 * Parameters                                              *
 *      start -- first scanline of the cursor              *
 *      end  -- last scanline of the cursor                *
 **********************************************************/
void change_cursor(int start, int end)
{
        union REGS regs;      /* Registers for an INT 21 call */

        regs.h.ah = CHANGE_SIZE;  /* Change cursor size function */
        regs.h.ch = start;
        regs.h.cl = end;
        (void)int86(INT_BIOS, &regs, &regs);
}
/**********************************************************
 * usage -- tell how to use the program                   *
 **********************************************************/
void usage(void)
{
        (void)fprintf(stderr,"Usage is: cursor <start> <end>\n");
        exit (1);
}
```

Modular Programming and Libraries

One of the great advantages of C is that it allows the programmer to create reusable program modules. A module is a group of functions that perform a single purpose. A library is a set of modules put together in a single library (`.LIB`) file. The library and associated header files that work together give the programmer a well-defined package that he can use.

For example, you are already familiar with the standard I/O package. The header file `<stdio.h>` defines the data structure and functions for this package, while functions such as `prinf`, `fopen`, `fread`, and `fwrite` do the work.

In this chapter we will create an extended strings package. Normal strings contain normal characters (A,q,z, etc.). Extended characters are just like normal characters except that they have a color attribute added. The characters each have their own foreground color, background color and blink attribute.

We will discuss the entire process of producing a module including the design, implementation and documentation. Good design practices are discussed including rules for data sharing and data hiding.

The Idea

Early computers had only a teletype for output. This was a printing terminal that could only type uppercase letters. ALTHOUGH UPPERCASE WAS UGLY AND DIFFICULT TO READ, THE TELETYPE WAS BETTER THAN NO TERMINAL AT ALL. When the first CRTs came out they emulated teletypes (some even output uppercase only). In fact they were known as glass teletypes. The cursor was forever positioned on the last line and the data scrolled up off the screen.

But soon terminal makers started coming out with CRTs with cursor control. The users discovered that they could do amazing things with the new machines, like create full screen editors.

The invention of the PC brought another innovation to the market: cheap color. Now terminals could not only output simply text, but text in color.

Unfortunately, language designers have not kept up with the hardware. ANSI standard C has a set of I/O functions for a teletype, but doesn't go any farther than allowing the programmer to output a line of text at the bottom of the screen.

Turbo C improved on this by adding a set of non-standard functions to handle cursor positioning, clear-screen, and other CRT-based functions. However the functions to handle text color leave much to be desired.

The functions `textattr`, `testbackground`, and `textcolor` allow the programmer to change the color of the output. The problem is that since these are separate function calls they are difficult to use. For example, to print "RED" in red letters and "BLUE" in blue letters, we need the following code:

```
#include <conio.h>
main()
{
    textcolor(RED);
    (void)cprintf("RED");
    textcolor(BLUE);
    (void)cprintf("BLUE\r\n");
    return (0);
}
```

Wouldn't it be better if we could just write something like:

```
ex_printf("~rRED ~bBLUE\r\n");
```

NOTE Turbo C requires both the return (\r) and line feed (\n) for its console output routines `cprintf` and `cputs`. We decided to follow that standard.

The second way is much simpler and easier to use. We decided to create a set of modules to let the programmer unleash the power of color.

Designing an Extended String

In designing a library you must keep the following question in mind: How do we expect it to be used?

The extended string package is designed for outputting color strings to the screen. It should be convenient to print strings, so some sort of `printf` function is required. It also should be easy to specify extended strings.

For this reason, we've decided to allow extended strings to be specified as regular C strings with special escape sequences added. C programmers are already familiar with the concept of escape characters; after all, the backslash (\) escape is used for special characters and the percent (%) escape is used for printf specifications.

We need an escape character for color, so we scan the keyboard to find an appropriate character. The tilde (~) is not widely used, so we decide to use it as our escape character. (When's the last time you saw a tilde in a sentence?)

To be as consistent as possible we decided to give each color a letter. The background colors will be given capital letters and the foreground colors lowercase. Assigning letters to the various colors we get ~r for red, ~b for blue, ~g for green and so on. But we quickly run into a problem, as there are 16 possible colors and only 26 letters of the alphabet. How are we going to assign each color a mnemonic letter? The colors LIGHTGRAY, LIGHTBLUE, LIGHTGREEN, LIGHTCYAN, LIGHTRED and LIGHTMAGENTA are particularly difficult.[1]

---

1   These colors are defined in the header file <conio.h>

Our solution is to use the escape ~1 for light colors and ~d for dark colors. This reduces our color set to only 10: BLACK, BLUE, GREEN, CYAN, RED, MAGENTA, BROWN, GRAY, YELLOW and WHITE. For most colors, the choice of letter is obvious. We had to stretch for BROWN, BLUE and BLACK. The only problem color is GRAY. "g" was taken for green, "y" for yellow, and "r" for red. Finally we chose the letter "x" for GRAY. It's not mnemonic, but there's no good letter left.

Our list of color to letter assignment is:

Text	Background	Color
~b	~B	blue
~k	~K	black
~n	~N	brown
~c	~C	cyan
~x	~X	gray
~g	~G	green
~m	~M	magenta
~r	~R	red
~w	N.A.	white
~y	N.A.	yellow

We have two light/dark shift characters

~1	choose colors from the light set
~d	choose colors from the dark set

Finally, we need something to handle blinking. Since the letters are reserved for colors, we decided to use plus (+) and minus (-) to turn blinking on and off.

The full list of letters used in this package can be found in the header file "x_string.h" at the end of this chapter.

~+	Blink on
~-	Blink off

Finally, we need a way of putting an escape character (tilde) in a string. Usually this is done by doubling

~~	tilde (~)

This completes our selection of color specifications.

There is one remaining problem. This book is written in black and white. There is no way we can show red text on a blue background.

Although we can't use color on monochrome monitors, we can use reverse video, underline, and blink. The additional characters for the monochrome attributes are:

~ (	Reverse video
~)	Normal video
~_	Underline
~.	Underline off

All the information about escape characters is now written into a header file `"x_string.h"` as C comments. (See listing at the end of this chapter.)

Designing Functions for Extended Strings

We need a type for our strings. A character is 8 bits and we have 8 bits of attributes; combined they make up 16 bits. So an extended character is 16 bits or a **short int**.

We define a type for our extended strings with the statement:

```
typedef short int x_char;
```

Now we need to decide what functions we are going to put in this package. First of all we need a function to convert normal strings (with color escapes) to extended strings.

There are two possible ways of defining this. The first is:

```
void standard_to_extended(x_char *extended, char *standard)
```

this would convert the standard string "standard" to the extended string "extended". The other method we might use is:

```
x_char *standard_to_extended(char *standard)
```

This routine uses an internal buffer to hold the converted string. This type of function has several problems. First of all, the size of the internal buffer must be big enough to hold the largest string we plan on using. Secondly, since we are returning a pointer to a static internal buffer, subsequent calls to this function will cause the new data to overwrite the old.

In the first definition, the call is responsible for allocating the output string and a different string can be used for each call.

The main advantage of the second definition is that by returning a pointer to the extended string, we can nest calls. For example, we can print an extended string with the statement:

```
(void)x_puts(standard_to_extend("~rError:~b Blue alert\r\n"));
```

Let's think about what this package is to be used for. It is designed for outputting lines of color text to the screen. Strings are not going to be long, probably about 80 characters maximum. (We will design for more to try to eliminate Murphy.)

However, this is not a heavy duty data processing package. For that reason we value ease of use far more than limited functionality, so the second form of the function:

```
x_char *standard_to_extended(char *standard)
```

is the one chosen. The functionality is very good and the limitations aren't too bad.

As we've already seen, we need a way to send the characters to the screen. One way is to write a function very similar to `puts`:

```
int x_puts(x_char *extend)
```

This writes an extended string to the screen. Like `puts`, it returns the number of characters printed.

Continuing on with our output routines we define the function:

```
int x_printf(x_char fmt, parameter-list);
```

which works like `printf`, only with extended strings. By now you may have noticed that we are defining a large number of routines that look like standard C functions. This is intentional. We want to give the user something familiar. It is always better to build on what is known than to start over from scratch. Our list of similar functions include:

Function	Extended Version	Purpose
strlen	x_strlen	Gets the length of a string
strcpy	x_strcpy	Copy a string
strcat	x_strcat	Concatenate two strings
strcmp	x_strcmp	Compare two strings
strncpy	x_strncpy	Copy a string (with limit)
strncat	x_strncat	Concatenate two strings (with limit)
strncmp	x_strncmp	Compare two strings (with limit)

Finally there are more functions that we need to finish our set. The first is the reverse of `stand_to_extend`. It is defined as:

```
char *extend_to_stand(x_char *extend);
```

Because of the way extended strings are implemented, we cannot say that processing a string through `stand_to_extend` and `extend_to_stand` will result in the original string. (For example: "~B~wNormal" may translate to "~w~BNormal".)

At this point, we have spent a great deal of time and effort thinking about how our extended string package is going to be used by the outside world. It is extremely important to take the time to do the external design right. Everything we have done has been written down inside the header file "x_string.h".

This file holds the public part of our module; that is, the part of the library that we present to the outside world. The user does not need to know the actual implementation details: That information is considered private. The user doesn't care how we implement our functions as long as they work.

Implementation

Once we have decided what we are going to do (the specification) we can do it (the implementation). This is actually the easiest part of the process.

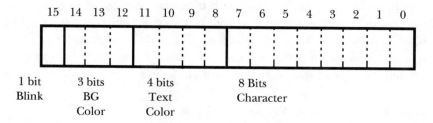

Figure 5-1. *Text Attributes*

There are two types of data used in constructing modules: *public* and *private*. Variables, types and function declarations are presented to the outside world (the user) are public. We have constructed a single header file "printout.h" to hold our public information. Private information is kept within the library. For example, how the extended characters are constructed is part of the private information. The user doesn't care which bits are the attributes and which are the data. As long as the library works, it doesn't matter to him. For the function in the library that has to manipulate these bits, it does matter. We will use the header file "x_param.h" to hold this private information.

The extended characters consist of 8 bits of attributes and 8 bits of characters. The attributes can further be broken down into 1 bit of blink, 3 bits of background color and 4 bits of text color. These are all combined into a 16-bit integer as illustrated by Figure 5-1.

Implementing stand_to_extend

We start the implementation phase with the function stand_to_extend. The attributes for the current character will be stored in the variable attrib. This is initialized so that by default our text starts out as white letters on a black background.

```
int attrib = ((BLACK << 4) | WHITE) << 8;
```

The main loop of this function loops through each character in the input string, adding an attribute byte and depositing the result in the output string. This loop also checks for the escape character, decoding all escape sequences.

```
for (in_ptr = standard; *in_ptr != '\0'; in_ptr++) {
    if (*in_ptr == X_CHAR) {
```

```
        ... handle escape sequence
} else {
    /* store character and attribute */
    *out_ptr = attrib | (*in_ptr & 0xFF);
    *out_ptr++;
}
}
```

Decoding the escape character is done through the use of a large **switch** statement. For most colors the implementation is rather simple, just set the color in the variable `attribute`. For example:

```
  /* Set the background to blue */
case X_BACK_BLUE:
    BACK(BLUE);
    break;
```

The macro `BACK` is used to set the background color bits in the variable `attrib`. We have defined similar macros to set the text color and blink attributes.

Some colors come in light and dark flavors. The variable `light_dark` is used to control which flavor is used. For example the string "~r" is decoded by the case:

```
  /* Set text color to red */
case X_TEXT_RED:
    if (light_dark == LIGHT)
        TEXT(LIGHTRED);
    else
        TEXT(RED);
    break;
```

That takes care of all the colors. Blinking is handled in a similar fashion.

All that's left is the monochrome attributes reverse and underline. Our Turbo C documentation completely describes the function `textattr` for color monitors, but tells us nothing about how the attributes function for monochrome monitors. As a professional programmer, you will get used to incomplete documentation.

In order to discover how the text attributes really work, we write a short program that displays all the attributes on the screen (see listing of `att.c`).

This program gives us enough information to select the proper set of attributes for a monochrome system and how they work.

Not too surprisingly, we learn that the attribute 0x70 (LIGHTGRAY text on BLACK background) represents normal video. Reverse video is attribute 0x07 (BLACK text on LIGHTGRAY background). What is surprising though is that underline is attribute 0x71 (BLUE text on BLACK background). There is also no way to underline reverse video.

So we add constants to represent these attributes in our stand_to_extend function and add a few more cases to our big **switch** statement. Our function is now complete. Next we need to compile it.

There are two methods of compiling programs under Turbo C. The first is to use the integrated development environment (IDE). The second is to use the utility "make" and the command line compiler "tcc".

The IDE provides a nice set of commands for the creation of projects; however, it is somewhat limited. Worse, it generates project files that are dependent on where you installed your copy of Turbo C. If you move to another machine, your project files will not work. Finally, there is no way to use the IDE to generate a library. For these reasons we will be using the utility "make". The Makefile for our extended string library is pretty standard except for the implicit rule:

```
.c.obj:
        $(CC) $(CFLAGS) -c $<
        tlib xstring.lib /E /C -+ $*.obj
```

The command "$(CC) $(CFLAGS) -c $<" is the standard compile command that turns our .c files into .obj files. The next line "tlib xstring.lib /E /C -+ $*.obj" is used to insert the newly compiled object file in the library. The tlib command is used to build and maintain libraries. The argument "xstring.lib" is the name of our library. The switch /E tells tlib to create an extended directory that will cause our library to load faster. The /C switch indicates that the function names in the object file are case sensitive. (**tlib** is also used with languages like Pascal where names are not case sensitive.) Finally the command "-+ $*.obj" tells tlib to insert our new object file in the library replacing any older version. (This generates a warning if there is no old version. This warning can safely be ignored.)

Using the make command we compile our first function and put it in the library. Now we need to test it. Unfortunately, testing will have to be deferred until we have some way of viewing the result. A HEX dump is possible, but difficult to read. We need a way of writing an extended string to the screen.

x_puts

The function x_puts will write an extended string to the screen. The implementation of the function is rather simple. It loops through each character of the string, and picks off the attribute byte. If the attributes have changed, the function will set them using textattr. Otherwise it just outputs the character. The implementation looks like:

```c
int x_puts(x_char *string)
{
    /*
     * cur_attrib starts out at an impossible value to force
     * a textattr call. We don't know what attributes the user
     * left set, so we make sure to start our own out right
     */
    int cur_attrib = -1;    /* current attribute for output */
    int char_count = 0;     /* # characters output so far */
    int new_attrib;         /* attribute of current character */

    /* Loop until we run out of string */
    while (*string != 0) {
        new_attrib = X_ATTRIB_PART(*string);

        /* If attributes changed -- then tell console */
        if (new_attrib != cur_attrib) {
            textattr(new_attrib);
            cur_attrib = new_attrib;
        }

        if (putch(X_CHAR_PART(*string)) < 0)
            return (-1);

        char_count++;
        string++;
    }
    return (char_count);
}
```

With these two functions we can now start testing. This is done with a short test routine to output various strings for monochrome monitors:

```
void test_1(void)
{
    x_puts(stand_to_extend("Test ~+blink~- non-blink\r\n"));
    x_puts(stand_to_extend("Test ~_Under~. ~(Reverse~)\r\n"));
    x_puts(stand_to_extend("Test ~+~(Rev/blink~)~- Norm\r\n"));
    x_puts(stand_to_extend(
                "Test ~_~+Under/blink~-~. Norm\r\n"));
     return (0);
}
```

This routine actually serves two functions: it tests out our routines as well as providing a short example of how to use our library.

A color version of this test is also written.

extend_to_stand

Now we can produce and output extended strings. It would be nice to take an extended string and turn it back into its standard equivalent. The function to do this is:

```
char *extend_to_stand(x_char *extended)
```

This is largely a table driven function. As you can see from the listing the tables take up more space than the code.

The main loop goes through each character checking each attribute (blink, text color, and background color) to see if they have changed. When a change is spotted, the appropriate escape sequence is generated by table lookup.

ex_printf

The ex_printf function is much like printf, except the format specification (which is a standard string) is converted to an extended string before printing.

The implementation is straightforward except that we must handle variable length argument lists. The header file <stdarg.h> defines macros to handle variable length argument lists. The macro va_start is used to set up the argument list. The macro va_end is used to perform any stack fixups that are needed so that the function can end normally. If the macro is not present, the function may behave strangely.

The function `ex_printf` is defined as:

```
int ex_printf(char *format, ...)
```

The ". . ." is used to indicate the variable argument list. Upon entry to the function we set up the list with the statement:

```
va_start(arg_list, format);
```

This initializes the variable `arg_list`. This macro needs to know the name of the last fixed parameter (in this case, format) so that it can find the argument list. Next the function `vsprintf` is called to do the bulk of the work. Since we are now finished with the argument list, we clean up with the macro `va_end`. To finish up, we convert and output the string.

Other Functions

The implementation of the string-related functions: `x_strlen`, `x_strcpy`, `x_strcat`, `x_strcmp` `x_strncpy`, `x_strncat`, and `x_strncmp` is simple and straightforward.

The two `printf` like functions `x_printf` and `x_sprintf` are implemented much like `ex_printf`.

Example

To show how to use the extended strings functions, we've created a short example in addition to our test routine. Our program prints "Hello world." using some of the extended strings functions. On a black & white screen, "Hello" will be reversed and "world." will be underlined. On color screens, "Hello" and "world." will be different colors.

Listing 5-1. "example.c"

```
/*********************************************************
 * example -- a simple example of x-string usage        *
 *                                                       *
 * Prints out "Hello world." with hello reverse and      *
 * world underlined.                                     *
 *********************************************************/
#include <stdio.h>
#include "x_string.h"

main(void)
{
    x_char x_hello[100];   /* "Hello" as an extended string */
    x_char x_world[100];/* " world.\n" as an extended string */
    x_char x_hello_world[200];   /* Both strings */

    ex_printf("~(Hello~) ~_world.~.\r\n");
    (void)x_strcpy(x_hello, stand_to_extend("~(Hello~)"));
    (void)x_strcpy(x_world, stand_to_extend(" ~_world.~.\r\n"));

    (void)x_strcpy(x_hello_world, x_hello);
    (void)x_strcat(x_hello_world, x_world);

    x_printf(x_hello_world);
    (void)printf("The text: %s\n",
                 extend_to_stand(x_hello_world));
    return (0);
}
```

Listing 5-2. "Makefile"

```
CC=tcc
CFLAGS=-ml -w -N -v -y
OBJS=\
        ex_printf.obj    \
        to_ascii.obj     \
        to_x.obj         \
        x_printf.obj     \
        x_puts.obj       \
        x_sprintf.obj    \
        x_strcat.obj     \
        x_strcmp.obj     \
        x_strcpy.obj     \
        x_strlen.obj     \
        xstrncat.obj     \
        xstrncmp.obj     \
```

continued

Listing 5-2 continued.

```
        xstrncpy.obj

all: xstring.lib example.exe

example.exe: example.c  xstring.lib
        $(CC) $(CFLAGS) -eexample.exe example.c xstring.lib

xstring.lib: $(OBJS)

$(OBJS): x_string.h x_param.h

.c.obj:
        $(CC) $(CFLAGS) -c $<
        tlib xstring.lib /E /C -+ $*.obj
```

Summary

We have just completed our extended-string library. This collection of functions demonstrates several good programming practices. First of all, it's useful. The functions are well documented in the header file "x_string.h". The design of our library is built on well-known string functions so that it is easy to understand and use.

Whenever possible, we made our design flexible. For example, if we wanted to change the escape character from tilde (~) to carat (^) all we have to do is change the definition of X_CHAR and recompile the library.

There is a good separation between the public and private parts of the library. Actual implementation details are hidden in the functions and the private header file "x_param.h".

The final result of all our work is a well-rounded set of reusable code that can easily be incorporated into other programs.

Listing 5-3. "x_string.h"

```
#ifndef _XSTRING_H
#define _XSTRING_H
#include <string.h>
/*************************************************************
 * x_string -- a package to handle extended strings         *
 *                                                           *
 * Extended characters are just like regular strings         *
 *      but with foreground color, background color,        *
 *      and blinking added.                                  *
 *                                                           *
 * Types defined                                             *
 *      x_char -- an extended character                     *
 *                                                           *
 * The extend character (~) is used to indicate a            *
 *   special function is to be performed                    *
 *                                                           *
 * Character            Special function                     *
 *      ~~              Put a tilde (~) in the string        *
 *                                                           *
 *              Text (foreground) colors                     *
 *                                                           *
 *      ~k              Set text color to black              *
 *      ~b              Set text color to blue               *
 *      ~g              Set text color to green              *
 *      ~c              Set text color to cyan               *
 *      ~r              Set text color to red                *
 *      ~m              Set text color to magenta            *
 *      ~n              Set text color to brown              *
 *      ~x              Set text color to gray               *
 *      ~y              Set text color to yellow             *
 *      ~w              Set text color to white              *
 *      ~l              Text colors come from light          *
 *                      set                                  *
 *      ~d              Text colors come from the            *
 *                      dark set                             *
 *                                                           *
 *              Background colors                            *
 *                                                           *
 *      ~K              Set background color to black        *
 *      ~B              Set background color to blue         *
 *      ~G              Set background color to green        *
 *      ~C              Set background color to cyan         *
 *      ~R              Set background color to red          *
 *      ~M              Set background color to magenta      *
 *      ~N              Set background color to brown        *
```

continued

Listing 5-3 continued.

```
 *       ~Y                  Set background color to gray      *
 ***********************************************************/


/***********************************************************
 * For monochrome monitors                                 *
 *       ~(                  Reverse video                  *
 *       ~)                  Normal video                   *
 *       ~_                  Underline                      *
 *       ~.                  Underline off                  *
 *                                                          *
 * Blinking                                                 *
 *       ~+                  Set blinking text              *
 *       ~-                  Set non-blinking text          *
 ***********************************************************/
typedef short int x_char;       /* extended character */


/***********************************************************
 * stand_to_extend -- converts standard char string        *
 *                to an extended version                   *
 *                                                          *
 * Parameters                                               *
 *      standard -- standard character string (in)         *
 *                                                          *
 * Returns                                                  *
 *      extended -- extended character string (out)        *
 *                                                          *
 *      Errors are ignored                                  *
 ***********************************************************/
x_char *stand_to_extend(char *standard);


/*
 * defines for all the extend character sequence
 */
#define X_CHAR          '~'  /* extended char escape sequence */

#define X_TEXT_BLACK    'k'  /* Set text color to black    */
#define X_TEXT_BLUE     'b'  /* Set text color to blue     */
#define X_TEXT_GREEN    'g'  /* Set text color to green    */
#define X_TEXT_CYAN     'c'  /* Set text color to cyan     */
#define X_TEXT_RED      'r'  /* Set text color to red      */
#define X_TEXT_MAGENTA  'm'  /* Set text color to magenta  */
#define X_TEXT_BROWN    'n'  /* Set text color to brown    */
#define X_TEXT_GRAY     'x'  /* Set text color to gray     */
#define X_TEXT_YELLOW   'y'  /* Set text color to yellow   */
```

continued

Listing 5-3 continued.

```
#define X_TEXT_WHITE   'w'  /* Set text color to white    */

#define X_TEXT_LIGHT   'l'  /* Text colors come from light set */
#define X_TEXT_DARK    'd'  /* Text colors come from dark set */
/*
 * Background colors
 */
#define X_BACK_BLACK   'K' /* Set background color to black  */
#define X_BACK_BLUE    'B' /* Set background color to blue    */
#define X_BACK_GREEN   'G' /* Set background color to green   */
#define X_BACK_CYAN    'C' /* Set background color to cyan    */
#define X_BACK_RED     'R' /* Set background color to red */
#define X_BACK_MAGENTA 'M' /* Set background color to magenta */
#define X_BACK_BROWN   'N' /* Set background color to brown   */
#define X_BACK_GRAY    'Y' /* Set background color to gray    */
/*
 * Blinking
 */
#define X_BLINK_ON  '+'    /* Set blinking text */
#define X_BLINK_OFF '-'    /* Set non-blinking text */
/*
 * For monochrome monitors
 */
#define REVERSE        '(' /* Reverse video */
#define NORMAL         ')' /* Normal video */
#define UNDERLINE_ON   '_' /* Underline    */
#define UNDERLINE_OFF  '.' /* Underline off */


/***********************************************************
 * extend_to_stand -- convert standard string to          *
 *             extended                                    *
 *                                                         *
 * Parameters                                              *
 *     extended -- extended character string (in)          *
 *                                                         *
 * Returns                                                 *
 *     standard character string                           *
 ***********************************************************/
char *extend_to_stand(x_char *extended);
/***********************************************************
 * these functions duplicate the standard strings          *
 * package.  They have a similar calling sequence and       *
 * return value.                                            *
 *                                                         *
```

continued

Listing 5-3 continued.

```
 * x_strcat -- extended version of strcat            *
 * x_strcmp -- extended version of strcmp            *
 *   (Note: This checks characters only, not attributes)*
 * x_strcpy -- extended version of strcpy            *
 *                                                    *
 * x_strncat -- extended version of strncat          *
 * x_strncmp -- extended version of strncmp          *
 *   (Note:This checks characters only, not attributes) *
 * x_strncpy -- extended version of strncpy          *
 *                                                    *
 * x_strlen -- extended version of strlen            *
 ****************************************************/
x_char *x_strcat(x_char *destination, x_char *source);
int     x_strcmp(x_char *s1, x_char *s2);
x_char *x_strcpy(x_char *destination, x_char *source);

x_char *x_strncat(x_char *destination, x_char *source,
                  size_t limit);
int     x_strncmp(x_char *s1, x_char *s2, size_t limit);
x_char *x_strncpy(x_char *destination, x_char *source,
                  size_t limit);

unsigned int x_strlen(x_char *string);

 /**********************************************************
 * x_printf -- extended version of print (actually    *
 *      cprintf).  Will take an extended string as     *
 *      format.  Parameters are the same as printf     *
 *                                                    *
 * x_sprintf -- extended version of sprintf           *
 * ex_printf -- convert to extended string and print  *
 * x_put -- output an extended string                 *
 ****************************************************/
int x_printf(x_char *fmt, ...);
int x_sprintf(x_char *string, x_char *fmt, ...);
int ex_printf(char *fmt, ...);
int x_puts(x_char *string);
/* is-functions */
#endif _XSTRING_H
```

Listing 5-4. "x_param.h"

```
#define MAX_STRING 1000 /* longest string to be used */

/*
 * Given an extended character -- return the character part
 */
#define X_CHAR_PART(ch)         ((ch) & 0xFF)
/*
 * Given an extended character -- return the attribute part
 */
#define X_ATTRIB_PART(ch)       (((unsigned int)(ch)) >> 8)
```

Listing 5-5. "ex_print.c"

```
/**********************************************************
 * Extended characters are just like regular strings      *
 *       but with foreground color, background color,      *
 *       and blinking added.                               *
 *                                                         *
 **********************************************************/
#include "x_string.h"
#include "x_param.h"
#include <conio.h>
#include <stdarg.h>
#include <stdio.h>

/**********************************************************
 * ex_printf -- convert string to extended and print      *
 *                                                         *
 * Parameters                                              *
 *      format -- standard character string with           *
 *               embedded extended escapes                 *
 *      parameter(s) -- printf style parameters            *
 *                                                         *
 * Returns                                                 *
 *      Number of characters output (just like printf)     *
 **********************************************************/
int ex_printf(char *format, ...)
{
    va_list arg_list;           /* argument list */

    /* formatted output string */
    char out_string[MAX_STRING];

    x_char *extend_out;         /* extended string to output */
```

continued

Listing 5-5 continued.

```
        va_start(arg_list, format);
        (void)vsprintf(out_string, format, arg_list);
        va_end(arg_list);

        extend_out = stand_to_extend(out_string);
        if (x_puts(extend_out) == 0)
            return (0);

        return(x_strlen(extend_out));
}
```

Listing 5-6. "to_ascii.c"

```
/***********************************************************
 * Extended characters are just like regular strings       *
 *       but with foreground color, background color,       *
 *       and blinking added.                                *
 *                                                          *
 ***********************************************************/
#include "x_string.h"
#include "x_param.h"
#include "conio.h"

/*
 * Store a character and move pointer up one
 */
#define STORE_CH(ch) {*out_ptr = (ch);out_ptr++;}
/***********************************************************
 * extend_to_stand -- convert extended string to           *
 *                     normal string                        *
 *                                                          *
 * Parameters                                               *
 *       extended -- extended character string              *
 *                                                          *
 * Returns                                                  *
 *       standard -- standard character string              *
 *                                                          *
 ***********************************************************/
char *extend_to_stand(x_char *extended)
{
    /* output string */
    static char out_string[MAX_STRING];
    char *out_ptr;              /* Pointer to next output character */
```

continued

Listing 5-6 continued. •

```
char ch;                        /* The actual character */

/* These start out at -1 to force output of color/blink
    selectors */
char cur_blink = -1;         /* current blink attribute */
char cur_back = -1;          /* current background */
char cur_text = -1;          /* current text color */
/* current light/dark part of text color */
char cur_light_dark = -1;
char this_blink;             /* blink attribute of this char */
char this_back;              /* background of this char */
char this_text;              /* text color of this char*/
char this_light_dark;        /* light/dark text color this char */

/* The blink attribute characters */
static char blink_array[] = {X_BLINK_OFF, X_BLINK_ON};

/* The background attributes */
static char back_array[] = {
    X_BACK_BLACK,            /* 0 */
    X_BACK_BLUE,             /* 1 */
    X_BACK_GREEN,            /* 2 */
    X_BACK_CYAN,             /* 4 */
    X_BACK_RED,              /* 5 */
    X_BACK_MAGENTA,          /* 6 */
    X_BACK_BROWN,            /* 7 */
    X_BACK_GRAY              /* 8 */
};


/* The text attributes */
static char text_array[] = {
    X_TEXT_BLACK,            /* 0 */
    X_TEXT_BLUE,             /* 1  (Dark) */
    X_TEXT_GREEN,            /* 2  (Dark) */
    X_TEXT_CYAN,             /* 3  (Dark) */
    X_TEXT_RED,              /* 4  (Dark) */
    X_TEXT_MAGENTA,          /* 5  (Dark) */
    X_TEXT_BROWN,            /* 6 */
    X_TEXT_GRAY,             /* 7  (Light) */
    X_TEXT_GRAY,             /* 8  (Dark) */
    X_TEXT_BLUE,             /* 9  (Light) */
    X_TEXT_GREEN,            /* 10 (Light) */
    X_TEXT_CYAN,             /* 11 (Light) */
    X_TEXT_RED,              /* 12 (Light) */
    X_TEXT_MAGENTA,          /* 13 (Light) */
```

continued

Listing 5-6 continued.

```
                X_TEXT_YELLOW,            /* 14 */
                X_TEXT_WHITE              /* 15 */
    };

#define ANY 'a'
    /* The light/dark part of text attributes */
    static char light_dark_array[] = {
        ANY,              /* BLACK    0 */
        X_TEXT_DARK,      /* BLUE     1  (Dark) */
        X_TEXT_DARK,      /* GREEN    2  (Dark) */
        X_TEXT_DARK,      /* CYAN     3  (Dark) */
        X_TEXT_DARK,      /* RED      4  (Dark) */
        X_TEXT_DARK,      /* MAGENTA  5  (Dark) */
        ANY,              /* BROWN    6 */
        X_TEXT_LIGHT,     /* GRAY     7  (Light) */
        X_TEXT_DARK,      /* GRAY     8  (Dark) */
        X_TEXT_LIGHT,     /* BLUE     9  (Light) */
        X_TEXT_LIGHT,     /* GREEN   10  (Light) */
        X_TEXT_LIGHT,     /* CYAN    11  (Light) */
        X_TEXT_LIGHT,     /* RED     12  (Light) */
        X_TEXT_LIGHT,     /* MAGENTA 13  (Light) */
        ANY,              /* YELLOW  14 */
        ANY               /* WHITE   15 */
    };


    out_ptr = out_string;
    while (*extended != 0) {
        this_blink = (*extended >> 15) & 0x1;
        this_back  = (*extended >> 12) & 0x7;
        this_text  = (*extended >> 8)  & 0xF;

        if (this_blink != cur_blink) {
            cur_blink = this_blink;
            STORE_CH(X_CHAR);
            STORE_CH(blink_array[cur_blink]);
        }

        if (this_back != cur_back) {
            cur_back = this_back;
            STORE_CH(X_CHAR);
            STORE_CH(back_array[cur_back]);
        }

        if (this_text != cur_text) {
```

continued

Listing 5-6 continued.

```
                    /* First see if the light/dark is correctly set */
                    this_light_dark = light_dark_array[this_text];

                    if ((this_light_dark != cur_light_dark) &&
                        (this_light_dark != ANY)) {

                        cur_light_dark = this_light_dark;
                        STORE_CH(X_CHAR);
                        STORE_CH(this_light_dark);
                    }

                    cur_text = this_text;
                    STORE_CH(X_CHAR);
                    STORE_CH(text_array[cur_text]);
                }

            ch = *extended & 0xFF;
            if (ch == X_CHAR)
                STORE_CH(X_CHAR);
            STORE_CH(ch);
            extended++;
        }
    STORE_CH('\0');
    return (out_string);
}
```

Listing 5-7. "to_x.c"

```
/***********************************************************
 * Extended characters are just like regular strings       *
 *      but with foreground color, background color,        *
 *      and blinking added.                                 *
 *                                                          *
 ***********************************************************/
#include "x_string.h"
#include "x_param.h"
#include "conio.h"

#define TEXT(color)\
    {attrib = (attrib & 0xf0ff) | ((color) << 8);}
#define BACK(color) \
    {attrib = (attrib & 0x8fff) | ((color) << 12);}
#define SET_BLINK(blink) \
    {attrib = (attrib & 0x7fff) | ((blink) << 8);}
```

continued

Listing 5-7 continued.

```
/* attribute for monochrome underline on */
#define A_UNDERLINE_ON  BLUE
/* attribute for monochrome underline off */
#define A_UNDERLINE_OFF WHITE
/* attribute for monochrome reverse video */
#define A_REVERSE       0x7000
/* attribute for monochrome normal video */
#define A_NORMAL        0x0700
/* Mask to isolate reverse video bits */
#define REV_MASK        0x7F00
/***********************************************************
 * stand_to_extend -- converts standard char string       *
 *              to an extended version                     *
 *                                                         *
 * Parameters                                              *
 *      standard -- standard character string (in)         *
 *                                                         *
 * Returns                                                 *
 *      extended -- extended character string (out)        *
 *                                                         *
 *      Errors are ignored                                 *
 ***********************************************************/
x_char *stand_to_extend(char *standard)
{
    /* place to put the output character */
    static x_char out_string[MAX_STRING];

    /* attributes of this char */
    /* Initially, white characters on black screen */
    int attrib = ((BLACK << 4) | WHITE) << 8;

    /* color flag for light/dark toggle */
    enum {DARK, LIGHT} light_dark = LIGHT;

    char *in_ptr;         /* pointer to input string */
    x_char *out_ptr;      /* pointer to output string */

    out_ptr = out_string;         /* start at the beginning */
    for (in_ptr = standard; *in_ptr != '\0'; in_ptr++) {

        /* check for escape character */
        if (*in_ptr == X_CHAR) {
            in_ptr++;          /* move to character after escape */

            switch (*in_ptr) {
```

continued

Listing 5-7 continued.

```
                    /* Escape/Escape -- put escape in output */
                    case X_CHAR:
                            /* Same as default */

                    /* Ignore errors */
                    default:
                        *out_ptr = attrib | (*in_ptr & 0xFF);
                        out_ptr++;
                        break;

                    /* Set text color to black              */
                    case X_TEXT_BLACK:
                        TEXT(BLACK);
                        break;

                    /* Set text color to blue               */
                    case X_TEXT_BLUE:
                        if (light_dark == LIGHT)
                            TEXT(LIGHTBLUE)
                        else
                            TEXT(BLUE)
                        break;

                    /* Set text color to green              */
                    case X_TEXT_GREEN:
                        if (light_dark == LIGHT)
                            TEXT(LIGHTGREEN)
                        else
                            TEXT(GREEN)
                        break;

                    /* Set text color to cyan               */
                    case X_TEXT_CYAN:
                        if (light_dark == LIGHT)
                            TEXT(LIGHTCYAN)
                        else
                            TEXT(CYAN)
                        break;

                    /* Set text color to red                */
                    case X_TEXT_RED:
                        if (light_dark == LIGHT)
                            TEXT(LIGHTRED)
                        else
                            TEXT(RED)
```

continued

Listing 5-7 continued.

```
                    break;

        /* Set text color to magenta    */
        case X_TEXT_MAGENTA:
            if (light_dark == LIGHT)
                TEXT(LIGHTMAGENTA)
            else
                TEXT(MAGENTA)
            break;

        /* Set text color to brown            */
        case X_TEXT_BROWN:
            TEXT(BROWN);
            break;


        /* Set text color to gray             */
        case X_TEXT_GRAY:
            if (light_dark == LIGHT)
                TEXT(LIGHTGRAY)
            else
                TEXT(DARKGRAY)
            break;

        /* Set text color to yellow           */
        case X_TEXT_YELLOW:
            TEXT(YELLOW);
            break;

        /* Set text color to white      */
        case X_TEXT_WHITE:
            TEXT(WHITE)
            break;

        /* text colors come from light set    */
        case X_TEXT_LIGHT:
            light_dark = LIGHT;
            break;

        /* text colors come from the dark set */
        case X_TEXT_DARK:
            light_dark = LIGHT;
            break;


        /* Set background color to black      */
        case X_BACK_BLACK:
```

continued

Listing 5-7 continued.

```
                                 BACK(BLACK);
                                 break;

                      /* Set background color to blue */
                      case X_BACK_BLUE:
                          BACK(BLUE);
                          break;

                      /* Set background color to green        */
                      case X_BACK_GREEN:
                          BACK(GREEN);
                          break;

                      /* Set background color to cyan */
                      case X_BACK_CYAN:
                          BACK(CYAN);
                          break;

                      /* Set background color to red  */
                      case X_BACK_RED:
                          BACK(RED);
                          break;

                      /* Set background color to magenta       */
                      case X_BACK_MAGENTA:
                          BACK(MAGENTA);
                          break;


                      /* Set background color to brown        */
                      case X_BACK_BROWN:
                          BACK(BROWN);
                          break;

                      /* Set background color to gray */
                      case X_BACK_GRAY:
                          BACK(LIGHTGRAY);
                          break;

                      /* Set blinking text */
                      case X_BLINK_ON:
                          SET_BLINK(BLINK);
                          break;

                      /* Set non-blinking text */
```

continued

Listing 5-7 continued.

```
                            case X_BLINK_OFF:
                                SET_BLINK(0);
                                break;

                            /*
                             * For monochrome monitors
                             */
                            /* Reverse video */
                            case REVERSE:
                                attrib = (attrib & (~REV_MASK)) | A_REVERSE;
                                break;

                            /* Normal video */
                            case NORMAL:
                                attrib = (attrib & (~REV_MASK)) | A_NORMAL;
                                break;

                            /* Underline      */
                            case UNDERLINE_ON:
                                TEXT(A_UNDERLINE_ON);
                                break;

                            /* Underline off */
                            case UNDERLINE_OFF:
                                TEXT(A_UNDERLINE_OFF);
                                break;
                        }
                } else {
                    /* character is not escaped */
                    *out_ptr = attrib | (*in_ptr & 0xFF);
                    out_ptr++;
                }
        }

        *out_ptr = 0;
        return (out_string);
}
```

Listing 5-8. "x_printf.c"

```c
#include "x_string.h"
#include "x_param.h"
#include <stdio.h>
#include <stdarg.h>

/***********************************************************
 * x_printf -- perform printf on an extended string       *
 *                                                         *
 * Parameters                                              *
 *      format -- the printf style format (extended        *
 *                              string)                    *
 *      arg(s) -- arguments to printf                      *
 *                                                         *
 * Returns                                                 *
 *      number of bytes output                             *
 ***********************************************************/
int x_printf(x_char *format, ...)
{
    va_list arg_list;               /* argument list */

    char out_string[MAX_STRING];/* str to send after sprintf */
    x_char *extend_out;             /* Extended string to output */

    va_start(arg_list, format);
    (void)vsprintf(out_string,
                    extend_to_stand(format), arg_list);
    va_end(arg_list);

    extend_out = x_puts(stand_to_extend(out_string));
    if (extend_out == 0)
        return (0);

    return(x_strlen(extend_out));
}
```

Listing 5-9. "x_puts.c"

```c
/***********************************************************
 * x_puts -- output a string to the console               *
 ***********************************************************/
#include "x_string.h"
#include "x_param.h"
#include <conio.h>
/***********************************************************
 * x_puts -- output a string to the console               *
```

continued

Listing 5-9 continued.

```
 *                                                         *
 * Parameters                                              *
 *      string -- extended string to output               *
 *                                                         *
 * Returns                                                 *
 *      # characters output if successful                  *
 *      -1 for error                                       *
 *                                                         *
 * Note: This routine does NOT add a newline like          *
 *       puts.  It works more like cputs and fputs          *
 ***********************************************************/
int x_puts(x_char *string)
{
    /*
     * cur_attrib starts out at an impossible value to force
     * a textattr call.  We don't know what attributes the user
     * left set, so we make sure to start our own out right
     */
    int cur_attrib = -1;    /* current attribute for output */
    int char_count = 0;     /* # characters output so far */
    int new_attrib;         /* attribute of current character */

    /* Loop until we run out of string */
    while (*string != 0) {
        new_attrib = X_ATTRIB_PART(*string);

        /* If attributes changed -- then tell console */
        if (new_attrib != cur_attrib) {
            textattr(new_attrib);
            cur_attrib = new_attrib;
        }

        if (putch(X_CHAR_PART(*string)) < 0)
            return (-1);

        char_count++;
        string++;
    }
    return (char_count);
}
```

Listing 5-10. "x_sprint.c"

```
#include "x_string.h"
#include "x_param.h"
#include <stdio.h>
#include <stdarg.h>


/************************************************************
 * x_sprintf -- perform sprintf on an extended string      *
 *                                                          *
 * Parameters                                               *
 *      out_string -- string to store result               *
 *      format -- the printf style format (extended         *
 *                                string)                   *
 *      arg(s) -- arguments to sprintf                      *
 *                                                          *
 * Returns                                                  *
 *      number of bytes output                              *
 ************************************************************/
int x_sprintf(x_char *out_string,x_char *format, ...)
{
    va_list arg_list;                /* argument list */

    char sprintf_string[MAX_STRING];   /* string after sprintf */

    va_start(arg_list, format);
    (void)vsprintf(sprintf_string,
                extend_to_stand(format), arg_list);
    va_end(arg_list);

    (void)x_strcpy(out_string, stand_to_extend(sprintf_string));

    return(x_strlen(out_string));
}
```

Listing 5-11. "x_strcat.c"

```
#include "x_string.h"
#include "x_param.h"
#include <limits.h>

/************************************************************
 * x_strcat -- concatenate an extended string              *
 *                                                          *
 * Parameters                                               *
 *      from -- string we copy from                        *
 *      to -- string we copy to                            *
```

continued

Listing 5-11 continued.

```
 *                                                         *
 * Returns                                                 *
 *       pointer to the result string                      *
 ***********************************************************/
x_char *x_strcat(x_char *to, x_char *from)
{
    return (x_strncat(to, from, UINT_MAX));
}
```

Listing 5-12. "x_strcmp.c"

```
#include "x_string.h"
#include "x_param.h"
#include <limits.h>

/***********************************************************
 * x_strcmp -- Compare extended string                     *
 *                                                         *
 * Parameters                                              *
 *       string1, string2 -- strings to check              *
 *                                                         *
 * Returns                                                 *
 *       0 -- strings equal                                *
 *       0< -- string1 < string2                           *
 *       0> -- string1 > string2                           *
 ***********************************************************/
int x_strcmp(x_char *string1, x_char *string2)
{
    return (x_strncmp(string1, string2, UINT_MAX));
}
```

Listing 5-13. "x_strcpy.c"

```
#include "x_string.h"
#include "x_param.h"
#include <limits.h>

/***********************************************************
 * x_strcpy -- copy an extended string                     *
 *                                                         *
 * Parameters                                              *
 *       from -- string we copy from                       *
 *       to -- string we copy to                           *
 *                                                         *
```

continued

Listing 5-13 continued.

```
 * Returns                                                        *
 *      pointer to the result string                             *
 ************************************************************/
x_char *x_strcpy(x_char *to, x_char *from)
{
    return (x_strncpy(to, from, UINT_MAX));
}
```

Listing 5-14. "x_strlen.c"

```
#include "x_string.h"
#include "x_param.h"

/************************************************************
 * x_strlen -- compute the length of an extended string *
 *                                                        *
 * Parameters                                             *
 *      string -- we want the length of this string       *
 *                                                        *
 * Returns                                                *
 *      length of the string                              *
 ************************************************************/
unsigned int x_strlen(x_char *string)
{
    /* pointer to the end of the string */
    register x_char *str_end;

    for (str_end = string; *str_end != 0; str_end++)
        /* do nothing */;

        return ((unsigned int)(str_end - string));
}
```

Listing 5-15. "xstrncat.c"

```
#include "x_string.h"
#include "x_param.h"

/************************************************************
 * x_strncat -- concatenate an extended string (limited)*
 *                                                        *
 * Parameters                                             *
 *      from -- string we copy from                       *
 *      to -- string we copy to                           *
```

continued

Listing 5-15 continued.

```
*        length -- maximum length                            *
*                                                            *
* Returns                                                    *
*        pointer to the result string                        *
*                                                            *
* Warning:                                                   *
*        This function is similar to strncat                 *
*        and will NOT copy a null if we run out              *
*        of length.                                          *
 ***********************************************************/
x_char *x_strncat(x_char *to, x_char *from, size_t length)
{
    x_char *old_to = to;           /* save to pointer */

    for (/* to from list */; *to != 0; to++)
        /* find end of string */;

    while (length > 0) {
        *to = *from;

        if (*to == 0)
            return (old_to);

        to++;
        from++;
        length--;
    }
    return (old_to);
}
```

Listing 5-16. "xstrncmp.c"

```
#include "x_string.h"
#include "x_param.h"

#define CHAR(x) ((x) & 0xFF)     /* Character part of x_char */
/***********************************************************
 * x_strncmp -- compare extended strings (chars only        *
 *                      not attributes)                      *
 *                                                           *
 * Parameters                                                *
 *        string1 -- one string to check against             *
 *        string2 -- the other string                        *
 *        length -- maximum length                           *
 *                                                           *
```

continued

Listing 5-16 continued.

```
 * Returns                                                         *
 *       0 -- strings equal                                        *
 *       <0 -- string1 < string2                                   *
 *       >0 -- string1 > string2                                    *
 ************************************************************/
int x_strncmp(x_char *string1, x_char *string2, size_t length)
{
    while (length > 0) {
        if (CHAR(*string1) != CHAR(*string2))
            break;

        /* if one string ends, get out */
        if (CHAR(*string1) == 0)
            break;

        if (CHAR(*string2) == 0)
            break;

        string1++;
        string2++;
        length--;
    }
    /*
     * At this point either we have a mismatch or we've reached
     * the end.
     */
    return (CHAR(*string1) - CHAR(*string2));
}
```

Listing 5-17. "xtrcncmp.c"

```
#include "x_string.h"
#include "x_param.h"

/*************************************************************
 * x_strncpy -- copy an extended string (limited)          *
 *                                                          *
 * Parameters                                               *
 *      from -- string we copy from                         *
 *      to -- string we copy to                             *
 *      length -- maximum length                            *
 *                                                          *
 * Returns                                                  *
 *      pointer to the result string                        *
 *                                                          *
```

continued

Listing 5-17 continued.

```
 * Warning:                                                    *
 *      This function is similar to strncpy                    *
 *      and will NOT copy a null if we run out                 *
 *      of length.                                             *
 ************************************************************/
x_char *x_strncpy(x_char *to, x_char *from, size_t length)
{
    x_char *old_to = to;           /* save to pointer */

    while (length > 0) {
        *to = *from;

        if (*to == 0)
            return (old_to);

        to++;
        from++;
        length--;
    }
    return (old_to);
}
```

Simple Interrupts and TSR Programming

Introduction

So far, we've been working with sequential programs. That is, where one instruction follows another in an orderly fashion. To really use the power of your computer, you need to understand interrupt level programming.

This is the most difficult and complex type of programming. Debugging an interrupt program can be very frustrating since problems can occur randomly.

One of the classic cases of an interrupt-related bug causing trouble concerned the software for the first space shuttle. There was an error in the code that had a 1 out of 32 chance of happening each time the computer was started. All through the extensive test phase of the project, the system worked. However, during the countdown for the first launch, the bug triggered and forced the first mission to be scrubbed.

In this chapter, we will introduce you to the interrupt and give you a set of rules for designing interrupt functions. By careful programming, you can greatly reduce the chance for errors and produce more reliable code.

What Is an Interrupt?

There are two main types of interrupts on the 8086 processor: software and hardware. Although they have a similar structure and share a common interrupt vector table, they are vastly different.

Software interrupts occur when a program executes an interrupt (INT) instruction. DOS programs use software interrupts to communicate with the operating system. You can think of software interrupts as a specialized type of function call.

Hardware interrupts occur when an I/O device needs servicing. For example, when you press a key, the keyboard generates an interrupt. These interrupts are event oriented. That is, they are caused by outside events such as a key being pressed, a disk read finishing, or a line printer printing a character. Interrupts can occur at any time during a program.

Software Interrupts

In DOS, software interrupts are used to perform operating system functions. For example, to send a character to the screen, you use interrupt 0x21.

```
Mov     AH,0x6      ;Function code 6
Mov     DL,Ch       ;Get character to send
Int     21h         ;Ask DOS to print the character
```

DOS was designed to be programmed in assembly language. The interface between DOS and the application is simple; while in C, we must go through many contortions to do the same thing. The equivalent code written in Turbo C is:

```
#include <dos.h>
send_ch(char ch)
{
    _AH = 6;
    _DL = ch;
    geninterrupt(0x21);
}
```

Let's examine in detail what happens when we execute a software interrupt. When the 8086 executes an interrupt instruction, it gets the address of the interrupt handler from an address table located at 0000:0000 through

0000:0400. Each entry in the table contains a far pointer to an interrupt routine.

The processor uses this address to call the interrupt function. In this case, the interrupt function is part of DOS which checks the AH register and performs the appropriate function. This may take some time. When DOS is finished, it puts any results in the registers and returns to the instruction after the interrupt.

The following rules apply to software interrupts:

1. They occur only when the program asks for them by executing an INT instruction.

2. The interrupt service routine can take a long time before it returns from the interrupt. In some cases, like a terminate request, it will never return.

3. Parameters are passed in registers. The interrupt service function inside DOS knows what the registers contain and uses registers like AH to hold function codes.

4. The interrupt service routine can change the registers before it returns.

Hardware Interrupts

Hardware interrupts are generated by I/O devices when they need service. For example, the keyboard generates an interrupt every time a key is pressed. This is the keyboard's way of telling the processor that it wants attention.

The 8086 services hardware interrupts just like software interrupts. Each interrupt number has its own interrupt service routine whose address is stored in the table at 0000:0000 through 0000:0400.

Hardware interrupts may occur at any time during the execution of a program. For that reason they must preserve all the registers and flags during their execution. Failure to do this may cause very strange programming problems. Suppose we had an interrupt routine that changed the value of AX to 5. Then the following code would not work (sometimes):

```
MOV      AX,offset 1              ;Initialize AX
ADD      BX,AX                    ;Increment BX
```

As long as we don't get an interrupt after the first instruction we are OK. But if an interrupt occurs the value of AX will be changed to five. So suddenly we are adding five to BX instead of one.

Hardware interrupt service routines should be short. This is for two reasons. During an interrupt, all interrupts are turned off. A device can wait a short time for service, but not long. For example, the COM port can hold one incoming character. If the port is not read within the time it takes to receive the next character, the first one is lost. The second reason is that interrupt level programming is extremely difficult and tricky. The shorter the routine, the less chance of something going wrong.

Finally, an interrupt routine cannot use any DOS services. DOS is designed to be used by programs, not interrupt service routines. A request from an interrupt service routine can be very confusing and easily result in a hard system crash.

A Very Simple Interrupt Routine

The system clock executes a level 8 interrupt 65,536 times an hour. We wish to time how long it takes to type in a line of text. Turbo C uses the non-standard keyword **interrupt** to indicate that a function is an **interrupt** handler. A special code for this function that saves all the registers and flags will be generated. Also, the function will end with an interrupt return (RETI) instruction instead of the normal return (RET).

NOTE   The state of the floating point unit is not saved so our interrupt routine should not use any floating point.

The interrupt routine for our clock interrupt is very simple:

```
int time = 0;          /* Time in ticks since we started */

void interrupt clock_interrupt();
{
    time++;
}
```

Now all we need to do is let DOS know that we want this function to be attached to interrupt 8. This is done through the setvect() routine.

```
void interrupt clock_interrupt(void);

main()
{
    disable();
    setvect(8, clock_interrupt);
    enable();

    ....
}
```

The `enable()` and `disable()` functions are required and will be discussed later.

However, there is one problem. DOS already had a clock interrupt handler and won't work if we overwrite it. Our solution is to have our interrupt routine call the old interrupt routine.

To get the address of the interrupt routine use the function `getvect()`. So our code now looks like:

```
int time = 0;            /* Time in ticks since we started */

/* Pointer to the interrupt old interrupt routine */
void interrupt (*dos_interrupt);

void interrupt clock_interrupt();
{
    time++;
    *dos_interrupt();        /* Call dos version of interrupt */
}

main()
{
    dos_interrupt = getvect(8);

    disable();
    setvect(8, clock_interrupt);
    enable();

    ....
```

Finally, before our program exits, we must restore the old interrupt routine with the code:

```
disable();
setvect(8, dos_interrupt);
enable();
```

One word of caution. Our program does not protect itself against the user typing ^C or Break and exiting the program abnormally. If this happens, then the interrupt routine will not be restored. The system will still call our interrupt routine, even though the program has exited. The next program to be run will wipe out this section of memory, the interrupt routine will suddenly become random code, and the system will crash. The full program follows:

Listing 6-1. "time-in.c"

```
/**********************************************************
 * Time-In -- Time how long it takes to input a line      *
 *                                                         *
 * Usage:                                                  *
 *      time-in                                            *
 *               Type a line and time appears              *
 *                                                         *
 * Warning: Don't ^C out of this or the system will        *
 *          crash                                          *
 **********************************************************/
#include <stdio.h>
#include <dos.h>

#define TIME_INTERRUPT 8

int time = 0;    /* Time since we started (in ticks) */

/* The DOS version of the timer interrupt routine */
void interrupt (*dos_interrupt)(void);
/**********************************************************
 * clock_interrupt -- handle a clock tick                 *
 **********************************************************/
void interrupt clock_interrupt()
{
time++;
(*dos_interrupt)();
}

main()
{
    char line[80];         /* Line for input */

    /* Get the old interrupt */
    dos_interrupt = getvect(TIME_INTERRUPT);
```

continued

Listing 6-1 continued.

```
        disable();
        setvect(TIME_INTERRUPT, clock_interrupt);
        enable();

        (void)printf(
          "Warning: Do not use ^C to exit from this program\n");
        (void)printf("Enter a line of text\n");

        (void)fgets(line, sizeof(line), stdin);
        (void)printf("That took %d ticks\n", time);

        /* Get out of here */
        disable();
        setvect(TIME_INTERRUPT, dos_interrupt);
        enable();

        return (0);
}
```

Critical Code

Suppose that instead of timing how long it takes to type one line of input, we want to time 10 and produce a time for each line, as well as a total for all 10. We could write the programs:

Listing 6-2. "time-10.c"

```
/**********************************************************
 * Time-10 -- Time how long it takes to input 10 lines   *
 *                  Print total and sub-total            *
 *                                                        *
 * Usage:                                                 *
 *      time-in                                           *
 *                  Type a line and time appears          *
 *                                                        *
 * Warning: Don't ^C out of this or the system will       *
 *      crash                                             *
 *                                                        *
 * Warning: This program contains a minor flaw.           *
 **********************************************************/
#include <stdio.h>
#include <dos.h>

#define TIME_INTERRUPT 8        /* Interrupt vector for clock
```

continued

Listing 6-2 continued.

```
*/ #define MAX_LINES       10     /* Number of lines to time */

volatile int   line_time = 0;   /* Time for this line */
/* Time since we started (total) */

volatile int   total_time = 0;
int   times[MAX_LINES]; /* Times on a per line basis */

/* The DOS version of the timer interrupt routine */
void  interrupt(*dos_interrupt) (void);


/***********************************************************
 * clock_interrupt -- handle a clock tick               *
 ***********************************************************/
void interrupt clock_interrupt()
{
    line_time++;
    total_time++;
    (*dos_interrupt) ();
}

main()
{

    char   line[80];/* Line of text in */
    int    line_number;  /* current line number */
    int    final_total;  /* time for final time */

/* Get the old interrupt */
dos_interrupt = getvect(TIME_INTERRUPT);

disable();
setvect(TIME_INTERRUPT, clock_interrupt);
enable();

(void) printf(
      "Warning: Do not use ^C to exit from this program\n");

for (line_number = 0; line_number < MAX_LINES;
    line_number++) {
    (void) printf("Enter line number %d\n", line_number + 1);

    (void) fgets(line, sizeof(line), stdin);
    times[line_number] = line_time;
    line_time = 0;
```

continued

Listing 6-2 continued.

```
}
/*
 * Freeze total time --
 *          the clock will tick while we write out
 * times
 */
final_total = total_time;

for (line_number = 0; line_number < MAX_LINES;
     line_number++) {
    (void) printf("Time for line %2d: %3d\n",
                 line_number + 1, times[line_number]);
}
(void) printf("Total time %d\n", final_total);

        /* Get out of here */
        disable();
        setvect(TIME_INTERRUPT, dos_interrupt);
        enable();

    return (0);
}
```

However, when we run this, we notice that sometimes something strange happens: The total time does not agree with the times for the individual lines. In the following run, the times for the individual lines add up to 127, but the total time is 128. Somehow we lost a clock interrupt.

```
Time for line 1: 3
Time for line 2: 15
Time for line 3: 14
Time for line 4: 25
Time for line 5: 12
Time for line 6: 11
Time for line 7: 12
Time for line 8: 11
Time for line 9: 13
Time for line 10: 11
Total time 128
```

Solving a mystery like this can be a very difficult, frustrating and time consuming task. Interrupt routines are especially hard to debug (that is another reason to keep them short). A debugger won't work on an interrupt routine.

(Special equipment like logic analyzers and emulators are needed to debug large interrupt routines.) `printf` statements are not allowed. The program does not fail consistently, so there's no reliable way of even reproducing the problem.

Solving this problem requires close inspection of the code. First, we inspect the interrupt routine. No problem there, it's very simple and there's very little that can go wrong with it. Next we go through the code line by line asking the question, "What happens if I get an interrupt here?"

Going through the code we come to the lines:

```
times[line_number] = line_time;
line_time = 0;
```

What happens if we get an interrupt here?

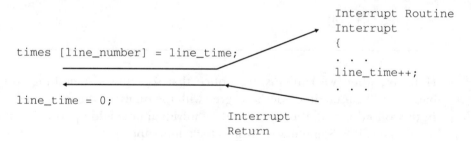

The variable `line_time` is stored before the interrupt. The interrupt occurs and it is incremented. The variable is then zeroed. The tick that occurred between these two lines is not credited to the current input time or the next input time, it is lost. This is how we can lose an interrupt.

These two lines must execute together if the program is to work properly. The technical term for a code like this is critical code or a critical section.

The function `disable()` turns off the interrupt system; the function `enable()` turns it on. Interrupts should only be turned off for short periods of time. Any interrupt that occurs while interrupts are disabled will be deferred until they are turned on again. One interrupt per device is stacked, so if interrupts are turned off for two clock ticks, the second interrupt will be lost. Our critical code looks like:

```
/*
 * Critical code (must execute without interrupt)
 */

disable();
times[line_number] = line_time;
line_time = 0;
enable();
```

You may have noticed that we have bracketed our calls to setvect() with disable() and enable(). This is because this function is considered critical code. An interrupt table entry is 4 bytes long. The function setvect() takes two instructions to store the new address. If it gets half way through the process when an interrupt occurs, the system will use the mangled interrupt vector address to branch off to an unknown location. So the process of changing the interrupt vector must not be interrupted.

The full code for our fixed timing routine is:

Listing 6-3. "time-10b.c"

```
/**********************************************************
 * Time-10 -- Time how long it takes to input 10 lines   *
 *               Print total and sub-total                *
 *                                                        *
 * Usage:                                                 *
 *      time-in                                           *
 *               Type a line and time appears             *
 *                                                        *
 * Warning: Don't ^C out of this or the system will       *
 *      crash                                             *
 **********************************************************/
#include <stdio.h>
#include <dos.h>

#define TIME_INTERRUPT 8       /* Interrupt vector for clock */
#define MAX_LINES      10       /* Number of lines to time */

int line_time = 0;      /* Time for this line */
int total_time = 0;     /* Time since we started (total) */
int times[MAX_LINES];   /* Times on a per line basis */

/* The DOS version of the timer interrupt routine */
void interrupt (*dos_interrupt)(void);

/**********************************************************
```

continued

Listing 6-3 continued.

```
 * clock_interrupt -- handle a clock tick                *

 ***********************************************************/
void interrupt clock_interrupt()
{
    line_time++;
    total_time++;
    (*dos_interrupt)();
}

main()
{
    char line[80];        /* Line of text in */
    int line_number;      /* current line number */
    int final_total;      /* time for final time */

    /* Get the old interrupt */
    dos_interrupt = getvect(TIME_INTERRUPT);

    disable();
    setvect(TIME_INTERRUPT, clock_interrupt);
    enable();

    (void)printf(
            "Warning: Do not use ^C to exit from this program\n");

    for (line_number = 0; line_number < MAX_LINES;
         line_number++) {
        (void)printf("Enter line number %d\n", line_number+1);

        (void)fgets(line, sizeof(line), stdin);

        /*
         * Critical code (must execute without interrupt)
         */
        disable();
        times[line_number] = line_time;
        line_time = 0;
        enable();
    }
    /*
     * Freeze total time --
     *   the clock will tick while we write out times
     */
    final_total = total_time;
```

continued

Listing 6-3 continued.

```
        for (line_number = 0; line_number < MAX_LINES;
            line_number++) {
            (void)printf("Time for line %2d: %3d\n",
            line_number + 1, times[line_number]);
    }
    (void)printf("Total time %d\n", final_total);

    /* Get out of here */
    disable();
    setvect(TIME_INTERRUPT, dos_interrupt);
    enable();

    return (0);
}
```

Context Switches

DOS is a single tasking operating system. That is, it executes only one program at a time. Multitasking executes many programs simultaneously. However, DOS does allow one program to run another program. This is done when the parent program calls the Turbo C `spwanl` (or related) function. DOS will put the parent into hibernation, and start executing the new program.

Each program has its own set of open files and other system dependent data. DOS saves this information in a Program Segment Prefix (PSP).

When a spawn request is made, DOS executes the following steps:

1. It creates a PSP for the new process.
2. The program is loaded into the free memory above the currently executing programs.
3. The new PSP becomes the current PSP.
4. DOS sets a new Data Transfer Address (DTA). (This address is used by DOS for all disk I/Os).
5. Control is transferred to the start address new program.

Suppose we had a menu program called "MENU". It, in turn, called various application programs like a word processor "WP". While WP is running, all other programs are suspended. Our memory map would look like:

```
┌─────────────────────────────┐
│      Interrupt Vectors      │
├─────────────────────────────┤
│            DOS              │
├─────────────────────────────┤
│        COMMAND.COM          │
├─────────────────────────────┤
│            MENU             │
├─────────────────────────────┤
│            WP               │
├─────────────────────────────┤
│                             │
│            FREE             │
│                             │
└─────────────────────────────┘
```

When the program exits, DOS does the following:

1. Returns the memory used by the program to the free pool.
2. Destroys the PSP.
3. Restores the old DTA.
4. Changes the current PSP to the PSP of the program that executed the spawn request.

In our previous example, when WP exits, the execution of "MENU" resumes.

```
┌─────────────────────────────┐
│      Interrupt Vectors      │
├─────────────────────────────┤
│            DOS              │
├─────────────────────────────┤
│        COMMAND.COM          │
├─────────────────────────────┤
│            MENU             │
├─────────────────────────────┤
│                             │
│            FREE             │
│                             │
└─────────────────────────────┘
```

It may seem like we are going into excessive detail about a simple DOS process, but when we take up Terminate and Stay Resident programs in the next chapter you'll see how important it is to understand this process.

TSR Programming

TSR (Terminate and Stay Resident) programs provide a number of useful functions, yet DOS was never designed to handle these types of programs.

DOS was designed to handle a single task at a time. One of the first TSR programs was the "PRINT" command, which is used to spool data to the line printer; however, the DOS interrupts used by this program were not documented because the designers of DOS did not think that ordinary users would ever write TSR programs.

Early hackers discovered these undocumented system calls and started writing programs which used them. Although the interfaces for TSR programs are well known, the support is still minimal, forcing the programmer to do a great deal of work to get their program to function properly.

A Minimal TSR Program

We work on several different computers with different keyboards. All are laid out the same, except that my PC keyboard has a "CAPS LOCK" key where the "CONTROL" key should be. This is most annoying.

On the PC-AT, PC-XT and later systems, the BIOS has a keyboard interrupt function. Every time a key is pressed, an INT 15 is generated with AH set to 0x4F and AL containing the scan code of the key. This interrupt is designed to be used by keyboard translators.

We want to translate the scan code for CAPS LOCK (0x3A) to CONTROL (0x1D). When a key is pressed the scan code will appear in AL. When the key is released, AL will contain the scan code plus 0x80.

Our TSR hooks a translation interrupt routine onto interrupt 15. Interrupt routines in Turbo C can take no parameters or the parameters `bp`, `di`, `si`, `ds`, `es`, `dx`, `cx`, `bx`, `ax`, `ip`, `cs`, `flags`.

The program uses the `keep` function to exit with a terminate and stay resident system call. This function takes two parameters, the return status and the size of the program. We will discuss how to compute this parameter later.

The program uses the Turbo C special variable `_stklen` to allocate a shorter than normal stack. After all, this is a very simple program. It uses no heap space, so the length of the heap is set to 2 by using the Turbo C special variable `_heaplen`. (We don't use zero for the heap length, because zero is a signal to Turbo C to make the heap as large as possible.)

The regular portion of the program ends with a call to the keep function. This function takes two arguments, an exit code and the size of the program in paragraphs. The exit code is easy, we use zero—normal exit. The size of the program must be computed.

Looking at a memory map for all models, we find that the stack segment is at the end sometimes followed by a heap segment. Since the heap is unusable in TSR programs, the Stack segment is the last useful segment. The variable _psp points to the program segment prefix for this program.

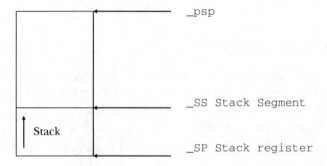

This is our first address. So we need to reserve the space from _psp:0000 to _SP:_SS plus a fudge factor to make sure that we allocate enough space. The result is the number of paragraphs (16-byte chunks) for the keep function.

```
keep_size = _SS - _psp + (_SP / 16) + 50;
```

This equation works for all models. The full program is:

Listing 6-4. "trans.c"

```
/*******************************************************
 * trans -- translate the CAPS-LOCK key into the       *
 *       control KEY.  A very simple TSR program.       *
 *******************************************************/
#include <dos.h>

/*******************************************************
 * Define Various Interrupt Vectors                     *
 *******************************************************/
#define KBD_INT        0x15      /* keyboard interrupt */
#define KBD_FUNCTION   0x4F      /* keyboard function code */

/* Scan codes */
```

continued

Listing 6-4 continued.

```
#define CAPS_LOCK   0x3A
#define CONTROL     0x1D

unsigned int _heaplen = 2;       /* Use no heap */
unsigned int _stlken = 1024;     /* Use almost no stack */

#define u_int unsigned int
#define INTERRUPT_REGS u_int bp,u_int di,u_int si, \
        u_int ds,u_int es,\
        u_int dx,u_int cx,u_int bx,u_int ax,\
        u_int ip,u_int cs,u_int flags
#define INTERRUPT_PARAM bp,di,si,ds,es,dx,cx,bx,ax,ip,cs,flags

/* Old keyboard interrupt routine */
static void interrupt (*old_keyboard)();
/***********************************************************
 * new_keyboard -- handle keyboard translate interrupt   *
 *                                                        *
 * Parameters                                             *
 *      interrupt registers                               *
 *                                                        *
 * Returns                                                *
 *      AX is changed if this is the CAPS_LOCK key        *
 ***********************************************************/
#pragma warn -par         /* Turn parameter checking off */
void interrupt new_keyboard(INTERRUPT_REGS)
{
if (_AH == KBD_FUNCTION) {
    /* Check for key pressed */
    if (_AL == CAPS_LOCK)
        _AL = CONTROL;

    /* Check for key release */
    if (_AL == (CAPS_LOCK|0x80))
        _AL = (CONTROL|0x80);

    /* Save results */
    ax = _AX;
}
_FLAGS = flags;
_AX = ax;
(*old_keyboard)();
ax = _AX;
flags = _FLAGS;
bx = _BX;
cx = _CX;
```

continued

Listing 6-4 continued.

```
       dx = _DX;
       si = _SI;
       di = _DI;
       es = _ES;
       }
#pragma warn .par          /* Turn parameter checking on */

int main(void)
       {
       /* Size of program in paragraphs */
       static unsigned keep_size;

       disable();
       old_keyboard = getvect(KBD_INT);
       setvect(KBD_INT, new_keyboard);
       enable();

       keep_size = _SS - _psp + (_SP / 16) + 50;
       keep(0, keep_size);

       /* Keep compiler happy  -- not really reached */
       return (0);
}
```

A Step Back

We have shown you the final program, but not the work that went into it.
Before creating this program we had to know the scan code for the CAPS
LOCK and CONTROL keys. If you are lucky you have a DOS reference book
which contains a list of scan codes. If you are typical, you don't and must resort
to experimentation.

So we write a short program to discover key codes:

Listing 6-5. "keys.c"

```
/**********************************************************
 * Keys -- a simple program to display the value          *
 *           scan and character codes                      *
 *                                                         *
 * This program establishes an interrupt handler for       *
 * interrupt 15 which prints out scan codes.               *
 *                                                         *
 * The main loop waits for keystrokes and prints           *
```

continued

Listing 6-5 continued.

```
 * keycodes.                                              *
 *                                                        *
 * Warning: This program should only be exited with the  *
 *      escape key.  Anything else will leave the         *
 *      interrupt handler turned on and cause             *
 *      a system crash                                    *
 *                                                        *
 * Note: This program does NOT follow the rules           *
 *      governing interrupts since it calls DOS from      *
 *      an interrupt routine                              *
 ********************************************************/
#define KBD_INT        0x15     /* keyboard interrupt */
#define KBD_FUNCTION   0x4F     /* keyboard function code */

#define ESC 0x1b                /* escape character */
#include <conio.h>
#include <dos.h>
#include <stdio.h>

/*
 * Register structure passed to an interrupt routine
 */
#define INTERRUPT_REGS int bp,int di,int si,int ds,int es,\
       int dx,int cx,int bx,int ax,int ip,int cs,int flags
#define INTERRUPT_PARAM bp,di,si,ds,es,dx,cx,bx,ax,ip,cs,flags

void interrupt kbd_interrupt(INTERRUPT_REGS);

/* old version of handler */
void interrupt (*old_interrupt)(INTERRUPT_REGS);

main(void)
{
    unsigned char ch;    /*  character from keyboard */

    disable();
    /* save old handler, establish new one */
    old_interrupt = getvect(KBD_INT);
    setvect(KBD_INT, kbd_interrupt);
    enable();

    while (1) {
        ch = getch();

        if (ch == ESC)
            break;
```

continued

Listing 6-5 continued.

```
            (void)printf("Char:%x\n", ch);
    }
    disable();
    setvect(KBD_INT, old_interrupt);
    enable();
    return (0);
    }
    /***********************************************************
     * kbd_interrupt -- keyboard interrupt handler          *
     ***********************************************************/
    void interrupt kbd_interrupt(INTERRUPT_REGS)
    {
    (void)printf("AX %x %x\n", ax);
    if ((ax >> 8) == KBD_FUNCTION) {
        (void)printf("Scan:%x\n", ax & 0xff);
    }
    (*old_interrupt)(INTERRUPT_PARAM);
}
```

This program has a problem. As long as we type single letters slowly, the program works. However, if we try the arrow keys on our extended keyboard, the system crashes. It's a hard crash, even Control-Alt-Delete won't work. (On some systems, even typing slowly won't work. You'll always crash.)

What's wrong? We broke the rules. One of the rules of an interrupt handler is that you can't execute a DOS function inside an interrupt handler. We have a `printf` in the middle of our interrupt function. That is illegal.

Why does the program work as long as we type single character? The simple answer is that we got lucky. However, the arrow keys on an extended keyboard send two scan codes resulting in two back to back interrupts. This results in the interrupt routine being interrupted, confusing the system so badly that only a power cycle will cure it.

The proper thing to do in our interrupt routine is to deposit the scan codes into an array for printing by the program's main loop. That way, our interrupt just moves data and the main program does the work.

That's the way most interrupt routines work. They stuff data into a memory so that they can be handled at a later time by a non-interrupt routine.

Listing 6-6 "keys2.c"

```
/**********************************************************
 * Keys -- a simple program to display the value         *
 *              scan and character codes                 *
 *                                                        *
 * This program establishes an interrupt handler for     *
 * interrupt 15 which prints out scan codes.             *
 *                                                        *
 * The main loop waits for keystrokes and prints         *
 * keycodes.                                             *
 *                                                        *
 * Warning: This program should only be exited with the  *
 *       escape key.  Anything else will leave the       *
 *       interrupt handler turned on and cause           *
 *       a system crash                                  *
 **********************************************************/
#define KBD_INT        0x15      /* keyboard interrupt */
#define KBD_FUNCTION   0x4F      /* keyboard function code */

#define ESC 0x1b                 /* escape character */
#include <conio.h>
#include <dos.h>
#include <stdio.h>

/*
 * Register structure passed to an interrupt routine
 */
#define INTERRUPT_REGS int bp,int di,int si,int ds,int es,\
        int dx,int cx,int bx,int ax,int ip,int cs,int flags
#define INTERRUPT_PARAMS bp,di,si,ds,es,dx,cx,bx,ax,ip,cs,flags

void interrupt kbd_interrupt(INTERRUPT_REGS);

/* old version of handler */
void interrupt (*old_interrupt)(INTERRUPT_REGS);

#define MAX_INDEX 10    /* Size of storage buffer */
unsigned char scan_buffer[MAX_INDEX];

int in_index = 0;
int out_index = 0;

main(void)
{
    unsigned char ch;   /*  character from keyboard */

    disable();
```

continued

Listing 6-6 continued.

```
        /* save old handler, establish new one */
        old_interrupt = getvect(KBD_INT);
        setvect(KBD_INT, kbd_interrupt);
        enable();

        while (1) {
            ch = getch();

            if (ch == ESC)
                break;

            (void)printf("Char:%x\n", ch);

            while (out_index != in_index) {
                (void)printf("Scan Code %x\n",
                             scan_buffer[out_index]);
                out_index = (out_index + 1) % MAX_INDEX;
            }
        }
        disable();
        setvect(KBD_INT, old_interrupt);
        enable();
        return (0);
}
/*************************************************************
 * kbd_interrupt -- keyboard interrupt handler             *
 *************************************************************/
void interrupt kbd_interrupt(INTERRUPT_REGS)
{
        static int ah;         /* Save register values */
        static int al;

        al = _AL;
        ah = _AH;

        if (ah == KBD_FUNCTION) {
            scan_buffer[in_index] = al;
            in_index = (in_index + 1) % MAX_INDEX;
        }
        (*old_interrupt)(INTERRUPT_PARAMS);
}
```

Argument Passing In Interrupt Routines

Argument handling in interrupt routines is completely different from normal C parameter passing. The calling routine puts the arguments in registers. It expects the software interrupt handler to return the data in the registers.

At the beginning of an interrupt routine, Turbo C pushes all the registers on the stack. At the end, they are restored from the stack. Unless special provisions are made, the function will not change the value of the registers.

To get to the registers returned to the caller, an interrupt routine must declare the registers as parameters:

```
#define u_int unsigned int    /* Shorthand */
void interrupt function(u_int bp, u_int di, u_int si,
                        u_int ds, u_int es, u_int dx,
                        u_int cx, u_int bx, u_int ax,
                        u_int ip, u_int cs, u_int flags)
```

Changing the value of these special parameters will cause the corresponding register to be when the function returns. For example, if the interrupt function sets ax=5 then the register AX will be set to five when the interrupt completes. Hardware interrupts handlers should never change registers; software interrupts handlers frequently change registers to return arguments to the caller.

Many interrupt routines are chained. An interrupt will be intercepted by one function and if it doesn't want to handle it, the data are passed on to the old interrupt routine. This means that our outer level interrupt routine must do some work. First, if the outer level interrupt routine executes any C code, it will destroy the registers, so it must shift the original registers from the parameters to the registers. Then it calls the inner level interrupt routine. This routine returns arguments in the registers. These must be stuffed back into the parameters so that they will reach the main program.

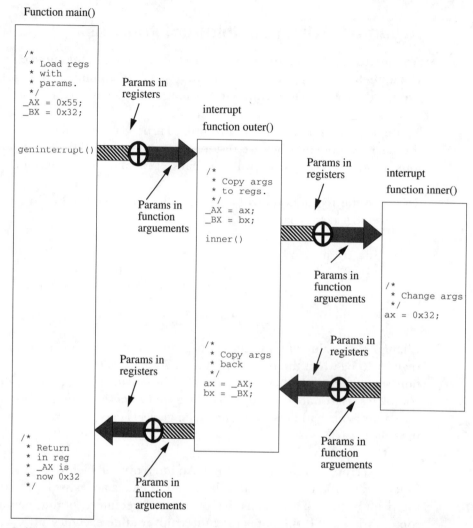

Calling the inner interrupt routine is a bit tricky. The arguments are passed in registers. No parameters are specified. But the actual function definition defines a long set of parameters. This may be confusing, but that's exactly how it's done. (This syntax also does a good job of confusing the Turbo C compiler.)

In order to understand parameter passing better, we've written a short program that demonstrates parameter passing through two levels of interrupt routines.

The program uses interrupt 0x77 (an unused interrupt) to call the function outer. This, in turn, calls another interrupt inner. inner returns the value one in register AX. outer returns two in register BX. At each stage the registers are dumped so we can see exactly what is happening.

The function inner is simple. After dumping the registers it sets the parameter ax and returns. This causes the register AX to be changed in the calling program.

The function outer is a little more complex. Printing the registers scrambles them. Registers are very volatile things and can easily be changed. We need to pass our register arguments from the main routine to the interrupt function inner. To do this we simply load the register from their stack versions:

```
_BX = bx;      /* Order is important */
_CX = cx;
_DX = dx;
_FLAGS = flags;
_AX = ax;
```

After executing the routine inner, the function outer must transfer the data left by inner (in the registers) to where the main function can get them (the parameters).

This is done with the code:

```
ax = _AX;      /* Order is important */
flags = _FLAGS:
bx = _BX;
cx = _CX;
dx = _DX;
```

A printout from our test looks like:

```
-----------Start
Regs    AX:0041 BX:0042 CX:0043 DX:0044
        BP:0045 SI:0046 DI:0047 DS:0048 ES:0049
----------Inside outer
Regs    AX:0041 BX:0042 CX:0043 DX:0044
        BP:1483 SI:0046 DI:0047 DS:0048 ES:0049
        Ip:ffa3 Cs:1483 Flags:f202
---------Inner Regs AX:0041 BX:0042 CX:0043 DX:0044
        BP:ff6e SI:0046 DI:0047 DS:1483 ES:0049
        Ip:03fb Cs:1483 Flags:f202
----------After inner
Regs    AX:0001 BX:0042 CX:0043 DX:0044
```

```
            BP:1483 SI:0046 DI:0047 DS:0048 ES:0049
            Ip:ffa3 Cs:1483 Flags:f202 ----------Final
    Regs    AX:0001 BX:0002 CX:0043 DX:0044
            BP:1483 SI:0046 DI:0047 DS:0048 ES:0049
```

From this we notice that everything is fairly straightforward, except that the parameter we passed in bp doesn't make it into the function outer. This register is used by C to point to the current temporary variable area (where things like parameters are stored). Don't use bp as a register or as a parameter.

A Nasty Surprise

When we first wrote this program we set the flags register last. After all, every arithmetic instruction changes the flags register, so it's the most volatile.

So initially we wrote:

```
_AX = ax;      /* Don't code like this */
_BX = bx;
_CX = cx;
_DX = dx;
_FLAGS = flag;
(*inner_ptr)();
```

but failed miserably. (Our TSR routine trans locked up and forced us to do a hard reset.)

The problem is with the line:

```
_FLAGS = flags;
```

The 8086 does not have an instruction to move the flags directly from the register to memory. Turbo C does an end run around this restriction by routing the flags register through the AX register. The assembly language for this assignment is (paraphrased):

```
;       _FLAGS = flags
        mov    ax,flag          ;Get flags into register AX
                                ;Destroy old contents of AX
        push   ax               ;Put AX on the stack
        popf                    ;Get FLAGS from stack
```

This is why the order of our statements is so important. Although the following two sections of code appear to be the same, they act very differently.

Good:

```
_FLAGS = flags;
_AX = ax;
```

Bad:

```
_AX = ax;
_FLAGS = flags;
```

Interrupt programming is extremely tricky. Surprises can lurk in even the most obvious code. Keep your interrupt routines small and simple. That way there's less to go wrong. Finally, keep in mind the programmer's version of the Harvard Law: "Under the most rigorously controlled conditions of program quality, style and testing, the computer will do as it pleases."

A Pop-up TSR

A pop-up TSR is a program that lurks in the background until it is activated by a hotkey. When active, it appears on the screen (pops up) and interacts with the user. The classic example of a pop-up TSR is Borland's Sidekick utility program.

DOS was not designed to handle pop-up TSR. There are a few undocumented hooks designed for TSR programs like PRINT and MODE that never pop up, so it is up to the programmer to do almost all the work himself.

We are going to write a very simple pop-up TSR, "Hello World". When the hotkey (F12 for this program) is pressed the program will display "Hello World". Even though this program is one of the simplest programs, it will take about 650 lines of code to do this task.

Unfortunately, our program cannot just pop up when the hotkey is pressed. DOS might be running and we can't perform a context switch and pop up while DOS is active. Disk I/O is very tricky and time dependent. If there is disk I/O active, we can't pop up. If we did, it would screw up the disk timing.

The program activates when the hotkey is pressed. The routine `tsr_interrupt` is attached to interrupt 9 (INT_KEY). Whenever a key is pressed an interrupt nine is generated. The function `tsr_interrupt` is called. Because DOS may be busy or disk I/O may be in progress we can't pop up from this interrupt routine.

Our keyboard routine needs to know what key was pressed as well as what shift keys (SHIFT, CAPS, ALT, etc.) are active. The scan code for the key is found by directly reading the hardware. The shift flags are stored at location 0000:0147 (KEY_FLAGS).

If the correct key is pressed we can't immediately pop up. DOS may be active, or disk I/O may be in progress. All we can do at this point is set a flag to tell other interrupt routines that it's time to pop up. After setting this flag, we eat the character by doing direct I/O to the keyboard and the interrupt controller.

Finally, if we don't see the hotkey, we don't care what was pressed, so we call the normal interrupt handler to take care of the incoming character.

```
/************************************************************
 * tsr_keyboard -- keyboard interrupt                       *
 *                                                          *
 * Check to see if the hotkey was pressed and               *
 * set the flags accordingly                                *
 ************************************************************/
static void interrupt tsr_keyboard(void)
{
    /* Status information from the keyboard port */
    static int keyboard_status;
    static unsigned char far *key_flags = MK_FP(0, KEY_FLAGS);

    if (running == FALSE) {
        if ((inportb(KEYBOARD_DATA) == scancode) &&
            ((*key_flags & keymask) == keymask)) {

            hotkey_found = TRUE;

            /*
             * Strobe the top bit of the keyboard
             * status register
             */
            keyboard_status = inportb(KEYBOARD_STATUS);
            outportb(KEYBOARD_STATUS, keyboard_status | 0x80);
```

```
            outportb(KEYBOARD_STATUS, keyboard_status);
            /* Clear the interrupt */
            outportb(0x20, 0x20);
            return;
        }
    }
    /* It's not our key, let the system have it */
    (*norm_keyboard)();
}
```

The timer interrupt routine (`tsr_timer`) is called whenever the clock ticks (65,536 times an hour or about 18.2 times per second). First, the routine calls the normal timer interrupt routine, so anyone else who is waiting for the clock gets interrupted.

Then it checks to see if conditions are right to start the pop-up routine. All of the following conditions must be met:

1. The program must not already be running.
   The clock interrupt keeps on going even if the TSR is running. Starting to activate an active TSR can lead to great confusion, which will lock up the computer.

2. The hotkey must have been pressed.
   Obviously we don't want to pop up until we're wanted.

3. DOS is not active.
   We can't perform the context switch needed to pop up while DOS is active. The `dosbusy` flag is set when DOS is busy executing a system call. By checking it we make sure that it's safe to pop up.

4. No disk I/O may be in progress.
   Disk I/O is tricky and the timing is very critical. We don't want to pop up at the wrong time and disturb any disk I/O in progress. Later on we will discuss how our disk interrupt intercept routine sets the variable `diskflag` when I/O is in progress.

The full code for our clock interrupt routine (`tsr_timer`) follows:

```
/************************************************************
 * tsr_timer -- timer interrupt routine.                  *
 *                                                        *
 * If it's a good time to pop up and we want to pop up    *
 * this routine will cause us to appear                   *
 ************************************************************/
```

```
static void interrupt tsr_timer(void)
{
    (*norm_timer)();
    if (running == FALSE) {
      if (hotkey_found && (*dosbusy == 0)) {
          if (diskflag == 0) {
              do_it();
          }
      }
    }
}
```

This works fine as long as DOS doesn't remain busy for long periods of time. But what happens when someone executes a getch function? DOS waits for a keystroke and remains busy until it's typed. If we press the hotkey, our keyboard routine will intercept and set hotkey_flag, but DOS is running. (It's waiting for a character). We can't pop up because dosbusy is true.

But DOS comes to our rescue. Whenever DOS is waiting it repeatedly executes an interrupt 28 (INT_IDLE). Our idle interrupt is very similar to our timer interrupt, except we don't check the dosbusy flag.

```
/**********************************************************
 * tsr_idle -- idle interrupt handler                   *
 *                                                      *
 * This is called when DOS is not doing anything much   *
 * to allow TSR programs a chance to execute.           *
 **********************************************************/
static void interrupt tsr_idle(void)
{
    (*norm_idle)();
    if (running == FALSE) {
      if (hotkey_found) {
          if (diskflag == 0) {
              do_it();
          }
      }
    }
}
```

In order to pop up we must know if there is any disk I/O in progress. We get this information by intercepting the BIOS Disk I/O interrupt (0x13 or INT_DISK). Our interrupt routine increments a counter (diskflag) at the beginning of each I/O operation and decrements it when the operation is finished.

The reason that we use a counter instead of just a flag, is that it is possible for the disk I/O interrupt to be recursively called. So one interrupt can cause another. By counting, we can make sure that no disk I/O is in progress when diskflag is zero.

The disk I/O interrupt uses the registers to pass data back to the caller. Because of the way Turbo C handles interrupt registers we must explicitly transfer the data from the norm_disk handler to our caller using the statements:

```
ax = _AX;
bx = _BX;
```

and so on.

Finally, Turbo C generates a warning if a function doesn't use all its parameters. An interrupt routine is special. We get all the registers as parameters whether we want them or not. Since we don't use them all, we generate a warning message. To turn this warning message off, we put the line:

```
#pragma warn -par
```

before the beginning of the function and

```
#pragma warn .par
```

after the end. This turns off the warning for this function only. The complete version of our disk routine is:

```
/*************************************************************
 * tsr_disk -- called for each disk interrupt              *
 *                                                         *
 * This routine keeps track of all the disk interrupts     *
 * so that we don't pop up during a disk operation.        *
 *************************************************************/
#pragma warn -par /* We know that we don't use all the params */
static void interrupt tsr_disk(INTERRUPT_REGS)
{
    diskflag++;
    (*norm_disk)();
    ax = _AX;       /* Now pass back all the registers */
    bx = _BX;
    cx = _CX;
```

```
        dx = _DX;
        si = _SI;
        di = _DI;
        es = _ES;
        flags = _FLAGS;
        diskflag--;
    }
    #pragma warn .par    /* Restore warning */
```

Now that we've taken care of the routines that take care of deciding to pop up we need a function to do the actual popping up. Our function needs to:

- Save the context of the running program.
- Switch to the TSR context.
- Do whatever the TSR does. (In this case display "hello world.")
- Restore the original context.

A context switch is very difficult in DOS because the operating system was never designed to do multitasking. A context includes:

1. The registers. These are automatically saved on the stack at interrupt time.

2. The stack. The stack must be treated specially. Because it has such significance in C, changing it is very tricky and dangerous.

3. The program segment prefix (psp). This is a pointer used by DOS to indicate what program is currently running.

4. The data transfer address (dta). The dta is the address DOS uses for disk I/O, as well as other types of I/O. Since we don't want to do I/O to the program that was running when we popped up, we must save the dta and set our own.

5. Control-Break interrupt handler. A TSR program can never exit. (When it does, it greatly confuses DOS.) Control-Break must be disabled during the execution of the TSR so that the user can't hit it and force the TSR to exit.

6. Control-C interrupt handler. This must be saved for the same reasons as control-break.

7. Critical Error Interrupt. When DOS detects a critical error, like a disk error, it generates a critical error interrupt. By default, this causes the message:

```
Abort, Retry, Fail?
```

to appear on the screen. If the user selects abort, the program is stopped. Since a TSR can't stop, we can't give the user this option, so we must intercept the critical error handler.

8. Cursor size/location and video page. We want to restore the screen to its original appearance. In order to do this, we must save all the cursor information.

9. Control-Break Flag. Programs are allowed to turn on and off the control-break interrupt. Our TSR turns it off.

The data structure used to store the context is:

```
struct context {
    /* Stack location, segment, and register (SS, SP) */
    unsigned int stack_segment, stack_register;

    /* psp (Program Segment Prefix) */
    unsigned int psp;

    /* dta (Data transfer address)
     * Where DOS does its read/writes */
    char far *dta;

    /* Break interrupt handler */
    void interrupt (*int_break)(void);
    void interrupt (*int_control_c)();       /* ^C handler */
    /* Critical error handler */
    void interrupt (*int_crit)(INTERRUPT_REGS);
    unsigned int cursor_size;     /* The cursor size */
    unsigned int cursor_loc;     /* Cursor location */
    unsigned char video_page;      /* Page number for video */
    boolean control_break;     /* The control-break flag */
};
```

This structure is used to hold almost all the information we need to save. The one piece that's missing is the screen data. It is assumed that each pop up window will save the data under it and restore the screen when it is removed.

Obtaining the current context is a somewhat complex task. Our function to do this work (get_context) looks like:

```
void get_context(struct context *context)
{
    /* Get the PSP address */
    _AH = DOS_GET_PSP;
```

```
        geninterrupt(INT_DOS);
        context->psp = _BX;

        context->dta = getdta();
        context->control_break = getcbrk();

        context->int_crit = getvect(INT_CRITICAL);
        context->int_control_c = getvect(INT_CONTROL_C);
        context->int_break = getvect(INT_BREAK);

        _AH = VIDEO_GET_INFO;
        geninterrupt(INT_VIDEO);
        context->cursor_size = _CX;
        context->cursor_loc = _DX;
        context->video_page = _BH;
}
```

Getting the information is straightforward. There are library functions or DOS system calls to get the information we need.

This function does not take care of the stack. The stack must be saved before this function is called. That's because the act of calling a function changes the stack. Manipulating the stack in C is about as tricky as juggling knives blindfolded. You're working in the dark and have to be very careful.

Our function to set a new context set_context is a mirror image of get_context.

```
  void set_context(struct context *context)
  {
      /* Set the PSP address */
      _AH = DOS_SET_PSP;
      _BX = context->psp;
      geninterrupt(INT_DOS);

      setdta(context->dta);
      setcbrk(context->control_break);

      setvect(INT_CRITICAL, context->int_crit);
      setvect(INT_CONTROL_C, context->int_control_c);
      setvect(INT_BREAK, context->int_break);

      _AH = VIDEO_SET_CURSOR_SIZE;
      _CX = context->cursor_size;
      geninterrupt(INT_VIDEO);
```

```
        _AH = VIDEO_SET_CURSOR_POSITION;
        _DX = context->cursor_loc;
        _BH = context->video_page;
        geninterrupt(INT_VIDEO);
    }
```

Now we come to the routine to handle the popping up part of our program (do_it). It is responsible for the context and stack switches, as well as calling tsr_main, the function that actually displays the "Hello World" message.

This function also sets a number of flags, as well as checking the video mode so that we only pop up if the screen is in text mode. Finally, as it exits, it checks to see if the user has asked the TSR program to unload itself and called unload if needed.

```
    static void do_it(void)
    {
        static int mode;
        disable();

        normal_context.stack_segment = _SS;
        normal_context.stack_register = _SP;

        get_context(&normal_context);
        set_context(&tsr_context);

        _SS = tsr_context.stack_segment;
        _SP = tsr_context.stack_register;

        running = TRUE;
        hotkey_found = FALSE;

        enable();

        /*
         * Only show yourself in text modes
         */
        mode = *video_mode;

        if (((mode >= 0) && (mode <= 3)) ||
            (mode == 7))
            tsr_main();

        running = FALSE;
        disable();
        if (unloading)
            do_unload();
```

```
    set_context(&normal_context);
    _SP = normal_context.stack_register;
    _SS = normal_context.stack_segment;
    enable();
}
```

We have finally reached the part of the program that does the work, the function `tsr_main`. This function first saves the screen data for our "hello window" using the function `gettext`. Next it displays the "Hello World" message and waits for the user to type a key. If the key is 'u', it checks to see if it is possible to unload this TSR and sets the flag `unloading`. Then it puts the screen back the way it found it and returns.

```
static void tsr_main(void)
{
    int ch;

    (void)gettext(X1, Y1, X2, Y2, window_save);
    window(X1, Y1, X2, Y2);

    clrscr();
    drawbox(1, 1, X_WIDTH, Y_WIDTH-1);
    gotoxy(2,2);
    cputs(" Hello World");
    ch = bioskey(0);
    ch &= 0x7F;
    if (ch == 'u') {
        unloading = unload_ok();
    }
    (void)puttext(X1, Y1, X2, Y2, window_save);
}
```

Most TSR programs can be loaded only; once in memory there is no way to get them out (except reboot). Our TSR is a little nicer. If it is possible for it to leave, it will. To leave, we must restore all the interrupt vectors we hooked to their original values. This is fine if we were the last TSR loaded, but what happens if someone comes in after us and also hooks the interrupt vectors? Then it is not possible to leave.

The function `unload_ok` loops through our table of interrupt hooks checking to see if any have changed. If someone monkeyed with any one of them a FALSE is returned, indicating that we can't be unloaded. If everything is OK, a TRUE is returned.

```
static boolean unload_ok(void)
{
    struct hook_vect *cur_hook;    /* Current interrupt hook */

    for (cur_hook = hooks; cur_hook->vect != -1; cur_hook++) {
        if (getvect(cur_hook->vect) != cur_hook->tsr_vect)
            return (FALSE);
    }
    return (TRUE);
}
```

The function do_unload does the actual unloading. Actually, all we have to do at this point is to restore the interrupt vectors and free all the memory that belongs to our program.

Restoring the interrupt is straightforward. To return the memory, we loop through every memory segment, looking for any that are owned by us. (See Chapter 3, 8086 Details, for a description of DOS memory.) When we find one, we use the standard function freemem to return it to DOS. Finally, we destroy the magic number. This number is used to make sure that we don't load twice. We'll discuss the magic number more a little further on.

```
static void do_unload(void)
{
    struct hook_vect *hook;      /* Current interrupt hook */

    /* Current memory segment */
    struct mcb far *current_mcb = mcb_start;

    for (hook = hooks; hook->vect != -1; hook++) {
        setvect(hook->vect, *hook->old_vect);
    }

    while (1) {
        if (current_mcb->owner == _psp)
            freemem(FP_SEG(current_mcb)+1);

        if (current_mcb->flag != 'M')
            break;

        current_mcb = MK_FP(FP_SEG(current_mcb) +
            current_mcb->size + 1, 0);
    }

    magic_number = 0;    /* Kill the number */
}
```

A TSR program should be loaded once. Rather than trust the user to remember if he loaded us or not, our program checks to see if it is already loaded. It does this through a magic number. This is a 4-byte value that should be unique for each program. For this program we chose the characters "TSRX" (0x54535258L). (We were going to choose the first four characters of "Hello", but our editor didn't like that idea.)

The function `is_loaded` checks to see if this program has already been loaded. This is done by looping through each memory segment checking to see that it's owned by someone else (we don't want to check our own magic number). Next it makes sure it's a program segment by checking the first word against `PSP_MAGIC`. DOS always sets the first two bytes of a program segment to this value. Finally, it checks the other program's magic number.

Finding the other program's magic number is a bit tricky. It's at the same address (relative to the start of the program). The address calculation is done in two parts, the segment and the offset. The variable `_psp` points to the beginning of our program. (It is a segment.) The pseudo-variable `_DS` points to our data segment. So our relative segment offset is `_DS` - `_psp`. This is added to the segment address of the other program (`FP_SEG(block_ptr)`) to get the segment address of the magic number. The offset of the magic number is the same for both programs and can be gotten by the simple equation `&magic_number`. Combining them with the macro `MK_FP` gives us a far pointer to the other program's magic number.

The function to check to see if the program is loaded looks like:

```
static boolean is_loaded(void)
{
    /* Current item in the mcb chain */
    struct mcb far *current_mcb = mcb_start;

    /* Pointer to current memory block */
    int far *block_ptr;
    /* Segment and offset of a possible magic number */
    unsigned int magic_seg, magic_off;

    /* Pointer to the magic number */
    long unsigned int far *magic_ptr;

    while (1) {
            if ((current_mcb->owner != NULL) &&
                (current_mcb->owner != _psp)) {
                block_ptr = MK_FP(current_mcb->owner, 0);
```

```
            if (*block_ptr == PSP_MAGIC) {
                magic_seg = FP_SEG(block_ptr) + _DS - _psp;
                magic_off = (int)&magic_number;
                magic_ptr = MK_FP(magic_seg, magic_off);
                if (*magic_ptr == magic_number)
                        return (TRUE);
            }
        }

        if (current_mcb->flag != 'M')
                break;

        current_mcb = MK_FP(FP_SEG(current_mcb) +
            current_mcb->size + 1, 0);
    }
    return (FALSE);
}
```

Finally, there are a few details remaining. We have two interrupt routines
designed to catch the break interrupt and the critical error interrupt and do
nothing. Our break interrupt looks like:

```
static void interrupt tsr_break(void)
{
    return;
}
```

Our critical error handler must return an ignore code to the caller. It does this
by assigning zero to ax. Since we don't use all the registers and we don't want
C to fuss at us, this routine is surrounded by #pragma warn -par and
#pragma warn .par.

```
#pragma warn -par    /* We know that we don't use all the
params */
static void interrupt tsr_critical(INTERRUPT_REGS)
{
    ax = 0;
}
#pragma warn .par    /* Restore warning */
```

Finally there is our main function. This initializes various data structures,
saves the TSR context, installs our interrupt hooks, and exits using the keep
function.

Summary

DOS was never designed to handle TSR type programs, but these utilities can be extremely useful. Because of the limited DOS support provided, the programmer must do a great deal of work himself. The "Hello World" program presented in this chapter can easily be adapted to suit almost any need. Although tricky, TSR programming can generate very useful and needed applications.

Listing 6-7. "tsr_hello.c"

```c
#undef DEBUG
#include <dos.h>
#include <bios.h>
#include <stdlib.h>
#include <stdio.h>
#include <conio.h>

typedef char boolean;
#define TRUE 1
#define FALSE 0
/***********************************************************
 * Define Various Interrupt Vectors                        *
 ***********************************************************/
#define INT_TIMER       0x8     /* Timer interrupt */
#define INT_KEY         0x9     /* Keyboard character pressed */
#define INT_VIDEO       0x10    /* Video information interrupt */
#define INT_DISK        0x13    /* Raw disk I/O interrupt */
#define INT_BREAK       0x1B    /* Control-Break Handler */
#define INT_CONTROL_C   0x23    /* ^C error handler */
#define INT_CRITICAL    0x24    /* Critical Error Handler */
#define INT_IDLE        0x28    /* DOS Idle interrupt */
#define INT_DOS         0x21    /* DOS Calls */

/*
 * Function codes for video interrupt
 */
#define VIDEO_SET_CURSOR_SIZE       0x1  /* Set up cursor size */
#define VIDEO_SET_CURSOR_POSITION   0x2  /* Set cursor location */
#define VIDEO_GET_INFO              0x3 /* Get cursor size/location */
/*
 * Where the video mode is stored
 */
#define MODE_SEG 0x40
#define MODE_OFFSET 0x49
```

continued

Listing 6-7 continued.

```c
/*
 * Dos interrupt (INT_DOS) function codes
 */
#define DOS_GET_DOS_BUSY 0x34   /* Get address of DOS busy flag
*/
#define DOS_SET_PSP      0x50    /* Set current PSP address */
#define DOS_GET_PSP      0x51    /* Get current PSP address */
#define DOS_LIST_ADDRESS 0x52    /* Get address of DOS lists */


/*
 * Hardware ports we may need
 */
#define KEYBOARD_DATA    0x60    /* Keyboard data port */
#define KEYBOARD_STATUS  0x61    /* Keyboard status port */
/*
 * Place where bios stores shift values
 */
#define KEY_FLAGS        0x417
#define K_RIGHT          (1<<0)  /* Right shift pressed */
#define K_LEFT           (1<<1)  /* Left shift pressed */
#define K_CONTROL        (1<<2)  /* Control pressed */
#define K_ALT            (1<<3)  /* Alt pressed */
#define K_SLOCK          (1<<4)  /* Scroll lock on */
#define K_NLOCK          (1<<5)  /* Num lock on */
#define K_CAPS           (1<<6)  /* Caps lock on */
#define K_INSER          (1<<7)  /* Insert on */
/*
 * Register structure passed to an interrupt routine
 */
#define INTERRUPT_REGS int bp,int di,int si,int ds,int es,\
        int dx,int cx,int bx,int ax,int ip,int cs,int flags

static unsigned scancode = 0x58;        /* Numeric pad minus */
static unsigned keymask = 0;            /* No shifts */
unsigned _stklen = (2 * 1024);
unsigned _heaplen = 2;                  /* we don't use the heap */

/* unsigned int _stklen = (16 *1024); /* Increase stack size */

/* The following is used to see if we are currently loaded */
static unsigned long int magic_number = 0x54535258L;


/* True if we are in the process of unloading the routine */
static boolean unloading = FALSE;
/* Where video mode stored */
```

continued

Listing 6-7 continued.

```
static unsigned char far *video_mode;

/***********************************************************
 * The following three interrupts are grabbed only        *
 * when the pop-up portion of the TSR is executing so      *
 * that the program won't exit.                            *
 ***********************************************************/
static void interrupt tsr_critical(INTERRUPT_REGS);
static void interrupt tsr_break(void);
#define tsr_control_c tsr_break

void interrupt (*norm_break)(void);
void interrupt (*norm_control_c)(void);
void interrupt (*norm_critical)(void);

static char far *dosbusy;       /* DOS's I'm busy flag */
static int diskflag = 0;        /* Non-zero means disk active */

struct mcb {
    char flag;        /* 'M' -- normal block, 'Z' -- last block */
    unsigned int owner; /* Psp of the owner of this block */
    unsigned int size;    /* Size of the block in paragraphs */
    unsigned char not_used[3];  /* Padding */
    char name[8];             /* Name of who is using us */
};
static struct mcb far *mcb_start;

static boolean hotkey_found = FALSE;

/* True if we are currently executing the TSR */
static boolean running = FALSE;


/***********************************************************
 * This is a list of the interrupt vectors permanently     *
 * hooked by the TSR to control when it pops up.           *
 ***********************************************************/
void interrupt tsr_timer(void);          /* Timer interrupt */
void interrupt tsr_idle(void);           /* Dos idle interrupt */
void interrupt tsr_keyboard(void);     /* Key pressed interrupt */
void interrupt tsr_disk(INTERRUPT_REGS);/* Disk I/O request */

/* Places to save the old versions of the interrupts */
void interrupt (*norm_timer)(void);
void interrupt (*norm_keyboard)(void);
```

continued

Listing 6-7 continued.

```
void interrupt (*norm_idle)(void);
void interrupt (*norm_disk)(void);
/************************************************************
 * Table containing a list of all interrupt vectors       *
 *      that are always hooked so that we can pop up       *
 ************************************************************/
struct hook_vect {
    int vect;           /* Vector number of interrupt to intercept */
    void interrupt (*tsr_vect)(void);/* Ptr to new int routine */
    void interrupt (**old_vect)(void);/* Where to put the old */
} hooks[] = {
    /*Vect       Tsr              Old */
    {INT_TIMER, tsr_timer,        &norm_timer},
    {INT_IDLE,  tsr_idle,         &norm_idle},
    {INT_KEY,   tsr_keyboard,     &norm_keyboard},
#pragma warn -sus  /* Turn off pointer warning */
/* Turbo C thinks that interrupt routine
 *          with registers is different */
/* From a normal interrupt routine */
    {INT_DISK,  tsr_disk,         &norm_disk},
#pragma warn .sus  /* Restore warning */
    /* End of list indicator */
    {-1,        NULL,             NULL}
};



/************************************************************
 * context -- structure to hold almost all the             *
 *      information needed for a context switch.            *
 *                                                          *
 * Information stored                                       *
 *      stack segment: stack_register                       *
 *      psp, dta                                            *
 *      Interrupt handlers (break, control_c,               *
 *                      critical error handler)             *
 *                                                          *
 * Information not stored:                                  *
 *      registers -- these are stored on the                *
 *                          interrupt stack                 *
 *      floating point registers -- not saved.  It is       *
 *              assumed that the program will not use        *
 *              them.                                        *
 *      screen data -- it is assumed that any window         *
 *                      will save what's under it            *
 *                      before appearing                     *
 ************************************************************/
```

continued

Listing 6-7 continued.

```
struct context {
    /* Stack location, segment and register (SS, SP) */
    unsigned int stack_segment, stack_register;

    /* psp (Program Segment Prefix) */
    unsigned int psp;

/* dta (Data transfer address) Where DOS does its read/writes
*/
    char far *dta;

    void interrupt (*int_break)(void);  /* Break int handler */
    void interrupt (*int_control_c)();  /* ^C handler */
    /* Critical Error Handler */
    void interrupt (*int_crit)(INTERRUPT_REGS);
    unsigned int cursor_size;   /* The cursor size */
    unsigned int cursor_loc;    /* Cursor location */
    unsigned char video_page;   /* Page number for video */
    boolean control_break;      /* The control break flag */
};
/*
 * Context for this program (the TSR)
 */
static struct context tsr_context = {
    0, 0,               /* Stack segment, register */
    0,                  /* Psp */
    0,                  /* Dta */
    tsr_break,          /* int_break */
    tsr_control_c,      /* int_control_c */
    tsr_critical,       /* int_crit */
    0x0B0C,             /* Cursor size */
    0x0102,             /* Cursor position */
    0,                  /* Video Page */
    0,                  /* Control break flag */
};

/* Context of the program that calls us */
static struct context normal_context;

/***********************************************************
 * do_unload -- unload the TSR.                            *
 *      Assumes that we unload_ok has been called          *
 *      before this.                                       *
 ***********************************************************/
static void do_unload(void)
```

continued

Listing 6-7 continued.

```
{
    struct hook_vect *hook;       /* Current interrupt hook */

    /* Current memory segment */
    struct mcb far *current_mcb = mcb_start;

    for (hook = hooks; hook->vect != -1; hook++) {
        setvect(hook->vect, *hook->old_vect);
    }

    while (1) {
        if (current_mcb->owner == _psp)
            freemem(FP_SEG(current_mcb)+1);

        if (current_mcb->flag != 'M')
            break;

        current_mcb =
            MK_FP(FP_SEG(current_mcb) + current_mcb->size + 1, 0);
    }

    magic_number = 0;    /* Kill the number */
}

/**********************************************************
 * unload_ok -- true if we are allowed to unload          *
 *                                                         *
 * Returns                                                 *
 *      True -- we can unload.                             *
 *      False -- forget about unloading                    *
 *                                                         *
 * This checks to see if the interrupt vectors we          *
 * overwrote have been stomped on by someone else.         *
 * If so, then we can't restore them, so we can't unload*
 **********************************************************/
static boolean unload_ok(void)
{
    struct hook_vect *cur_hook; /* Current interrupt hook */

    for (cur_hook = hooks; cur_hook->vect != -1; cur_hook++) {

        if (getvect(cur_hook->vect) !=  cur_hook->tsr_vect)
            return (FALSE);
    }
```

continued

Listing 6-7 continued.

```
    return (TRUE);
}


/***********************************************************
 * drawbox -- draws a box using double lines              *
 *        from (x1,y1) to (x2,y2)                         *
 ***********************************************************/
static void drawbox(int x1, int y1, int x2, int y2)
{
    int x, y; /* Current location */

    /* Draw top */
    gotoxy(x1+1, y1);
    for (x = 1; x < x2; x++)
        putch(0xCD);                /* Horizontal line */

    /* Draw bottom */
    gotoxy(x1+1, y2);
    for (x = 1; x < x2; x++)
        putch(0xCD);                /* Horizontal line */

    /* Draw Sides */
    for (y = 1; y < y2; y++) {
        gotoxy(x1, y);              /* Vertical Line */
        putch(0xBA);

        gotoxy(x2, y);
        putch(0xBA);                /* Vertical Line */
    }
    gotoxy(x1, y1);
    putch(0xC9);                    /* Top left corner */

    gotoxy(x1, y2);
    putch(0xC8);                    /* Bottom left corner */

    gotoxy(x2, y1);                 /* Top right corner */
    putch(0xBB);

    gotoxy(x2, y2);                 /* Bottom right corner */
    putch(0xBC);
}

/* These constants define the box to draw on the screen */
#define X1      20
#define Y1      10
```

continued

Listing 6-7 continued.

```
#define X2      34
#define Y2      13
/*
* Note: We save an extra line so that the window won't
*       scroll when we write the last character.
*/


#define X_WIDTH (X2-X1+1)
#define Y_WIDTH (Y2-Y1+1)
/* 2 bytes per character (1 attribute/1 character) */
static char *window_save [(X_WIDTH * Y_WIDTH * 2)];
/***********************************************************
 * tsr_main -- body of the tsr pop-up routine            *
 *                                                        *
 * Display a window with "hello world" in it and          *
 * wait for user input.  If "U" try to unload program    *
 ***********************************************************/
static void tsr_main(void)
{
    int ch;

    (void)gettext(X1, Y1, X2, Y2, window_save);
    window(X1, Y1, X2, Y2);

    clrscr();
    drawbox(1, 1, X_WIDTH, Y_WIDTH-1);
    gotoxy(2,2);
    cputs(" Hello World");
    ch = bioskey(0);
    ch &= 0x7F;
    if (ch == 'u') {
        unloading = unload_ok();
    }
    (void)puttext(X1, Y1, X2, Y2, window_save);
}


/***********************************************************
 * Get_Context -- get the context of the current         *
 *                process                                 *
 *                                                        *
 * Parameter                                              *
 *      context -- the context to get                     *
 *                                                        *
 * Note: This does *NOT* handle the getting of the        *
 *       stack segment:register.  Stacks are difficult    *
```

continued

Listing 6-7 continued.

```
 *        to work with and must be saved at the highest     *
 *        level.                                            *
 ************************************************************/
void get_context(struct context *context)
{
    /* Get the PSP address */
    _AH = DOS_GET_PSP;
    geninterrupt(INT_DOS);
    context->psp = _BX;

    context->dta = getdta();
    context->control_break = getcbrk();

    context->int_crit = getvect(INT_CRITICAL);
    context->int_control_c = getvect(INT_CONTROL_C);
    context->int_break = getvect(INT_BREAK);

    _AH = VIDEO_GET_INFO;
    geninterrupt(INT_VIDEO);
    context->cursor_size = _CX;
    context->cursor_loc = _DX;
    context->video_page = _BH;
}


/************************************************************
 * set_context -- Set the context to the given values      *
 *                                                          *
 * Parameters                                               *
 *      context -- context to save                          *
 *                                                          *
 * Note: We don't save the stack pointer because it's       *
 * tricky to handle and must be done carefully              *
 * elsewhere.                                               *
 ************************************************************/
void set_context(struct context *context)
{
    /* Set the PSP address */
    _AH = DOS_SET_PSP;
    _BX = context->psp;
    geninterrupt(INT_DOS);

    setdta(context->dta);
    setcbrk(context->control_break);

    setvect(INT_CRITICAL, context->int_crit);
```

continued

Listing 6-7 continued.

```
        setvect(INT_CONTROL_C, context->int_control_c);
        setvect(INT_BREAK, context->int_break);

        _AH = VIDEO_SET_CURSOR_SIZE;
        _CX = context->cursor_size;
        geninterrupt(INT_VIDEO);

        _AH = VIDEO_SET_CURSOR_POSITION;
        _DX = context->cursor_loc;
        _BH = context->video_page;
        geninterrupt(INT_VIDEO);
}

/***********************************************************
 * do_it -- save context and execute the TSR program      *
 ***********************************************************/
static void do_it(void)
{
        static int mode;
        disable();

        normal_context.stack_segment = _SS;
        normal_context.stack_register = _SP;

        get_context(&normal_context);
        set_context(&tsr_context);

        _SS = tsr_context.stack_segment;
        _SP = tsr_context.stack_register;

        running = TRUE;
        hotkey_found = FALSE;

        enable();

        /*
         * Only show yourself in text modes
         */
        mode = *video_mode;

        if (((mode >= 0) && (mode <= 3)) ||
            (mode == 7))
            tsr_main();

        running = FALSE;
```

continued

Listing 6-7 continued.

```
        disable();

        if (unloading)
            do_unload();

        set_context(&normal_context);

        _SP = normal_context.stack_register;
        _SS = normal_context.stack_segment;
        enable();
}

#define PSP_MAGIC      0x20CD   /* This begins each PSP segment
*/
/***********************************************************
 * is_loaded -- returns true if we are already loaded    *
 *                                                        *
 * This routine walks the memory chain looking for        *
 * any segment that is a PSP.                             *
 *                                                        *
 * When it finds another program, it checks to see        *
 * if that program has the same magic number              *
 * in the same place as we do.                            *
 *                                                        *
 * Warning: This works only for TINY, SMALL xxxx          *
 * memory models.                                         *
 ***********************************************************/
static boolean is_loaded(void)
{
    /* Current item in the mcb chain */
    struct mcb far *current_mcb = mcb_start;

    /* Pointer to current memory block */
    int far *block_ptr; /*


    /* Segment and offset of a possible magic number */
    unsigned int magic_seg, magic_off;

    /* Pointer to the magic number */
    long unsigned int far *magic_ptr;


    while (1) {
        if ((current_mcb->owner != NULL) &&
            (current_mcb->owner != _psp)) {
```

continued

Listing 6-7 continued.

```c
            block_ptr = MK_FP(current_mcb->owner, 0);

            if (*block_ptr == PSP_MAGIC) {
                magic_seg = FP_SEG(block_ptr) + _DS - _psp;
                magic_off = (int)&magic_number;
                magic_ptr = MK_FP(magic_seg, magic_off);
                if (*magic_ptr == magic_number)
                    return (TRUE);
            }
        }

        if (current_mcb->flag != 'M')
            break;

        current_mcb =
            MK_FP(FP_SEG(current_mcb) + current_mcb->size + 1, 0);
    }
    return (FALSE);
}


/************************************************************
 * tsr_break -- break interrupt handler                     *
 *                                                          *
 * Since we are a TSR program, we can not stop for          *
 * any reason, so ignore all breaks.                        *
 ************************************************************/
static void interrupt tsr_break(void)
{
    return;
}
/************************************************************
 * tsr_critical -- critical error handler                   *
 *                                                          *
 * Returns                                                  *
 *      AX = 0  -- tell DOS to ignore the error             *
 ************************************************************/
#pragma warn -par  /* We know that we don't use all the params */
static void interrupt tsr_critical(INTERRUPT_REGS)
{
    ax = 0;
}
#pragma warn .par         /* Restore warning */
/************************************************************
 * tsr_disk -- called for each disk interrupt.              *
 *                                                          *
```

continued

Listing 6-7 continued.

```
 * This routine keeps track of all the disk interrupts  *
 * so that we don't pop up during a disk operation.      *
 ********************************************************/
#pragma warn -par/* We know that we don't use all the param */
static void interrupt tsr_disk(INTERRUPT_REGS)
{
    diskflag++;
    (*norm_disk)();
    ax = _AX;   /* Now pass back all the registers */
    bx = _BX;
    cx = _CX;
    dx = _DX;
    si = _SI;
    di = _DI;
    es = _ES;
    flags = _FLAGS;
    diskflag--;
}
#pragma warn .par        /* Restore warning */


/*********************************************************
 * tsr_keyboard -- keyboard interrupt                    *
 *                                                       *
 * Check to see if the hotkey was pressed and            *
 *  set the flags accordingly.                           *
 ********************************************************/
static void interrupt tsr_keyboard(void)
{
    /* Status information from the keyboard port */
    static int keyboard_status;
    static unsigned char far *key_flags = MK_FP(0, KEY_FLAGS);

    if (running == FALSE) {
        if ((inportb(KEYBOARD_DATA) == scancode) &&
            ((*key_flags & keymask) == keymask)) {

            hotkey_found = TRUE;

        /* Strobe the top bit of the keyboard status register */
            keyboard_status = inportb(KEYBOARD_STATUS);
            outportb(KEYBOARD_STATUS, keyboard_status | 0x80);
            outportb(KEYBOARD_STATUS, keyboard_status);
            /* Clear the interrupt */
            outportb(0x20, 0x20);
            return;
```

continued

Listing 6-7 continued.

```
        }
}
    /* It's not our key, let the system have it */
    (*norm_keyboard)();
}
/************************************************************
 * tsr_timer -- timer interrupt routine.                    *
 *                                                          *
 * If it's a good time to pop up and we want to pop up      *
 * this routine will cause us to appear.                    *
 ************************************************************/
static void interrupt tsr_timer(void)
{
    (*norm_timer)();
    if (running == FALSE) {
        if (hotkey_found && (*dosbusy == 0)) {
            if (diskflag == 0) {
                do_it();
            }
        }
    }
}
/************************************************************
 * tsr_idle -- idle interrupt handler                       *
 *                                                          *
 * This is called when DOS is not doing anything much       *
 * to allow TSR programs a chance to execute.               *
 ************************************************************/
static void interrupt tsr_idle(void)
{
    (*norm_idle)();
    if (running == FALSE) {
        if (hotkey_found) {
            if (diskflag == 0) {
                do_it();
            }
        }
    }
}

int main(void)
{
    struct hook_vect *hook;      /* Current vector for hookup */
    unsigned int far *table_ptr;/* Pointer to DOS tables */
```

continued

Listing 6-7 continued.

```
        _AH = DOS_GET_DOS_BUSY;
        geninterrupt(INT_DOS);
        dosbusy = MK_FP(_ES, _BX);

        _AH = DOS_LIST_ADDRESS;
        geninterrupt(INT_DOS);
        table_ptr = MK_FP(_ES, _BX);

        /* Entry -1 = start of memory chain */
        mcb_start = MK_FP(*(table_ptr - 1), 0);

#pragma warn -rch /* The following code should be
                   * unreachable if compiled
                   * Correctly, however if word
                   * aligned structures
                   *  are used, it will
                   * kick in and warn the programmer. */
        if (sizeof(struct mcb) != 16) {
            (void)cputs(
             "Compile error: Don't compile with word alignment\n\r");
            exit (1);
        }
#pragma warn .rch        /* Restore warning */

        video_mode = MK_FP(MODE_SEG, MODE_OFFSET);

#ifdef DEBUG
        tsr_main();

#else DEBUG
        if (is_loaded() == FALSE) {
            tsr_context.stack_segment = _SS;
            tsr_context.stack_register = _SP;
            tsr_context.psp = _psp;
            tsr_context.dta = getdta();

            for (hook = hooks; hook->vect != -1; hook++) {
                *hook->old_vect = getvect(hook->vect);
                setvect(hook->vect, hook->tsr_vect);
            }

            {
                /* Size of program in paragraphs */
```

Listing 6-7 continued.

```
            static unsigned keep_size;

            keep_size = _SS - _psp + (_SP / 16) + 50;
            keep(0, keep_size);
        }
    }
    (void)cputs("Program already loaded\n\r");
#endif DEBUG
    return (0);
}
```

I/O Drivers

This chapter describes how to use C to access the hardware directly. Most of the time, the operating system handles the hardware for you. However, there are times when you must access the devices directly. (Like, for example, when you are writing an operating system.)

Direct I/O programming is the most tricky and difficult type of programming there is. Hardware tends to follow its own set of rules, which are vastly different from anything you've seen in software. Part of this chapter will help you translate hardware talk into C code.

Interrupt programming is the most difficult of all. Because of the random nature of interrupts, failures are not predictable. To make it worse, debugging an interrupt routine is extremely difficult since almost all of our debugging tools don't work with interrupts.

This chapter discusses ways that you can make your programs more bullet proof, as well as several techniques that you can use to debug your programs in the absence of any good debugging tools.

We will begin by constructing a very simple keyboard-to-screen program that demonstrates the use of *polling*. We will then discuss the serial I/O hardware and translate a hardware data sheet into C code. This will be used to construct a simple, low speed, terminal program. The final program is the most difficult of all, an interrupt driven terminal program.

Accessing the Devices

There are two common methods of accessing I/O devices, *memory-mapped* and *separate I/O address space*. Memory-mapped devices are special locations in memory. A keyboard, for example, may put the last character typed in location 0xFFFFFF00. (This is not the method used on the PC.) The following code will read the last character typed on the keyboard on this memory-mapped machine:

```
        /* location of the keyboard input */
        volatile char *keyboard_in;
   . . .
        /* point to keyboard memory */
        keyboard_in = (char *) 0xFFFFFF00;
        /* get character */ ch = *keyboard_in;
```

The keyword **volatile** is used to tell C that keyboard_in points to a special memory location that can change at any time. The optimizer will normally feel free to eliminate apparently useless code, for example:

```
char *keyboard_control = (char *)0xFFFFFF01;
*keyboard_control = KEY_ON; /* turn keyboard on */
*keyboard_control = KEY_FUNCT; /* allow function keys */
*keyboard_control = KEY_NUM_LOCK; /* turn num_lock on */
```

would be optimized to:

```
char *keyboard_control = 0xFFFFFF01;
*keyboard_control = KEY_NUM_LOCK; /* turn num_lock on */
```

After all, this code doesn't make sense if *keyboard_control is a normal memory location. In this case, it is an I/O device, and assigning it three values is actually sending it three commands. We must tell C, "even though this code looks crazy, we know what we're doing." The keyword **volatile** does this.

The 68000 class CPUs and the DEC VAX computers use only memory-mapped I/O. The PC uses a combination of memory-mapped and separate I/O space. The screen is memory-mapped, while devices like the keyboard and serial I/O use a separate I/O space. In assembly language, special instructions are needed to access device space. Device numbers (ports) run from 0 to 0xFFFF. C does not have any provisions for dealing with input/output instructions. However, Turbo C provides four non-standard subroutines for handling device input/output. They are:

```
void outportb(int port, int data);
void outport(int port, int data);
int inportb(int port);
int inport(int port);
```

The function `outportb` sends a byte of data to the given output port. The function `outport` does the same thing, only a word is sent.

The function `inportb` reads a byte from an input port. To read a word, use the function `inport`.

If you try to write to a non-existent device, the operation will be ignored. Reading a non-existent device will give you a random number.

Polling

Most output devices work in the following manner:

- A character is written to the device output port.
- The device sets the busy flag.
- The device outputs the character. (This may take some time.)
- The device clears the busy flag.

Polling is done by repeatedly testing the busy flag until the device indicates that it is ready for more commands (goes "not busy"). The program then sends another character to the device. Data sent while the device is still busy will be ignored. Polling is a way of asking: "Are you ready? Are you ready? Are you ready? ......" until the device answers "yes".

In C, a typical polling loop looks like:

```
while (1) {
    status = inportb(STATUS_PORT);

    /* if not busy break */
    if ((status & BUSY) == 0)
```

```
        break;
    } /* end of busy wait */
    outportb(OUTPUT_PORT, ch);
```

We will describe this in more detail when we construct our polling serial I/O driver below.

Keyboard and Screen

Our serial I/O program will use three devices: the keyboard, the screen and the serial I/O. The serial I/O will be accessed directly while we will let the operating system handle the keyboard and screen.Turbo C provides the following functions for use with the keyboard.

```
status = kbhit()
```

kbhit returns true (1) if there is a character ready to be read from the keyboard.

```
ch = getch();
```

This reads a single character from the keyboard.

```
putch(ch);
```

The function putch will output characters to the screen. Notice that there is no function to see if the screen is ready. The screen is so fast that by the time putch returns, it's ready for the next character.

In order to demonstrate polling further, we're going to construct a very simple program that takes input from the keyboard and sends it to the screen. Although this program isn't very useful, it does illustrate a very simple use of polling.

The program waits in a loop executing the statement "/* do nothing */;" until a key is pressed (kbhit == 1). It then obtains a character from the keyboard and sends it to the screen. We will expand on this simple concept later in the chapter when we create a simple terminal program.

Listing 7-1. "echo program"

```
/***********************************************************
 * echo -- take what's typed on the keyboard and put      *
 * it on the screen                                       *
 *                                                        *
 * Limited to MS-DOS machines only                        *
 *                                                        *
 * Usage:                                                 *
 *          echo                                          *
 ***********************************************************/
#include <conio.h>
main() {
    char ch; /* character from keyboard */
    /* loop forever */
    while (1) {
        /* wait something on keyboard */
        while (kbhit() == 0)
            /* do nothing */;

        /* get character from keyboard */
        ch = getch();

        /* send it to the screen */
        putch(ch);
    }
}
```

Serial I/O Hardware

The Serial I/O chip controls a data input signal, a data output signal, and five special control signals. The programs in this chapter ignore the control signals and concentrate on just sending and receiving characters.

Serial I/O on a PC is done with a National 8250 UART (or equivalent) chip. (UART stands for Universal Asynchronous Receiver Transmitter, a fancy way of saying serial I/O.) The specification for this device (called a data sheet) is available from many chip manufacturers or electronic distributors.

A page from the National's data sheet is reproduced in Figure 7-1.

As you can easily see, this is not in a format that is easily used by a C programmer. Our job is to translate this into a data structure that can be used in programming.

8.0 Registers

The system programmer may access any of the UART registers summarized in Table II via the CPU. These registers control UART operations including transmission and reception of data. Each register bit in Table II has its name and reset state shown.

8.1 LINE CONTROL REGISTER

The system programmer specifies the format of the asynchronous data communications exchange and sets the Divisor Latch Access bit via the Line Control Register (LCR). The programmer can also read the contents of the Line Control Register. The read capability simplifies system programming and eliminates the need for separate storage in system memory of the line characteristics. Table II shows the contents of the LCR. Details on each bit follow:

Bits 0 and 1: These two bits specify the number of bits in each transmitted or received serial character. The encoding of bits 0 and 1 is as follows:

Bit 1	Bit 0	Character Length
0	0	5 Bits
0	1	6 Bits
1	0	7 Bits
1	1	8 Bits

Bit 2: This bit specifies the number of Stop bits transmitted and received in each serial character. If bit 2 is a logic 0, one Stop bit is generated or checked in the serial data. If bit 2 is a logic 1 when a 5-bit word length is selected via bits 0

TABLE II. Summary of Registers

Bit No.	0 DLAB=0 Receiver Buffer Register (Read Only) RBR	0 DLAB=0 Transmitter Holding Register (Write Only) THR	1 DLAB=0 Interrupt Enable Register IER	2 Interrupt Ident. Register (Read Only) IIR	3 Line Control Register LCR	4 MODEM Control Register MCR	5 Line Status Register LSR	6 MODEM Status Register MSR	0 DLAB=1 Divisor Latch (LS) DLL	1 DLAB=1 Division Latch (MS) DLM
0	Data Bit 0 (Note 1)	Data Bit 0	Received Data Available	"0" if Interrupt Pending	Word Length Select Bit 0 (WLS0)	Data Terminal Ready (DTR)	Data Ready (DR)	Delta 0 Clear to Send (DCTS)	Bit 0	Bit 8
1	Data Bit 1	Data Bit 1	Transmitter Holding Register Empty	Interrupt ID Bit (0)	Word Length Select Bit 1 (WLS1)	Request to Send (RTS)	Overrun Error (OE)	Delta Data Set Ready (DDSR)	Bit 1	Bit 9
2	Data Bit 2	Data Bit 2	Receiver Line Status	Interrupt ID Bit (1)	Number of Stop Bits (STB)	Out 1	Parity Error (PE)	Trailing Edge Ring Indicator (TERI)	Bit 2	Bit 10
3	Data Bit 3	Data Bit 3	MODEM Status	0	Parity Enable (PEN)	Out 2	Framing Error (FE)	Delta Data Carrier Detect (DDCD)	Bit 3	Bit 11
4	Data Bit 4	Data Bit 4	0	0	Even Parity Select (EPS)	Loop	Break Interrupt (BI)	Clear to Send (CTS)	Bit 4	Bit 12
5	Data Bit 5	Data Bit 5	0	0	Stick Parity	0	Transmitter Holding Register (THRE)	Data Set Ready (DSR)	Bit 5	Bit 13
6	Data Bit 6	Data Bit 6	0	0	Set Break	0	Transmitter Shift Register Empty (TSRE)	Ring Indicator (RI)	Bit 6	Bit 14
7	Data Bit 7	Data Bit 7	0	0	Divisor Latch Access Bit (DLAB)	0	0	Data Carrier Detect (DCD)	Bit 7	Bit 15

Note 1: Bit 0 is the least significant bit. It is the first bit serially transmitted or received.

Figure 7-1. *National 8250 Data Sheet. Reprinted with permission of National Semiconductor Corporation.*

Actually, things aren't too bad, they've just written everything sideways. The chip has seven registers numbered 0 through 6. (Some registers are named more than once.) Each entry in the table is listed with a long name at the top and just under it a TLA (three letter abbreviation). Rewriting this table vertically yields:

Number	TLA	Name
0	RBR	Receiver Buffer Register
0	THR	Transmitter Holding Register
1	IER	Interrupt Enable Register
2	IIR	Interrupt Identification Register
3	LCR	Line control register
4	MCR	Modem control register
5	LSR	Line Status Register
6	MSR	Modem Status Register
0	DLL	Divisor Latch (Least Significant Byte)
0	DLM	Divisor Latch (Most Significant Byte)

Our job is to translate this into a C structure. The first problem we have is that the "Receive Buffer Register" and the "Transmitter Holding Register" have the same number. How can two registers occupy the same place? The answer can be found by reading the fine print in the data sheet. The "Receive Buffer Register" is a read only register while the "Transmitter Holding Register" is a write only register. So if we read it, it's one thing, but if we write it, it's another. Rather than go through all the confusion of using two names, we'll just call it "data". It's 1 byte wide (8 bits) so we declare it using the character type.

Going through the rest of the registers to the "Modem Status Register" we get the following C structure:

```
/*
 * define the register structure for the serial I/O
 */
struct sio {
    char data;              /* data register */
    char interrupt_enable;  /* interrupt enable register */
    /* what kind of interrupt is going on */
    char interrupt_id;
    char format;            /* communications format */
    char out_control;       /* modem control lines */
    char status;            /* status byte */
    char i_status;          /* input status */
    char scratch;           /* extra pad */
};
```

Now most of the work is done. We only have two more registers to deal with. The hardware people overloaded registers 0 and 1. They can change from data and interrupt registers to divisor latches depending on something called "**DLAB=1**". Reading through the data sheet we find that DLAB stands for

"Divisor Latch Access Bit" and is assigned to the Line Control Register (#3) bit 7. This bit acts like a toggle switching the function of the first two registers between normal operation and acting as a divisor register. Overloading of registers in this way is quite common in hardware design, although it tends to drive the software people nuts.

We've decided to handle this problem by using "**#define**" to create alternate names for our first two registers.

```
#define baud_l data /* alias for sending baud rate */
#define baud_h interrupt_enable /* alias part 2 */
```

Defining the registers is only half the work. We now have to define names for each field. This is somewhat complicated by the fact that almost every register consists of eight single bit fields. We'll start with the register "format" (Line Control Register or LCR). Each format define begins with F_ to indicate that it belongs to the format register. Bit 7 is the Divisor Latch Access Bit. When set, registers 0 and 1 are the baud rate divisor. When 0 the registers operate normally. So create the two defines:

```
#define F_BAUD_LATCH    (1 << 7) /* enable baud rate registers */
#define F_NORMAL        (0 << 7) /* normal registers enabled */
```

(Here we use a trick (1<<7) to easily define the 7th bit).

The full definition of the fields in this register are:

```
#define F_BAUD_LATCH    (1 << 7) /* enable baud rate registers */
#define F_NORMAL        (0 << 7) /* normal registers enabled */
#define F_BREAK         (1 << 6) /* set a break condition */
#define F_NO_BREAK      (0 << 6) /* no break condition */
#define F_PARITY_NONE   (0 << 3) /* no parity on output */
#define F_PARITY_ODD    (1 << 3) /* odd parity on output */
#define F_PARITY_EVEN   (3 << 3) /* even parity on output*/
#define F_PARITY_MARK   (5 << 3) /* parity bit is always 1 */
#define F_PARITY_SPACE  (7 << 3) /* parity bit is always 0 */
#define F_STOP1         (0 << 2) /* Use one stop bit */
#define F_STOP2         (1 << 2) /* Use two stop bits */
#define F_DATA5         (0)      /* 5 data bits on output */
#define F_DATA6         (1)      /* 6 data bits on output */
#define F_DATA7         (2)      /* 7 data bits on output */
#define F_DATA8         (3)      /* 8 data bits on output */
```

The actual value for some of these fields, like the output data width, comes from tables within the 8250 data sheet.

We define similar constants for the other registers. See the listing at the end of this chapter for a complete listing of the header *serial.h.*

According to a PC technical manual the first serial port (COM1) is located at address 0x3f8. So the definition:

```
static struct sio near *com1 = (struct sio near *)0x3f8;
```

defines the variable *com1* so that it points to the COM1 port.

On a PC there are 16-bit and 32-bit pointers. 16-bit pointers are called **near** pointers. 32-bit pointers are called **far** pointers. The keyword near tells Turbo C to treat the pointer com1 as a 16-bit pointer. All pointers to I/O devices must be 16 bits.

Before we can use the device, we must initialize it. The procedure serial_init writes the appropriate control values to the device. We also clear the character waiting bit (S_RxRDY) by reading any old character data that may have been lingering around in the device with the statement:

```
(void)inportb(int)&sio->data);
```

Our initialization routine is:

```
/*
 * init -- initialize a port
 *
 * Parameters
 *        speed -- the speed (from table IV of the datasheet)
 *                 to send to the device
 */
void init(int speed)
{
    /* disable all serial interrupts */
    outportb((int) &COM->interrupt_enable, 0);

    /* Define the format of the serial I/O */
    outportb((int) &COM->format,
        F_BAUD_LATCH | F_NO_BREAK | F_PARITY_NONE |
        F_STOP1 | F_DATA8);
```

```
    /* Turn on all the control lines */
outportb((int) &COM->out_control, 0xf);
    /* DTR/RTS/GP01/GP02 */

 /* set the speed */
outportb((int) &COM->baud_l, speed & 0xFF);
outportb((int) &COM->baud_h, speed >> 8);

 /* tell the format register we are done with speed setting */
outportb((int) &COM->format,
    F_NORMAL | F_NO_BREAK | F_PARITY_NONE |
    F_STOP1 | F_DATA8);

/*
 * read the serial input data, thus clearing
 * the data-ready flag
 */
(void) inportb((int) &COM->data);
/*
 * Clear all of the other readable registers
 */
(void) inportb((int) &COM->interrupt_enable);
(void) inportb((int) &COM->interrupt_id);
(void) inportb((int) &COM->status);
}
```

Once we have set up the serial I/O device, we can use it. Our main loop just
moves characters from place to place. It moves characters from the keyboard
to the serial output and characters from the serial input to the screen.

In order to move a character from the keyboard to the serial output, two
things must happen. First, the keyboard must have a character, and second,
the serial output must be ready to receive it. If there is a character waiting at
the keyboard, but the serial output is not ready, we ignore it. This could cause
data loss if we typed very fast, but in actual practice, no one can type that fast.

To send data from the serial input to the screen, only the serial chip must be
ready. As we've said before, the screen is always ready.

Our main loop looks to see if it can move a character from the keyboard to the
serial output, then checks to see if it can move one from the serial input to the
screen. It also looks for characters coming in from the keyboard or the serial
I/O. The main loop sends the keyboard to the serial out and the serial in to
the screen.

```
while (1) {
    if (kbhit()) {
        /*
         * Keyboard ready
         * (check to see if serial out ready)
         */
        status = inportb((int)&sio->status);
        if ((status & S_TBE) != 0) {
            /* Keyboard and Serial Out both ready */
            ch = getch();
            outportb((int)&sio->data, ch);
        }
    }

    /* Incoming character? */
    status = inportb((int)&sio->status);
    if ((status & S_RxRDY) != 0) {
        ch = inportb((int)&sio->data);
        print_ch(ch);
    }
}
```

This type of I/O is somewhat limited. Sending a character to the screen can take some time. It may take so long that two characters come in over the serial line. The second character overwrites the first and causes an overrun error.

So at high speeds, this program will drop data. We need a better, faster way of doing I/O.

Hardware Interrupts

It would be nice if we could automatically call a procedure every time a character came. We can do this through the use of an interrupt procedure.

The concept of a hardware interrupt is simple. Suppose you are talking to someone in your office and the phone rings. You stop your conversation and pick it up. You have been interrupted. The ringing of the phone is the interrupt request and by picking it up you are servicing the interrupt. When you finish with the phone, you hang up and continue your conversation where you left off.

Hardware interrupts on the computer work much the same way. First you tell the device (in this case the serial I/O) that you want to be interrupted when it has data ready. You provide it with a special function to be called to service the interrupt. When the data arrive, an interrupt is generated. The hardware will stop the normal execution of your program, and execute the interrupt function. When the function is through, normal execution will resume as though nothing had happened.

```
         Normal Code                 Serial I/O interrupt

start = &buffer[0];                        Save machine state
end =                                  void interrupt get_it(void)
&buffer[sizeof(buffer)];               {
while (start < end) {                      in_ch = inportb(PORT);
   if (*start == '\0')                 }
      break;                           Interrupt done
   *start += 5;                        Restore machine state
   if (*start > max)
      max = start;
   start++;
}
length = end - start;
stats[STAT_LEN] = length;
```

Interrupts can occur at any time. It is the job of the interrupt routine to save the entire state of the machine, do its work, and restore the machine completely. The program which was interrupted has no idea that an interrupt occurred.

Because of their nature, interrupt routines should follow these guidelines:

- An interrupt should be as short as possible. Interrupts are processed with the interrupt system turned off and some other device may want to interrupt.

- Interrupt routines should be extremely simple. This is because they are extremely difficult to debug.

- An interrupt routine may not execute any DOS calls. After all, it may be DOS itself that was interrupted.

Turbo C uses the keyword **interrupt** to indicate that a function is to be used as an interrupt routine. Interrupt routines must save all registers and status. This keyword tells Turbo C to generate the necessary code.

Turbo C also defines the routine setvect to tell the hardware which interrupt function to use for a given interrupt. The functions enable and dis-

`able` are used to turn on and off interrupts. For a full listing of the interrupt driven terminal program, refer to the listing at the end of the chapter.

To tell Turbo C we want the routine `sio_interrupt` to be called when the serial I/O interrupts, we use the following code:

```
disable();
setvect(SIO_INTERRUPT_VECTOR, sio_interrupt);
enable();
```

`disable` is used to turn off interrupts. `setvect` installs an interrupt routine. In this case we install an interrupt routine to catch serial I/O interrupts. `enable` turns on interrupts.

Interrupts are disabled during the call to `setvect` because it is possible to get an interrupt at any time. A very bad time to get an interrupt is when `setvect` is half finished. The computer would not know that we were half done, would use the incomplete function address and branch off into nowhere.

The function `init` from our old program has been changed to allow the serial I/O to interrupt us when it receives a character. Also the main routine must tell the PC interrupt control device that we want serial I/O interrupts enabled. This is done with the code:

```
outportb(0x21, inportb(0x21) & 0xE7);
outportb(0x20, 0x20);
```

The interrupt routine (`sio_interrupt`) first checks the status register to make sure that we really have data. Sometimes flaky hardware or something else will cause an unexpected interrupt. This is a bit of bullet-proofing just to make sure.

The data are then read from the serial I/O and the interrupt_id register is read to tell the device that we have serviced the interrupt.

The character is stored in a buffer for future use.

Main Loop for the Interrupt Routine

The main loop is similar to the previous version, except the section dealing with input from the serial I/O has been changed. Instead of checking the status register, we now check the count of the number of characters in the buffer.

`count` is never incremented in the main loop. It can only be increased by the interrupt routine. When there are data in the buffer, the main loop will send them to the screen. During screen updates, interrupts are enabled and characters can be received.

Critical code is a set of instructions that must be executed without interruption. The call to `setvect` is one example. In our main loop, the statement

```
count--
```

is critical. This compiler actually translates this into the machine language instructions:

```
MOV COUNT,AX      ;AX = count;
SUB #1,AX         ;AX--
MOV AX,COUNT      ;count = AX
```

If we did not disable interrupts during this section, then the following might occur:

1. An interrupt puts a character in the buffer (count=1).
2. `if (count > 0)` is executed and `count > 0`.
3. The character is taken from the buffer and printed.
4. We execute the machine language instruction:

```
MOV COUNT,AX ;AX = count
```

at this point count is 1 and AX is 1.

5. An interrupt occurs. The interrupt routine reads the character, stores it in the buffer and increments `count` (count=2).
6. When the interrupt routine finishes, it returns to the instruction after the move and executes

```
SUB #1,AX      ;AX was 1, it is now 0
MOV AX,COUNT   ;Count is now 0
```

But a character came in and was not printed. Therefore count should be 1 and instead it is 0. The problem is that both the main loop and the interrupt routine both use count. Care must be taken to see that they don't interfere with each other.

Whenever the main loop wants to change count, it needs to tell the interrupt routine "hands off." It does this by disabling interrupts until it is finished with count.

Debugging Interrupt Routines

Interrupt routines are the most difficult and frustrating thing that a programmer has to deal with. Unlike other programs, those using interrupts will not act the same, given the same set of data. Programs have the most disconcerting habit of breaking at the worst time.

One of the problems in dealing with interrupt routines is that in most cases you can't use the debugger on them. There are hardware devices like emulators and logic analyzers that you can hook up to your machine, which will tell you what's going on. These are expensive.

The other way of debugging is to leave tracks. That is, have the interrupt routine set some debug variables that are read and printed by non-interrupt code. For example:

```
int serial_in_seen = 0;
interrupt serial_in()
{
    serial_in_seen = 1;    /* so far so good */
    . . .
}

main()
{
    . . . /* wait till interrupt happened */
    (void)printf("Interrupt seen? %d", serial_in_seen);
```

Unfortunately, in the absence of any specialized hardware or software, that's about all you can do. A more sophisticated version of this is the message buffer. That is a section of memory reserved for messages from the interrupt routine. For example:

```
#define BUF_SIZE (10*1024)        /* size of messages */
char message_buffer[BUF_SIZE];    /* place to put data */
char *msg_out = message_buffer;   /* put message here */

/*
 * send_msg -- put a message in the buffer'
 *          this should only be called from an interrupt routine
 * Parameters
 *        msg -- thc message to send
 */
void send_msg(char *msg)
{
    int len = strlen(msg);        /* the length of the message */
    (void)strcpy(msg_out, msg);   /* send message */
    msg_out += len;               /* move current message ptr */
}
```

The main routine can examine the message buffer and print any new message that has come in. This method has one drawback. It is relatively slow and a lot of messages can cause an interrupt to take a long time (for an interrupt).

The secret in debugging interrupts is to get the right amount of information out. Too little, and you don't know what's going on. Too much, and you slow down the system and cause trouble.

Summary

Direct I/O programming is one of the most difficult coding jobs. We've seen how the programmer must start with a hardware data sheet, translate it into C and then code from there. Whenever possible, the programmer should take the time to thoroughly check his assumptions. The data sheet is written in almost a completely different language. It is easy to translate it wrong.

Be especially careful when working with interrupts. They are difficult to design and very difficult to debug.

On the other hand, if you're careful, take it slowly and pay attention to the details, direct I/O programming can be a very interesting experience.

Listing 7-2. "serial.h"

```
/*********************************************************
 * serial.h -- define the structures and bits for the    *
 *       serial i/o hardware                              *
 *********************************************************/
/*
 * define the register structure for the serial i/o
 */
struct sio {
    char    data;             /* data register */
    char    interrupt_enable;/* interrupt enable register */
    /* what kind of interrupt is going on */
    char    interrupt_id;
    char    format;           /* communications format */
    char    out_control;      /* modem control lines */
    char    status;           /* status byte */
    char    i_status;         /* input status */
    char    scratch;          /* extra pad */
};
#define baud_l data             /* alias for sending baud rate */
#define baud_h interrupt_enable /* alias part 2 */


/*
 * Defines for Interrupt Enable Register (interrupt_enable)
 */
#define I_STATUS (1 << 3) /* interrupt on modem status changed */
/* interrupt on receive. status changed */
#define I_REC_STATUS (1 << 2)
#define I_TRANS_EMPTY   (1 << 1) /* interrupt on trans. empty */
#define I_CHAR_IN    (1 << 0) /* interrupt on character input */


/*
 * Defines for Line control register  (format)
 */
#define F_BAUD_LATCH    (1 << 7) /* enable baud rate registers */
#define F_NORMAL        (0 << 7) /* normal registers enabled */

#define F_BREAK         (1 << 6) /* set a break condition */
#define F_NO_BREAK      (0 << 6) /* no break condition */

#define F_PARITY_NONE   (0 << 3)  /* no parity on output */
#define F_PARITY_ODD    (1 << 3)  /* odd parity on output */
#define F_PARITY_EVEN   (3 << 3)  /* even parity on output*/
#define F_PARITY_MARK   (5 << 3)  /* parity bit is always 1 */
#define F_PARITY_SPACE  (7 << 3)   /* parity bit is always 0 */

#define F_STOP1         (0 << 2)   /* Use one stop bit */
```

continued

Listing 7-2 continued.

```
#define F_STOP2          (1 << 2)    /* Use two stop bits */

#define F_DATA5          (0)         /* 5 data bits on output */
#define F_DATA6          (1)         /* 6 data bits on output */
#define F_DATA7          (2)         /* 7 data bits on output */
#define F_DATA8          (3)         /* 8 data bits on output */

/*
 * Defines for the MODEM control register (out_control)
 */
#define O_LOOP           (1<<4)          /* loopback test */
#define O_OUT1           (1<<3)          /* Extra signal #1 */
#define O_OUT2           (1<<2)          /* Extra signal #2 */
#define O_RTS            (1<<1)          /* Request to send */
#define O_DTR            (1<<0)          /* Data terminal ready */

/*
 * Line Status register (Status)
 */
#define S_TXE            (1 << 6)
#define S_TBE            (1 << 5)    /* Transmitter buffer empty */
#define S_BREAK          (1 << 4)    /* Break detected on input */
#define S_FR_ERROR       (1 << 3)    /* Framing error on input */
#define S_PARITY_ERROR   (1 << 2)    /* Input parity error */
#define S_OVERRUN        (1 << 1)    /* Input overrun */
#define S_RxRDY          (1 << 0)    /* Receiver has character ready */
/*
 * Modem Status Register (i_status)
 */
#define I_DCD       (1 << 7)          /* DCD control line is on */
#define I_RI        (1 << 6)          /* RI control line is on */
#define I_DSR       (1 << 5)          /* DSR control line is on */
#define I_CTS       (1 << 4)          /* CTS control line is on */
#define I_DEL_DCD        (1 << 3)         /* DCD line changed */
#define I_DEL_RI         (1 << 2)         /* RI line changed */
#define I_DEL_DSR        (1 << 1)         /* DSR line changed */
#define I_DEL_CTS        (1 << 0)         /* CTS line changed */


/*
 * constants are used to define the
 * baud rate for the serial i/o chip
 * (Selected entries from Table-III of the National 8250
 *  data sheet)
 */
```

continued

Listing 7-2 continued.

```
#define B1200    96
#define B2400    48
#define B9600    12


/*
 * The location of the i/o registers on the IBM PC
 */
#define COM1    ((struct sio near *)0x3f8)
#define COM2    ((struct sio near *)0x2f8)


/*
 * Use COM1 for this program
 */
#define COM      COM1
#define SPEED    B9600
```

Listing 7-3. "termpoll.c"

```
/*********************************************************
 * term-poll -- simulate a terminal.                    *
 *             Send keyboard data to the serial output *
 *             Send serial input to screen             *
 *                                                      *
 * Warning: This routine uses polling so it may miss    *
 *     characters on input if they arrive too fast      *
 *********************************************************/
#include <dos.h>
#include <stdlib.h>      /* ANSI Standard only */
#include <conio.h>
#include <stdio.h>
#include "serial.h"

#define SPEED B9600      /* use 9600 baud */
#define COM COM1         /* use com1 for input and output */

#ifndef TRUE
#define FALSE 0
#define TRUE 1
#endif TRUE

#ifndef NULL
#define NULL ((char *)0)
#endif NULL
```

continued

Listing 7-3 continued.

```
main()
{
        /* routine to simulate a stupid terminal */
        void    term(void);
        term();
        return (0);
}

/*
 * init -- initialize a port
 */
void init()
{

        /* disable all interrupts */
        outportb((int)&COM->interrupt_enable,   0);

        /* Define the format of the serial i/o */
        outportb((int)&COM->format,
          F_BAUD_LATCH|F_NO_BREAK|F_PARITY_NONE|F_STOP1|F_DATA8);

        /* Turn on all the control lines */
        outportb((int)&COM->out_control,
                O_OUT1|O_OUT2|O_RTS|O_DTR);

        /* set the speed */
        outportb((int)&COM->baud_l, SPEED & 0xFF);
        outportb((int)&COM->baud_h, SPEED >> 8);

        /* tell the format register we are
         * done with speed setting */
           outportb((int)&COM->format,
            F_NORMAL|F_NO_BREAK|F_PARITY_NONE|F_STOP1|F_DATA8);

        /*
         * read the serial input data,
         * thus clearing the data ready flag
         */
        (void)inportb((int)&COM->data);
        /*
         * Clear all of the other readable registers
         */
        (void)inportb((int)&COM->interrupt_enable);
        (void)inportb((int)&COM->interrupt_id);
        (void)inportb((int)&COM->status);
```

continued

Listing 7-3 continued.

```
        }

    /**********************************************************
     * term -- act like a terminal                           *
     **********************************************************/
    void term()
    {
            char ch;            /* character we are working on */
            int status = 0; /* current status */
            void empty_buffer(void);        /* dump the data buffer */
                void init(void);            /* start the sio */

            init();

            while (1) {
                    if (kbhit()) {
                            ch = getch();
                            outportb((int)&COM->data, ch);
                    }
                    /* get the status */
                    status = (inportb((int)&COM->status));

                    if ((status & S_RxRDY) != 0) {
                            putch(inportb((int)&COM->data) & 0x7F);
                    }


            }
    }
```

Listing 7-4. "term-int.c"

```
    /**********************************************************
     * term-int -- interrupt version of the terminal         *
     *             program.                                  *
     *                                                       *
     * Usage:                                                *
     *      term-int                                         *
     **********************************************************/

    #include <dos.h>
    #include <stdlib.h>        /* ANSI Standard only */
    #include <conio.h>
    #include <stdio.h>
```

continued

Listing 7-4 continued.

```
#include "serial.h"
#ifndef TRUE
#define TRUE 1
#define FALSE 0
#endif TRUE

/* size of the buffer to use for string incoming characters */
#define COM_BUF_SIZE (62 * 1024)

static char *buffer_start;      /* beginning of the buffer */
static char *buffer_end;        /* end of the buffer */

/* pointer to next place to put character in */
static char *buffer_in;
static char *buffer_out;    /* place to get next character from */

static int count = 0;          /* number of characters in buffer */

main()
{
        /* input character handler */
        void    interrupt serial_interrupt();

        /* routine to simulate a stupid terminal */
        void    term(void);

        /* set up the input buffer */
        void    init_buf(void);

        init_buf();
        disable();
        setvect(0xC, serial_interrupt);
        enable();

        /* enable interrupts */
        outportb(0x21, inportb(0x21) & 0xE7);
        outportb(0x20, 0x20);

        term();
        return (0);
}
/************************************************************
 * init_buf -- initialize the buffer pointers              *
 ************************************************************/
void init_buf(void)
{
        buffer_start = malloc(COM_BUF_SIZE);
```

continued

Listing 7-4 continued.

```
        buffer_in = buffer_start;
        buffer_out = buffer_start;
        buffer_end = buffer_start + COM_BUF_SIZE - 10;
}

/***********************************************************
 * init -- initialize the port                            *
 ***********************************************************/
void init(void)
{
        /* don't allow interrupts while we do this */
        disable();
        /* receive interrupts */
        outportb((int)&COM->interrupt_enable,   I_CHAR_IN);

        outportb((int)&COM->format,
          F_BAUD_LATCH|F_NO_BREAK|F_PARITY_NONE|F_STOP1|F_DATA8);

        /* now that we have the baud latch set, send baud */
        outportb((int)&COM->baud_l, SPEED & 0xFF);
        outportb((int)&COM->baud_h, SPEED >> 8);

        outportb((int)&COM->format,
            F_NORMAL|F_NO_BREAK|F_PARITY_NONE|F_STOP1|F_DATA8);

        outportb((int)&COM->out_control,
                O_OUT1|O_OUT2|O_RTS|O_DTR);

        /* read the input registers
         * to clear their i-have-data flags */
        (void)inportb((int)&COM->data);
        (void)inportb((int)&COM->interrupt_enable);
        (void)inportb((int)&COM->interrupt_id);
        (void)inportb((int)&COM->status);

        outportb(0x20, 0x20);                   /* clear interrupts */
        enable();
}

/***********************************************************
 * buf_getch -- get a character from the buffer           *
 *              Update buffer_out                         *
 *                                                        *
 * Returns                                                *
 *      the character or ? if none                        *
 ***********************************************************/
char buf_getch(void)
```

continued

Listing 7-4 continued.

```
{
        char ch;            /* character we got */

        if (count == 0)
                return ('?');

        ch = *buffer_out;
        buffer_out++;

        if (buffer_out == buffer_end)
                buffer_out = buffer_start;

        disable();
        count--;
        enable();

        return(ch);
}
/**********************************************************
 * serial_interrupt -- interrupt handler for serial      *
 *      input                                             *
 *                                                        *
 * Called in interrupt mode by the hardware when          *
 * a character is received on the serial input            *
 **********************************************************/
void interrupt serial_interrupt()
{
        int     int_status;     /* status during interrupt */
        disable();

        int_status = inportb((int)&COM->status);

        /* tell device we have read interrupt */
        (void)inportb((int)&COM->interrupt_enable);
        (void)inportb((int)&COM->interrupt_id);

        if ((int_status & S_RxRDY) == 0) {
                enable();
                return;
        }
        *buffer_in = inportb((int)&COM->data) & 0x7F;
        buffer_in++;

        if (buffer_in == buffer_end)
                buffer_in = buffer_start;

        count++;
```

continued

Listing 7-4 continued.

```
        outportb(0x20, 0x20);
        enable();
}

/**********************************************************
 * term -- emulate a simple terminal                      *
 **********************************************************/
void term(void)
{
        char ch;          /* character we are working on */
        void empty_buffer(void);      /* dump the data buffer
*/

        init();

        while (1) {
                if (kbhit()) {
                        ch = getch();
                        outportb((int)&COM->data, ch);
                }
                empty_buffer();
        }
}

/**********************************************************
 * empty_buffer -- dump all the data buffered by          *
 *                 the interrupt routine                  *
 **********************************************************/
void empty_buffer()
{
        while (count > 0) {
                fputc(*buffer_out, stdout);

                buffer_out++;
                if (buffer_out == buffer_end)
                        buffer_out = buffer_start;
                disable();
                count--;
                enable();
        }
}

void interrupt get_it(void)
{
in_ch = inportb(PORT);
}
```

Real-Time and Event Driven Programming

This chapter introduces you to the concepts of Real-Time programming along with the design principles of Event Driven programs.

A real-time program is one which must complete its work within a certain time limit. Typical real-time programming tasks include data collection, transaction processing, process control, and games. Data collection can be very sensitive to timings. For example, if we have an instrument that sends the temperature of a chemical vat every 5 seconds, we can lose data if we take longer than 5 seconds to process a request. The data coming in are an event that must be processed in real time.

The design of event driven programs is quite different from simple linear programs. The programs we have seen so far are all linear programs. That is, A is followed by B, and C and so on. In other words, our program executes line by line (linear). Event driven programs react to external events like a mouse moving, a clock ticking, or a key pressed. They introduce the word "when" to programming.

For example:

```
when mouse moves do
    handle mouse
when key pressed do
    handle keyboard
```

Unfortunately, DOS provides almost no support for event driven programs. Larger systems like UNIX have a "wait for event" system call that puts the program to sleep until an event occurs. In DOS, we are forced to simulate this by using a spin-wait loop. This is a tight loop that repeatedly checks to see if an event occurred. So on DOS, our example looks like:

```
/* Loop forever */
while (1) {
    if mouse moved then
     handle mouse
     if key pressed then
     handle keyboard
}
```

On a single user system, like DOS, programming like this causes no problems. On a multi-user system, CPU time is wasted since the program keeps running even though no events occur. That's why most multi-user systems, like UNIX, provide some sort of "wait for event" support.

To demonstrate the principles of real-time and event driven programs, as well as to have a little fun, we are going to construct a game of Mouse and Cat. The game is simple; a cat appears on the screen and you chase it with the mouse. When you catch the cat, the game is over.

The Mouse

Back in the late 1960s and early 1970s computers finally got powerful enough so that they could do graphics. A pointing device was needed and many different devices were tried.

There were light pens, which were based on the idea that if you put a photo transistor against a CRT you can tell when the electron gun is sweeping across that spot. This will give you the position of the pen. Unfortunately, if the screen is black at that point, the electron gun is turned off, so this only worked on white areas.

One of the more exotic devices was the sound pen. When put against the CRT, it emitted a sound that was picked up by two strip microphones on the top and left side of the CRT. By measuring the time it took the sound to travel from the pen to the microphones you could compute the position of the pen. We operated one of them once, and it sputtered while it worked. It sounded like it was spitting at the CRT. Calibration was tricky. The speed of sound varies somewhat as the barometric pressure, temperature and humidity change. It's somewhat unnerving to point a pen at the CRT only to have the cursor appear $1/4$ inches to the right.

Some of the old style pointing devices survive today. They include the trackball and the digitizing tablet. Some of the more exotic devices include a foot pad, magic glove (just point your finger), and an eye tracker (look at where you want to point).

But by far, the most popular pointing tool is the mouse. Developed by Xerox, it is a relatively simple device consisting of a small ball with a couple of X-Y encoders. It's simple and easy to use. One of its main drawbacks is that it requires a clear desk space to work, and on our desk, clear space is at a premium. Also the ball can get dirty and begin to slip. But despite these drawbacks, the mouse is one of the most widely used pointing devices today.

The PC Mouse Interface

The software to control the mouse can be loaded in various ways depending on who manufactured your mouse. Some systems install a TSR program while others load a device driver through an entry in CONFIG.SYS.

The mouse software provided an interrupt, number 0x33, for communication with the application program. The driver takes care of not only the mouse, but also will put a mouse cursor on the screen and handle its movements. Unfortunately, in text mode, the mouse cursor is a solid block. Since we want to be a bit more creative for our mouse and cat game, we will handle the mouse cursor ourselves.

The first thing our game must do is initialize the mouse. This is done with the following system call:

Initialize mouse

Calling Registers	AX = 0
Interrupt	0x33
Return Registers	AX = 0 Mouse not installed
	AX = -1 Mouse installed
	BX = Number of buttons

Our game then enters the play loop, constantly polling the mouse to determine its location. The function to get the current mouse coordinates is:

Get mouse location

Calling Registers	AX = 3
Interrupt	0x33
Return Registers	BX - Button status
	CD - X Coordinate
	DX - Y Coordinate

The mouse reports its coordinates in units called *mickies*. These are unique units, unrelated to character or graphic positions. Also, the origin for the mouse is (0, 0) while the origin of the text screen is (1, 1). To convert a mouse location into a text location we use the following code:

```
text_x = (column * 8) - 1
text_y = (row * 8) - 1
```

Program Details

Our program begins by parsing the command line. The program takes two options: -d turns on debugging and the time between cat moves (in hundredths of seconds) can be specified with the option -t *time*. Because this is a demonstration program the default update time is set to 1 second (100 hundredths). This makes the game somewhat slow. The -t option allows the user to make the game more of a challenge by specifying a faster mouse.

We then enter the play routine. This function initializes the screen, mouse and cat, then enters the event loop.

This while loop checks for the following events: key pressed, mouse moved, the cat got caught, or time passes.

When a key is pressed, we read the keyboard and check for a legal command. The "d" command toggles debug, the "q" command aborts the program.

```
/*
 * Wait for an event to happen
 */

while ((!quit) && (!caught)) {
    /* Keyboard event */
    if (kbhit()) {
        ch = getch();

      switch (ch) {
          case 'q':
              quit = 1;
              break;
          case 'd':
              debug = !debug;
              break;
          default:
              putch(BELL);
              break;
      }
    }
}
```

Next we check to see if the mouse moved. If it did, we erase the "M" at the old location and put it in the new location. At this point, we also check to see if we caught the cat.

```
/* Mouse event */
_AX = MOUSE_GET_POSITION;
geninterrupt(INT_MOUSE);
raw_mouse_x = _CX;
raw_mouse_y = _DX;

/*
 * Correct mouse location
 */
mouse_x = raw_mouse_x / 8 +1;
mouse_y = raw_mouse_y / 8 +1;

if ((mouse_x != old_mouse_x) ||
    (mouse_y != old_mouse_y)) {
    /* Move mouse */
    if (old_mouse_x != -1) {
        gotoxy(old_mouse_x, old_mouse_y);
        putch(' ');     /* Erase old mouse */
```

```
        }
        gotoxy(mouse_x, mouse_y);
        putch('M');
    }

    caught = (mouse_x == cat_x) && (mouse_y == cat_y);
```

Finally, we check to see if it's time to move the cat. The cat is moved in a random direction and we reset the timer.

```
    /* Time event */
    gettime(&current_time);

    if (time_diff() > update_time) {
        int diff_x;    /* Cat Delta in X direction */
        int diff_y;    /* Cat Delta in Y direction */

      /* ... Compute new cat position .... */

      gotoxy(cat_x, cat_y);
      putch('C');

      start_time = current_time;
    } /* End of while loop */
```

At the end of the while loop is some debug code that displays the mouse information in the upper right corner of the screen.

Summary

Although simple, this program provides a good demonstration of how to program the mouse, as well as many of the principles of game programming. Since DOS has no built-in functions to handle events, we must design our own event loop.

The mouse cursor (the "M") must be updated in real time. It wouldn't do for the player to move the mouse and have the "M" move several seconds later. This is our first introduction to Real-Time programming. As we will see later in the breakout program, this type of programing can be somewhat tricky.

But in this example, we have a simple and easy way to understand some difficult programming concepts.

Listing 8-1. "mouse.c"

```
/***********************************************************
 * Mouse -- a game of mouse and cat                        *
 *                                                         *
 * How to play:                                            *
 *      A cat appears on the screen.  Use the mouse        *
 *      to catch it.                                       *
 *                                                         *
 *      Type 'Q' to exit                                   *
 *      Type 'D' to toggle debug mode                      *
 *                                                         *
 * Usage:                                                  *
 *      mouse [-d] [-t<time>]                              *
 *                                                         *
 *      -d -- turn debugging on                            *
 *      -t<time> -- set time between cat movements         *
 *                  in 100ths of seconds                   *
 ***********************************************************/
#include <stdio.h>
#include <dos.h>
#include <conio.h>
#include <stdlib.h>

#define INT_MOUSE          0x33    /* Mouse function */
#define MOUSE_INIT         0x00    /* Initialize the mouse */
#define MOUSE_SHOW         0x01    /* Show the mouse cursor */
#define MOUSE_HIDE         0x02    /* Hide the mouse cursor */
#define MOUSE_X_LIMIT      0x07   /* Set the X range of the mouse */
#define MOUSE_Y_LIMIT      0x08   /* Set the Y range of the mouse */
#define MOUSE_GET_POSITION 0x03 /* Get current mouse position */


#define INT_VIDEO          0x10    /* Video interrupt */
#define CURSOR_SET         0x01    /* Set cursor size/shape */
#define CURSOR_GET         0x03    /* Get cursor information */


#define BELL 7                     /* Turn on the bell */

int debug = 0;                     /* True if we are debugging */
int update_time = 100;             /* Time between mouse movements */

main(int argc, char *argv[])
{
    int mouse_buttons;   /* Number of buttons on the mouse */
    int mouse_status;    /* Status from init mouse call */
    char status;         /* Status of last game */
```

continued

Listing 8.1 continued.

```c
void usage(void);    /* Tell user how we work */
char play_game(void);/* Play one game of mouse and cat */

while ((argc > 1) && (argv[1][0] == '-')) {
    switch (argv[1][1]) {
        case 'd':
            debug = 1;
            break;
        case 't':
            update_time = atoi(&argv[1][2]);
            break;
        default:
            usage();
    }
    argc--;
    argv++;
}


if (argc != 1)
    usage();

/* Initialize the mouse */
_AX = MOUSE_INIT;
geninterrupt(INT_MOUSE);
mouse_status = _AX;
mouse_buttons = _BX;

if (mouse_status != -1) {
    (void)fprintf(stderr,"Mouse driver not present\n");
    exit (1);
}

if (debug)  {
    (void)printf(
            "Mouse present, %d buttons\n", mouse_buttons);
}
while (1) {
    status = play_game();
    if (status == 'q')
        break;
}


return (0);
}
static struct time current_time;        /* Time now */
```

continued

Listing 8.1 continued.

```
     /* Time when we started this move */
     static struct time start_time;

#define CONVERT(ti) ((((ti.ti_hour) * 60) + \
                     (ti.ti_min) * 60) + \
                     (ti.ti_sec) * 100) + \
                     (ti.ti_hund)
/***********************************************************
 * time_diff -- return the time difference between        *
 *              start and current times.                  *
 *                                                        *
 * Returns                                                *
 *      time difference in hundredths of seconds.         *
 ***********************************************************/
static unsigned long int time_diff(void)
{
     unsigned long int start;   /* Start time as hundredths */
     unsigned long int current; /* Current time as hundredths */

     start = CONVERT(start_time);
     current = CONVERT(current_time);

     return (current - start);
}
/***********************************************************
 * play_game -- play a single game                        *
 ***********************************************************/
static char play_game(void)
{
     char ch;                    /* Character from keyboard */
     int  cat_x, cat_y;          /* Cat location */
     int  mouse_x, mouse_y;      /* Location of mouse */
     int  raw_mouse_x, raw_mouse_y;/* Loc. of mouse (raw form) */
     int  quit;                  /* True if we need to exit */
     int  caught;                /* True if we got the mouse */
     int  cursor_size;           /* Size of the cursor */
     int  old_mouse_x, old_mouse_y;/* old mouse location */
     int  old_cat_x, old_cat_y;  /* old cat location */

     clrscr();

     _AH = CURSOR_GET;
     geninterrupt(INT_VIDEO);
     cursor_size = _CX;
```

continued

Listing 8.1 continued.

```
_AH = CURSOR_SET;
_CX = 0x0F0F;                    /* Turn off cursor */
geninterrupt(INT_VIDEO);

old_mouse_x = -1;
old_mouse_y = -1;
old_cat_x = -1;
old_cat_y = -1;

ch = 'x';                /* Set ch to an innocent character */
cat_x = random(80) +1;
cat_y = random(24) +1;
gotoxy(cat_x, cat_y);
putch('C');
quit = 0;
caught = 0;

gettime(&start_time);

/*
 * Wait for an event to happen
 */

while ((!quit) && (!caught)) {
    /* Keyboard event */
    if (kbhit()) {
        ch = getch();

        switch (ch) {
            case 'q':
                quit = 1;
                break;
            case 'd':
                debug = !debug;
                break;
            default:
                putch(BELL);
                break;
        }
    }
    /* Mouse event */
    _AX = MOUSE_GET_POSITION;
    geninterrupt(INT_MOUSE);
    raw_mouse_x = _CX;
    raw_mouse_y = _DX;
```

continued

Listing 8.1 continued.

```
/*
 * Correct mouse location
 */
mouse_x = raw_mouse_x / 8 +1;
mouse_y = raw_mouse_y / 8 +1;

if ((mouse_x != old_mouse_x) ||
    (mouse_y != old_mouse_y)) {
    /* Move mouse */
    if (old_mouse_x != -1) {
        gotoxy(old_mouse_x, old_mouse_y);
        putch(' ');         /* Erase old mouse */
    }
    gotoxy(mouse_x, mouse_y);
    putch('M');
}

caught = (mouse_x == cat_x) && (mouse_y == cat_y);

/* Time event */
gettime(&current_time);

if (time_diff() > update_time) {
    int diff_x; /* Cat Delta in X direction */
    int diff_y; /* Cat Delta in Y direction */

    diff_x = random(3) -1;
    diff_y = random(3) -1;

    gotoxy(cat_x, cat_y);        /* Erase old cat */
    putch(' ');

    cat_x += diff_x;
    cat_y += diff_y;

    /*
     * Check limits
     */
    if (cat_x < 1)
        cat_y = 1;

    if (cat_x < 1)
        cat_y = 1;

    if (cat_x > 80)
```

continued

Listing 8.1 continued.

```
                cat_x = 80;

            if (cat_y > 25)
                cat_y = 25;

            gotoxy(cat_x, cat_y);
            putch('C');

            start_time = current_time;
        }
        if (debug) {
            if ((old_cat_x != cat_x) ||
                (old_cat_y != cat_y) ||
                (old_mouse_x != mouse_x) ||
                (old_mouse_y != mouse_y)) {
                gotoxy(40, 1);
                cprintf("Cat location (%d,%d)    \n",
                        cat_x, cat_y);
                gotoxy(40, 2);
                cprintf("Mouse location (%d, %d)    \n",
                        mouse_x, mouse_y);
                gotoxy(40, 3);
                cprintf("Raw Mouse location (%d, %d)    \n",
                        raw_mouse_x, raw_mouse_y);

                old_cat_x = cat_x;
                old_cat_y = cat_y;
            }
        }
        old_mouse_x = mouse_x;
        old_mouse_y = mouse_y;
    }

    if (caught) {
        gotoxy(1,1);
        cputs("Got it!");
        ch = getch();
        quit = ch == 'q';
    }

    _AH = CURSOR_SET;
    _CX = cursor_size;              /* Restore cursor */
    geninterrupt(INT_VIDEO);
    clrscr();
```

continued

Listing 8.1 continued.

```
    return (ch);
}


/**********************************************************
 * usage -- tell the user how to use us                   *
 **********************************************************/
static void usage(void)
{
    (void)fprintf(stderr,"Usage is:\n");
    (void)fprintf(stderr,"      mouse [-d] [-t<time>\n");
    exit (1);
}
```

Chapter 9

A Breakout Game

Introduction

Game programming is not easy. Even a very simple game, like breakout, requires new knowledge of advanced graphics, animation, sound, and real-time programming. Our breakout program will make use of all these features, as well as provide you with a nice game to play.

Real-Time Graphics

Graphics are very CPU intensive. Even the basic graphics used in our breakout program will tax the power of our small 8086 class processor, with just two moving elements on the screen. Arcade games, which are filled with missiles, fireballs, aliens, and lasers uses specialized hardware to accelerate the graphics. Also, if you look carefully at the Arcade games, you will notice that they use two-dimensional graphics. Real-time good quality, three-dimensional graphics require computing power beyond what even the fastest supercomputer can supply. But the good news is that even with single color, two-dimensional graphics, we can create a lot of fun games.

Designing the Game

The first step in game design is to lay out the screen. Our screen will have two rows of bricks at the top and a paddle at the bottom. As we have said before, the comment is the most important statement in C. Rather than sketch our layout on a piece of paper that can be lost or thrown away, we put it in a comment:

```
/***********************************************************
 * Screen layout                                           *
 *                                                         *
 * (0,0)+-------------------------------+                  *
 *      |                               |                  *
 *ROW1->|***** ***** ***** ***** ***** *****|              *
 *      |***** ***** ***** ***** ***** *****|              *
 *      |                               |                  *
 *ROW2->|***** ***** ***** ***** ***** *****|              *
 *      |***** ***** ***** ***** ***** *****|              *
 *      |                               |                  *
 *      |                               |                  *
 *      |                               |                  *
 *      |                               |                  *
 *      |                               |                  *
 *      |                               |                  *
 * +->  |              *****            |                  *
 * |    +-------------------------------+                  *
 * |                                    ^                  *
 * +-paddle.top                 (MAX_X, MAX_Y)             *
 ***********************************************************/
```

Our layout not only shows where the important elements of the screen are located, but also lets us define the location of important variables. The two rows are located at ROW1 and ROW2. (We use uppercase variable names for things that will be defined at initialization time, and remain constant throughout the rest of the program.) We call these types of variables "semi-constants," because after they are initialized, they are treated as constants.

Initializing the Turbo C Graphics

Turbo C provides the user with a large library filled with a rich assortment of graphics functions. This library is excellent except for one major problem — it requires an external file containing the graphics driver to be present before anything will work. (Note: Microsoft uses a completely different graphics library. The programs presented in this chapter are highly Turbo C specific.)

The driver is loaded through the `initgraph` function call. This function is defined as:

```
initgraph(int *driver, int *mode, char *path)
```

where

`driver`   is a pointer to a constant indicating the type of graphics device present on the system. If this is set to the constant `DETECT`, the library will figure out what type of graphics device you have and load the appropriate driver.

                If an error occurs, `driver` will be set to a negative number.

`mode`   is the graphics mode to use. Different modes determine size and number of colors supplied by the graphics device. Each device interprets the mode number a little differently. We decided on using mode zero since it works reasonably across all devices.

`path`   is the path to the graphics driver. A value of `NULL` indicates that the driver is in the current directory.

Since we don't want to copy all the drivers to each program directory we need to point `initgraph` at the directory where Turbo C first puts the drivers. (This happens to be the directory where Turbo C is installed.) But Turbo C can be installed on any driver or any directory; how do we figure out where it is installed on this computer?

In this case, we decided to have the user execute a set command that sets the environment variable "TC" to the Turbo C install directory. For example, many people put their Turbo C compiler in C:\TC, so they would put the line:

```
SET TC=C:\TC
```

in their `AUTOEXEC.BAT` file. We can get the value of this environment variable using standard function `getenv`. So to initialize our graphics system we use the C code:

```
int graphic_driver = DETECT;   /* Detect graphics adaptor */
int graphic_mode = 0;          /* Default is mode 0 */
```

```
initgraph(&graphic_driver, &graphic_mode, getenv("TC"));
if (graphic_driver < 0) {
    (void)fprintf(stderr,
        "Graphics Initialization error %d\n",
                graphic_driver);
    exit (1);
}
```

After starting the graphics system, we compute the sizes (in pixels) of various objects on the screen. Unfortunately, starting the graphics systems causes us to lose one of our best diagnostic tools, the `printf` call. Graphics mode and text mode are mutually exclusive, so printing characters to a graphics screen causes a strange, unrecognizable collection of dots to appear on the screen.

This is especially annoying since we want to print some debug information at the end of this function. The solution is to stick our diagnostic message in a file for later review. The main program will open a file identified by the variable `debug_file` if the `-d` command line option is present.

At the end of `init_graphics`, we check to see if a debug file has been opened and then dumps the diagnostic data into it.

Drawing the Screen

One thing you might have noticed about our screen layout: everything is a rectangle. The two rows of bricks are rectangles, the paddle is a rectangle, and the ball is a rectangle. Why a square ball? Why not a round one? Computers make squares easily; circles take time and we can't afford the time.

Because everything is a box shape, we've defined a special data structure to handle this type of data:

```
struct box {
        int        left, top,
                   right, bottom;  /* Where it is */
        int        visible;        /* Is the box there? */
};
```

To initialize the screen, we put up two rows of boxes and a paddle. The ball will be created later when we begin to play a round.

Putting a row of boxes on the screen is not as simple as it sounds. We have a problem. A Hercules Graphics Adapter is 720 pixels wide and we're going to put a row of 14 equal-size boxes across the top of the screen. So that means that the width of each box must be 720⁄14 or 51.5 pixels wide. The graphics card can't handle half a pixel so we round down and each of our boxes is 51 pixels wide. But that leaves a gap of 6 pixels at the edge of our screen.

6 Pixel Gap

The gap is almost the size of the ball and looks ugly. How do we get rid of it? The answer is to distribute the 6 pixel error among six boxes. This will result in eight boxes, 51 wide, and six boxes, 52 wide. Distributed this way, the extra pixel will not be noticed.

The size of each box is computed based on the width remaining. The expression:

```
<width remaining> / <boxes remaining>
```

yields an integer number of pixels + a fractional error. For example, if the width remaining is 618 and the number of boxes left is 12, the ideal box size is 51.5. In real life, this is a 51-wide box with a 0.5 error. If the error is more than half a pixel, we make the box a pixel wider. (Rounding up is accomplished by adding 0.5 to the floating point expression before we convert the result to an integer.)

Our algorithm for computing the size of each box is:

```
for (boxes_remaining = BOXES_ACROSS;
                boxes_remaining > 0;
                boxes_remaining--) {
    box_width = ((float)width_remaining) /
            ((float)boxes_remaining) + 0.5;
        if (debug_file) {
                (void)fprintf(debug_file,
"Box place:Width %2d Width Remaining %3d Box Remaining %3d\n",
```

```
                        box_width, width_remaining,
                        boxes_remaining);
        }
        width_remaining -= box_width;
        last_box->left = box_x;
        last_box->top = where_y;
        last_box->right = box_x + box_width - border;
        last_box->bottom = where_y + BOX_HEIGHT;
        last_box->visible = 1;   /* We can see the box */
        draw_box(last_box);
        last_box++;
        box_x += box_width;
    }
```

The result of this algorithm is to distribute our wide boxes throughout the line. As we can see from the output of our debug statements, the wide boxes are correctly placed.

```
Box place: Width 51 Width Remaining 720 Box Remaining 14
Box place: Width 51 Width Remaining 669 Box Remaining 13
Box place: Width 52 Width Remaining 618 Box Remaining 12
Box place: Width 51 Width Remaining 566 Box Remaining 11
Box place: Width 52 Width Remaining 515 Box Remaining 10
Box place: Width 51 Width Remaining 463 Box Remaining 9
Box place: Width 52 Width Remaining 412 Box Remaining 8
Box place: Width 51 Width Remaining 360 Box Remaining 7
Box place: Width 52 Width Remaining 309 Box Remaining 6
Box place: Width 51 Width Remaining 257 Box Remaining 5
Box place: Width 52 Width Remaining 206 Box Remaining 4
Box place: Width 51 Width Remaining 154 Box Remaining 3
Box place: Width 52 Width Remaining 103 Box Remaining 2
Box place: Width 51 Width Remaining 51 Box Remaining 1
```

The actual drawing of the boxes is left to the routine draw_box. We use the standard Turbo C function bar to draw the box. (There is a standard function rectangle, but this draws a hollow rectangle.)

The definition of this function is:

```
void bar(int left, int top, int right, int bottom)
```

where:

left, top, right, bottom define bar to be drawn.

The bar is drawn using the current fill style and color. In order to draw solid color boxes, we set the fill style to SOLD_FILL and the color to 1 using the standard function setfillstyle. The definition of this function is:

```
void setfillstyle(int pattern, int color)
```

where

pattern is one of the fill styles defined in *graphic.h*.

color is the color to use.

The full function for drawing boxes is:

```
static void draw_box(struct box *box_ptr)
{
        setfillstyle(SOLID_FILL, 1); /* Visible boxes */
        bar(box_ptr->left, box_ptr->top,
            box_ptr->right, box_ptr->bottom);
```

Playing the Game

The actual game algorithm can be written as:

```
while (playing) {
        <wait a while>
        <check to see if ball hit something>
        <move the ball>
}
```

Waiting around is not a simple operation. At any time the user can move the mouse and the paddle should move with it. So we must constantly monitor the mouse.

We move the paddle by erasing it and redrawing it. This method was chosen because it is simple, not because it is good. The problem is that our computer is not fast enough to perform these operations without the user noticing a little flash as the paddle disappears and reappears. In an amateur game like this one, this is acceptable. A more professional effort would require a more sophisticated movement routine. We'll discuss advanced graphics techniques at the end of this chapter.

Hitting Things

The ball can hit a variety of things: the edge of the screen, a brick, or the paddle. Each of these must be checked individually.

The edges of the screen are easy to check. When the left side of the ball passes the right side of the screen, we have a hit. We cause the ball to bounce by reversing its movement in the X direction. Similar algorithms handle the other two edges.

```
if (ball.left <= 0)
        ball_xv = -ball_xv;
```

The bottom of the screen is different. Here we don't bounce unless we hit the paddle. The paddle itself is divided into three zones. The right zone increases the ball's velocity to the right. The middle leaves the velocity alone and the left increases the velocity to the left.

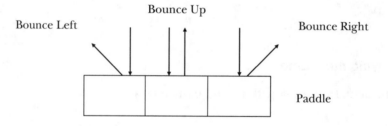

```
/* Middle of the ball */
    int ball_middle = (ball.left + ball.right)/2;

    /* Middle of the paddle */
    int paddle_middle = (paddle.left + paddle.right)/2;

    if (dist < PADDLE_MIDDLE_SIZE) {
       /* Middle zone -- reflect ball */
       ball_yv = -ball_yv;
    } else if (dist < ((PADDLE_WIDTH + BALL_SIZE) /2)) {
       /* Size zone, reflect ball and increase xv */
       ball_yv = -ball_yv;

       /* Increase XV */
       if (paddle_middle < ball_middle)
         ball_xv++;
    else
         ball_xv--;
```

If we missed the paddle, the round is over and the function exits.

Next we must check each of the bricks to see if the ball hit them. If the ball is in range in both the X and Y directions, then we've hit the brick. We erase the brick and determine which side we hit, adjusting the velocity of the ball accordingly.

Finally, after we handle all collisions, we update the ball and loop, waiting for the next movement.

Finishing Details

Sound is very important to a video game. We supply minimal sound. Every time the player hits a brick we output a beep. The first version of the game used the code:

```
putch(BELL);
```

to sound the beep. The problem was that the screen would freeze until the console had finished beeping. The solution was to start the beep with the line:

```
sound(700);          /* Start a 700 hz beep */
```

and at the same time start a 10-tick timer that controls when the sound will be turned off:

```
sound_left = 10;
```

This counter is decremented each clock tick by the function `cycle_wait`. When it becomes zero, the sound is turned off.

```
if (sound_left > 0) {
    sound_left--;
    if (sound_left <= 0)
        no_sound();      }
```

Finally, there is the displaying of the all-important score. We can't do a `printf` to the screen while it is in graphics mode; we must draw the text. This is done with the standard function `outtext`. It is defined as:

```
void outtext(char *string)
```

where

string   is the string to output. The string will be plotted at the
                 current position, using the current text width and text
                 height.

The standard function moveto is used to position us to the upper right
corner of the screen. Then we write the score. The definition of moveto is:

```
void moveto(int x, int y)
```

where

x,y   are the new current graphics position.

In text mode, writing a string to the screen will cause the new string to replace
the old. In graphics, the new string will overwrite the old, yielding something
like:

OЕ̃Ð

We need to erase the old score before writing the new one. This is accomplished by plotting the string again, this time using the background color. (It's
pretty hard to see white text on a white page.) This effectively erases the old
string.

Our full function for updating the score is:

```
void output_score(void)
{
    static int old_score = -1;    /* Last score we output */
    static int old_life = -1;     /* Last life we output */
    static char string[30] = "";    /* String to display */

    if ((score != old_score) || (life != old_life)) {
        if (string[0] != '\0') {
        setcolor(0);           /* Set color to background */
            moveto(10, 1);
            outtext(string);
        }
        (void)sprintf(string, "Balls left: %d Score: %d",
                life, score);
        setcolor(1);           /* Set color to foreground */
```

```
    moveto(10, 1);
    outtext(string);

    old_life = life;
    old_score = score;
    line(1, TOP_MARGIN-1, MAX_X, TOP_MARGIN-1);
  }
}
```

Graphics Tricks

Our game moves objects like the paddle and ball by erasing them and redrawing. The problem is that this causes a flash as the objects disappear and reappear.

One way around this problem is to intelligently update the paddle by only erasing and drawing the sections that change. For example, if the paddle moves 10 pixels to the left, we erase the right 10 pixels and draw in 10 left pixels.

How to Improve the Game

This program is a pretty good demonstration program; however, it's a very limited and tame game. We have programmed for the lowest common denominator and not made full use of the color available on some of our graphics systems. There is only one sound, a simple beep. The better games have music and other sound effects. Even with the limited speaker on the PC, you can generate some fairly good sounds.

Our game has one screen, one skill level, and one speed. Most games offer the player a chance to advance to different levels where things are more challenging.

Even with its limitations, though, this can be the beginning of a fairly good game.

Listing 9-1. "breakout.c"

```c
#undef KEYBOARD /* Use a keyboard timer instead of clock */
/************************************************************
 * Breakout -- a breakout game                            *
 *                                                        *
 * Usage:                                                 *
 *      breakout [-d]                                     *
 *                                                        *
 * Options                                                *
 *      -d -- write debug information to breakout.log     *
 ************************************************************/
#include <stdlib.h>
#include <graphics.h>
#include <stdio.h>
#include <dos.h>
#include <conio.h>



/************************************************************
 * Screen layout                                          *
 *                                                        *
 * (0,0)+----------------------------------+              *
 *      |                                  |              *
 *ROW1->|***** ***** ***** ***** ***** *****|             *
 *      |***** ***** ***** ***** ***** *****|             *
 *      |                                  |              *
 *ROW2->|***** ***** ***** ***** ***** *****|             *
 *      |***** ***** ***** ***** ***** *****|             *
 *      |                                  |              *
 *      |                                  |              *
 *      |                                  |              *
 *      |                                  |              *
 *      |                                  |              *
 *      |                                  |              *
 * +-> |                  *****          |                *
 * |   +----------------------------------+              *
 * |                                     ^                *
 * +-paddle.top                   (MAX_X, MAX_Y)*
 ************************************************************/
#define INT_MOUSE       0x33    /* Mouse function */
#define MOUSE_INIT      0x00    /* Initialize the mouse */
#define MOUSE_SHOW      0x01    /* Show the mouse cursor */
#define MOUSE_HIDE      0x02    /* Hide the mouse cursor */
/* Set the X range of the mouse */
#define MOUSE_X_LIMIT   0x07
/* Set the Y range of the mouse */
#define MOUSE_Y_LIMIT   0x08
```

continued

Listing 9-1 continued.

```
#define MOUSE_GET_POSITION 0x03 /* Get current mouse position */

/* Biggest X for mouse movements */
#define MOUSE_MAX_X     639

#define BOXES_ACROSS 14
/* Number of boxes across the screen */
#define TOP_MARGIN 10
/* We reserve this much at the top */

static int MAX_X, MAX_Y;           /
* Size of graphics screen in pixels */
static int BOX_WIDTH, BOX_HEIGHT;
/* Size of a breakout box */
static int ROW_1, ROW_2;
/* Location of the rows of boxes */
static int PADDLE_WIDTH, PADDLE_HEIGHT;/*Paddle size */
static int BALL_SIZE;              /* # pixels in the ball */
static int PADDLE_MIDDLE_SIZE;
/* Size of middle region of paddle */
static int MAX_BALL_XV = 5;
/* Biggest speed in X direction */

static FILE *debug_file = NULL; /* File for debug data */
static void byebye(void);        /* Get us out of here */

struct box {
        int     left, top,
                right, bottom;   /* Where it is */
        int     visible;         /* Is the box there */
};

#define MAX_BOXES  40
/* Max number of boxes on the screen */
static struct box boxes[MAX_BOXES];/* Boxes to hit */
/* Pointer to last box in the list */
static struct box *last_box = boxes;
static struct box ball;          /* Where the ball is */
static struct box paddle;        /* Where the paddle is */
static int paddle_debug = 0;
/* True if we are debugging paddle handler */
static int update_time = 4;      /* Update every 2/1000 seconds */
static int sound_left = 0;       /* Time left for sound */
```

continued

Listing 9-1 continued.

```c
#define MAX_LIFE 5              /* Number of balls */
static int life;               /* Number of balls left */
static int score = 0;          /* Current score */

main(int argc, char *argv[])
{
    int mouse_status;     /* Did we properly init the mouse? */

    void usage(void);
    void init_graphics(void);
    void init_screen(void);
    void do_paddle_debug(void);
    void do_round(void);
    void erase_box(struct box *);

    while ((argc > 1) && (argv[1][0] == '-')) {
        switch (argv[1][1]) {
            case 'd':
                debug_file = fopen("breakout.log", "w");
                if (debug_file == NULL) {
                    (void)fprintf(stderr,
                                "Unable to open breakout.log\n");
                    exit (1);
                }
                break;
            case 'p':
                paddle_debug = 1;
                break;
            default:
                usage();
                /*NOTREACHED*/
        }
        argc--;
        argv++;
    }

    /* Initialize the mouse */
    _AX = MOUSE_INIT;
    geninterrupt(INT_MOUSE);
    mouse_status = _AX;

    if (mouse_status != -1) {
        (void)fprintf(stderr,"Mouse driver not present\n");
        exit (1);
    }
```

continued

Listing 9-1 continued.

```
        init_graphics();
        init_screen();

        if (paddle_debug)
            do_paddle_debug();

        for (life = MAX_LIFE; life > 0; life--) {
            do_round();
            erase_box(&ball);           /* Clear old ball */

            if (kbhit())                /* Exit on user command */
                break;
        }
        byebye();
        return (0); /* Not reached */
}
static struct time current_time;            /* Time now */
/* Time when we started this move */
static struct time start_time;

#define CONVERT(ti) (((((ti.ti_hour) * 60) + \
                       (ti.ti_min) * 60) + \
                       (ti.ti_sec) * 100) + \
                       (ti.ti_hund)
/*************************************************************
 * time_diff -- return the time difference between        *
 *              start and current times.                  *
 *                                                        *
 * Returns                                                *
 *      time difference in hundredths of seconds.         *
 *************************************************************/
static unsigned long int time_diff(void)
{
    unsigned long int start;   /* Start time as hundredths */
    unsigned long int current; /* Current time as hundredths */

    start = CONVERT(start_time);
    current = CONVERT(current_time);

    return (current - start);
}
/*************************************************************
 * init_graphics -- Initialize the graphics system        *
 *************************************************************/
```

continued

Listing 9-1 continued.

```
static void init_graphics(void)
{
    int graphic_driver = DETECT;    /* Detect graphics adaptor */
    int graphic_mode = 0;                 /* Default is mode 0 */

    initgraph(&graphic_driver, &graphic_mode, getenv("TC"));
    if (graphic_driver < 0) {
        (void)fprintf(stderr,
            "Graphics Initialization error %d\n",
            graphic_driver);
        exit (1);
    }
    MAX_X = getmaxx();
    MAX_Y = getmaxy();

    BOX_HEIGHT = MAX_Y / 20;
    BOX_WIDTH = MAX_X / BOXES_ACROSS;

    ROW_1 = BOX_HEIGHT * 2;
    ROW_2 = BOX_HEIGHT * 5;

    PADDLE_WIDTH = BOX_WIDTH;
    PADDLE_HEIGHT = BOX_HEIGHT / 2;
    PADDLE_MIDDLE_SIZE = PADDLE_WIDTH / 6;

    BALL_SIZE = PADDLE_HEIGHT;

    if (debug_file != NULL) {
        (void)fprintf(debug_file,"MAX_X %d MAX_Y %d\n",
                        MAX_X, MAX_Y);
        (void)fprintf(debug_file,"BOX_HEIGHT %d BOX_WIDTH %d\n",
                BOX_HEIGHT, BOX_WIDTH);
        (void)fprintf(debug_file,
            "PADDLE_WIDTH %d PADDLE_HEIGHT %d\n",
            PADDLE_WIDTH, PADDLE_HEIGHT);
    }
}
/***********************************************************
 * erase_box -- remove a box from the screen              *
 *                                                        *
 * Parameters                                             *
 *      box_ptr -- the box we are to remove.              *
 *      (We assume that the box is no longer visible)     *
 ***********************************************************/
```

continued

Listing 9-1 continued.

```c
static void erase_box(struct box *box_ptr)
{
    setfillstyle(EMPTY_FILL, 0); /* Visible boxes */
    bar(box_ptr->left, box_ptr->top,
        box_ptr->right, box_ptr->bottom);
}
/***********************************************************
 * draw_box -- put a box on the screen                     *
 *                                                         *
 * Parameters                                              *
 *      box_ptr -- the box we are to draw.                 *
 *      (We assume that the box is visible)                *
 ***********************************************************/
static void draw_box(struct box *box_ptr)
{
    setfillstyle(SOLID_FILL, 1); /* Visible boxes */
    bar(box_ptr->left, box_ptr->top,
        box_ptr->right, box_ptr->bottom);
}
/***********************************************************
 * output_score -- write the score to the screen.         *
 ***********************************************************/
void output_score(void)
{
    static int old_score = -1;    /* Last score we output */
    static int old_life = -1;     /* Last life we output */
    static char string[30] = "";  /* String to display */

    if ((score != old_score) || (life != old_life)) {
        if (string[0] != '\0') {
            setcolor(0);             /* Set color to background */
            moveto(10, 1);
            outtext(string);
        }
        (void)sprintf(string, "Balls left: %d Score: %d",
            life, score);
        setcolor(1);                 /* Set color to foreground */
        moveto(10, 1);
        outtext(string);

        old_life = life;
        old_score = score;

        line(1, TOP_MARGIN-1, MAX_X, TOP_MARGIN-1);
    }
}
```

continued

Listing 9-1 continued.

```
/***********************************************************
 * Setup_row -- setup a row of boxes                       *
 *                                                         *
 * Parameters                                              *
 *      where_y -- the y location of the row               *
 *                                                         *
 * Note: We use a special algorithm to decide how          *
 * wide the boxes are.  This is because we want to          *
 * fill the screen across with boxes.                       *
 *                                                         *
 * That means that some boxes must be one pixel wider       *
 * than others.                                             *
 *                                                         *
 * The algorithm computes the size of the box as           *
 * the width remaining/#boxes remaining.                    *
 *                                                         *
 * A short width (due to truncation) will result in a      *
 * bigger width remaining for the next box.  So when        *
 * the next one is computed, it will sop up the excess     *
 * width.                                                  *
 ***********************************************************/
static void setup_row(int where_y)
{
    int box_x;          /* X location of the box */
    int border = 3;     /* Width of border between boxes */
    int box_width;      /* Width of this box */
    int width_remaining;/* Number of pixels remaining to try */
    int boxes_remaining;/* Number of boxes remain to be done */

    box_x = 0;
    width_remaining = MAX_X +1;
    for (boxes_remaining = BOXES_ACROSS; boxes_remaining > 0;
        boxes_remaining--) {
        box_width = ((float)width_remaining) /
                    ((float)boxes_remaining) + 0.5;
        if (debug_file) {
            (void)fprintf(debug_file,
    "Box place: Width %2d Width Remaining %3d Box Remaining %3d\n",
                box_width, width_remaining, boxes_remaining);
        }
        width_remaining -= box_width;
        last_box->left = box_x;
        last_box->top = where_y;
        last_box->right = box_x + box_width - border;
        last_box->bottom = where_y + BOX_HEIGHT;
```

continued

Listing 9-1 continued.

```
            last_box->visible = 1;   /* We can see the box */
            draw_box(last_box);
            last_box++;
            box_x += box_width;
        }
}
#define LONG(x)   ((long) (x))
int  old_mouse_x = -1;  /* Last location of the mouse */
/***********************************************************
 * cycle_wait -- wait for a cycle to complete.            *
 *              A cycle is finished after the proper      *
 *              time has elapsed or a character is        *
 *              typed.                                    *
 *                                                        *
 *      Update paddle during the cycle.                   *
 ***********************************************************/
static void cycle_wait(void)
{
    int  mouse_x;        /* Location of mouse */
    int  raw_mouse_x;    /* Location of mouse (raw form) */

    /* Time event */
    gettime(&current_time);
    start_time = current_time;

#ifdef KEYBOARD
    while (!kbhit())
#else KEYBOARD
    while ((time_diff() < update_time) && (!kbhit()))
#endif KEYBOARD
    {
        gettime(&current_time);

        /* Mouse event */
        _AX = MOUSE_GET_POSITION;
        geninterrupt(INT_MOUSE);
        raw_mouse_x = _CX;

        /*
         * Correct mouse location --
         *   Covert mouse coordinates into pixel coordinates.
         *   (Long must be used to avoid overflow on multiply.)
         */
        mouse_x = (int)((LONG(raw_mouse_x) * LONG(MAX_X)) /
                        LONG(MOUSE_MAX_X));
```

continued

Listing 9-1 continued.

```
            /*
             * Correct for the size of the paddle and
             * check for limits
             */
            mouse_x -= (PADDLE_WIDTH/2);

            if (mouse_x < 0)
                mouse_x = 0;



            if (mouse_x > (MAX_X - PADDLE_WIDTH))
                mouse_x = MAX_X - PADDLE_WIDTH;

            if (old_mouse_x != mouse_x) {
                old_mouse_x = mouse_x;

                erase_box(&paddle);
                paddle.left = mouse_x;
                paddle.right = mouse_x + PADDLE_WIDTH;
                draw_box(&paddle);

                if (debug_file)
                    (void)fprintf(debug_file,
                        "Mouse loc. raw %d Adj. %d\n",
                        raw_mouse_x, mouse_x);
            }
        }
        if (sound_left > 0) {
            sound_left--;
            if (sound_left <= 0)
                nosound();
        }
}
/***********************************************************
 * do_paddle_debug -- Allow paddle handlers to be         *
 *                    debugged.                            *
 *      Basically, just wait enabling paddle movement.    *
 *      Exits when a character is types.                   *
 ***********************************************************/
static void do_paddle_debug(void)
{
    while (!kbhit())
        cycle_wait();
    (void)getch();          /* Grab the character */
```

continued

Listing 9-1 continued.

```
        byebye();
}
/************************************************************
 * init_screen -- put all the objects on the screen       *
 *                (at beginning of game.)                  *
 ************************************************************/
static void init_screen(void)
{
        last_box = boxes;
        setup_row(ROW_1);
        setup_row(ROW_2);

        paddle.top = MAX_Y - PADDLE_HEIGHT;
        paddle.bottom = MAX_Y;
        paddle.left = (MAX_X - PADDLE_WIDTH) / 2;
        paddle.right = paddle.left + PADDLE_WIDTH;


}
/************************************************************
 * byebye -- get us out of here.  This consists of        *
 *           going into text mode and closing files.      *
 ************************************************************/
static void byebye(void)
{
        closegraph();
        if (debug_file != NULL)
            (void)fclose(debug_file);

        if (kbhit())
            (void)getch();              /* Eat a character */
        exit (0);
}
/************************************************************
 * Usage -- tell the user what to do                       *
 ************************************************************/
static void usage(void)
{
        (void)fprintf(stderr,"Usage is: breakout [-d] [-p]\n");
        exit (1);
}
/************************************************************
 * kill_box -- remove a box from the screen               *
 *                                                        *
 * Parameter                                              *
 *      cur_box -- box to remove from the screen          *
 ************************************************************/
```

continued

Listing 9-1 continued.

```
void kill_box(struct box *cur_box)
{
    score += 20;              /* Add on to the score */
    cur_box->visible = 0;
    sound(700);               /* Turn on the sound */
    sound_left = 10;      /* Time for sound */
    erase_box(cur_box);
}
/************************************************************
 * do_round -- play a single round.                        *
 *                                                         *
 *     Ends when the player fails to hit the ball          *
 *     or we kill all the bricks.                          *
 ************************************************************/
static void do_round(void)
{
    int ball_xv = 4;                    /* Ball X velocity */
    int ball_yv = 4;                    /* Ball Y velocity */
    struct box *cur_box;                /* Box we are looking at */
    int ball_middle_x, ball_middle_y;   /* Ball location */
    int box_middle_x, box_middle_y;     /* Box location */

    /*
     * Initialize the ball
     */
    ball.top = ROW_2 + BOX_HEIGHT * 2;
    ball.left = BOX_WIDTH * 2;
    ball.bottom = ball.top + BALL_SIZE;
    ball.right = ball.left + BALL_SIZE;

    draw_box(&ball);
    old_mouse_x = -1;              /* Redraw paddle */

    output_score();
    while (!kbhit()) {
        /* Wait for a cycle to complete */
        cycle_wait();


        /*
         * Check for collisions
         * ===== === ==========
         */

        /* Did we hit the sides of the screen */
        if (ball.top <= TOP_MARGIN+1)
```

continued

Listing 9-1 continued.

```
        ball_yv = -ball_yv;

    if (ball.left <= 0)
        ball_xv = -ball_xv;

    if (ball.right >= (MAX_X-1))
        ball_xv = -ball_xv;

    /*
     * Did the ball hit the paddle?
     */
    /* Is ball at bottom of the screen (going down) */

    if ((ball.bottom >= (MAX_Y-1-PADDLE_HEIGHT)) &&
        (ball_yv > 0)) {
        /* Middle of the ball */
        int ball_middle = (ball.left + ball.right)/2;

        /* Middle of the paddle */
        int paddle_middle = (paddle.left + paddle.right)/2;

        /* Distance between the middle
                    of the ball and paddle */
        int dist = abs(ball_middle - paddle_middle);
        /*
         * The paddle is divided into three zones.
         *
         * The middle zone just reflects the ball at the
         * same speed.
         *
         * The side zones increase the sideways speed of the
         * ball (up to a maximum of MAX_BALL_XV
         *
         * The third zone is the miss zone.  The ball didn't
         * make it.
         *
         */
        if (debug_file != NULL)
            (void)fprintf(debug_file,"Paddle hit %d\n",
                        dist);

        if (dist < PADDLE_MIDDLE_SIZE) {
            /* Middle zone -- reflect ball */
            ball_yv = -ball_yv;
```

continued

Listing 9-1 continued.

```
                    if (debug_file != NULL)
                        (void)fprintf(debug_file,"Hit Middle\n");

            } else if (dist < ((PADDLE_WIDTH + BALL_SIZE) /2)) {
                /* Size zone, reflect ball and increase xv */
                ball_yv = -ball_yv;

                /* Increase XV */
                if (paddle_middle < ball_middle)
                    ball_xv++;
                else
                    ball_xv--;

                if (ball_xv > MAX_BALL_XV)
                    ball_xv = MAX_BALL_XV;

                if (ball_xv < -MAX_BALL_XV)
                    ball_xv = -MAX_BALL_XV;

                if (debug_file != NULL)
                    (void)fprintf(debug_file,"Hit Sides %d\n",
                            ball_xv);
            } else {
                /* Missed -- check for ball off screen */
                if (ball.bottom >= MAX_Y)
                    return;
            }
        }


    for (cur_box = boxes; cur_box < last_box; cur_box++) {
        if (! cur_box->visible)
            continue;

        /*
         * Decide if the ball hits a box
         * Since a ball has width and we check for touching
         * we must check an area bigger than the box itself.
         *
         *       +-----------------------+
         *       |                       |
         *       | *******************   |
         *       | *                 *   |
         *       | *******************   |
         *       |                       |
         *       +-----------------------+
```

continued

Listing 9-1 continued.

```
 *        ^   ^box-location
 *        |
 *        + Area where the ball can be
 */
ball_middle_x = (ball.left + ball.right) / 2;
box_middle_x = (cur_box->left + cur_box->right) / 2;

if (abs(ball_middle_x - box_middle_x) >=
    (((BOX_WIDTH + BALL_SIZE)/2)+abs(ball_xv))) {
    continue;
}

ball_middle_y = (ball.top + ball.bottom) / 2;
box_middle_y = (cur_box->top + cur_box->bottom) / 2;

if (abs(ball_middle_y - box_middle_y) >=
    (((BOX_HEIGHT + BALL_SIZE)/2)+abs(ball_yv))) {
    continue;
}

kill_box(cur_box);

if (abs(cur_box->left - ball.right) <
    (BALL_SIZE/2)+abs(ball_xv)) {
    ball_xv = -ball_xv;
} else
if (abs(cur_box->right - ball.left) <
    (BALL_SIZE/2)+abs(ball_xv)) {
    ball_xv = -ball_xv;
}

if (abs(cur_box->top - ball.bottom) <
    (BALL_SIZE/2)+abs(ball_yv)) {
    ball_yv = -ball_yv;
} else
if (abs(cur_box->bottom - ball.top) <
    (BALL_SIZE/2)+abs(ball_yv)) {
    ball_yv = -ball_yv;
}
/*
 * At this point, we've killed a box.  Don't allow
 * two kills in one move, so breakout out here.
 */
break;
}
```

Listing 9-1 continued.

```
        /*
         * Move the ball
         */
        erase_box(&ball);
        /* Output score and fix any damage */
        output_score();

        ball.top += ball_yv;
        ball.bottom += ball_yv;
        ball.left += ball_xv;
        ball.right += ball_xv;
        draw_box(&ball);
    }
}
```

A Simple Menu System

Introduction

We're now going to leave the world of games and get back to the world of serious programming. Menus are a basic element of user friendly programming. In this chapter, we will create a general purpose menu package.

We will define routines to handle two basic types of menus, selection menus and fill-in-the-blank menus. In a selection menu, the user is presented with a list of items. The user then uses the cursor keys to choose an item. For example:

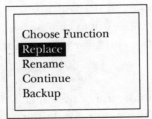

In a fill-in-the-blank menu, the user is presented with a series of questions and blanks. The user enters data into the blanks to complete the menu. An example of a fill-in-the-blank menu is:

Selection Menu

But what do we do when an item is selected? At first, we might be tempted to have the package just return the select number. The code to call this type of function looks like:

```
switch (select_menu_number(menu)) {
    case 0:
        do_replace();
        break;
    case 1:
        do_backup();
        break;
    case 2:
        do_cancel();
        break;
    default:
        /* Abort - Do nothing */
        break;        }
```

It looks like everyone who calls our selection menu package will follow it with a **switch** statement. This type of programming bothers us. First of all, this is a maintenance problem. If we add a selection to the menu (for example, a rename selection), we've got to change a bunch of case labels. Secondly, every time we see repetitive code, we wonder if there isn't some way of automating it.

The solution is to make use of a item called a "callback" routine. In our data structure defining the menu, we define a function for each item. When the user selects an item for the menu, the menu handler calls the "callback" function for that item. We've essentially moved the functionality of the **switch** into the menu package. But what's more important, the controlling information (which function to call for each menu item) remains with the definition of the menu. The result is a much cleaner and easier to maintain program.

When we add a new item to the menu, we automatically add information that tells the program which function to call. We don't have to edit a switch statement somewhere else in the program. (Or worse, edit several switch statements.)

The structure for each item in the menu is:

```
/*
 * One of these is defined for each item in the
 * selection list.
 */
struct select_item {
    char *name;             /* Name of the item */
    void (*call_back)(void);/* Function to call when selected */
};
```

name is the string to display in the menu. The function call_back will be called when this item is selected.

As you can see this structure is extremely simple, and yet groups the most useful information in one spot.

We need to put together a list of select_items along with some other information to form a select menu. This consists of a box somewhere on the screen containing a title and a list of items to select.

The data structure to store this information is:

```
struct select_menu {
    /* Location of upper left corner of menu */
    int loc_x, loc_y;

    /* Title of this menu */
    char *title;

    /* Pointer to the list of items to select */
    struct select_item *item_list;
};
```

The fields loc_x and loc_y are used to place the menu on the screen. The size of the menu will be computed from the size of the title and items in the menu.

The actual routine to handle the selection menu is defined as:

```
/********************************************************
 * select_menu -- handle a selection menu              *
 *                                                      *
 * Parameter                                            *
 *      menu -- menu to process                         *
 *      selection -- default selection                  *
 *      after -- call the callback routine after        *
 *                        destroying the window         *
 *                                                      *
 * Returns                                              *
 *      MENU_OK -- item selected.  Callback routine     *
 *              executed.                                *
 *      MENU_ERROR -- error occurred in system          *
 *      MENU_ABORT -- user typed in ESC to abort        *
 ********************************************************/
int select_menu(struct select_menu *menu, int selection,
                int after);
```

The following program uses the selection menu function to create a simple menu with the items "Replace", "Backup", and "Cancel". The callback routines merely display a message in the upper right corner of the screen, but in a real program they would do real work.

Listing 10-1. "select.c"

```
/********************************************************
 * select -- test menu system                          *
 ********************************************************/
#include <stdio.h>
#include <stdlib.h>
#include <conio.h>
#include "menu.h"

static void do_replace(void);    /* Replace callback routine */
static void do_backup(void);     /* Backup callback routine */
static void do_cancel(void);     /* Cancel callback routine */

struct select_item list1[] = {
  {"Replace", do_replace},
  {"Overwrite", do_backup},
  {"Cancel", do_cancel},
  {NULL, NULL}
};

struct select_menu select1 = {
```

continued

Listing 10-1 continued

```
    10, 10,                  /* Location */
    "Test Menu",
    list1
};

main()
{
    clrscr();
    select_menu(&select1, 0, 0);
    /*
     * Show result and wait for user to finish us
     */
    (void)getch();
    return (0);
}
/***********************************************************
 * do_replace -- callback function for replace selection *
 ***********************************************************/
void do_replace(void)
{
    gotoxy(1,1);
    cputs("Replace called");
}
/***********************************************************
 * do_backup -- callback function for backup selection    *
 ***********************************************************/
void do_backup(void)
{
    gotoxy(1,1);
    cputs("Overwrite called");
}
/***********************************************************
 * do_cancel -- callback function for cancel selection    *
 ***********************************************************/
void do_cancel(void)
{
    gotoxy(1,1);
    cputs("Cancel called");
}
```

One final detail, the callback routine can be called before or after we destroy the window. This allows us to created nested windows by letting the callback routine call the menu package again. For example, an "Insert" selection could easily pop up a new menu with the selection "Insert Before" and "Insert After".

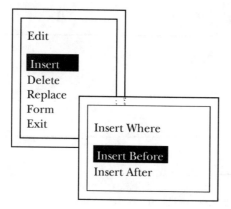

Limitations

One of the biggest limitations of our select_menu function is that it contains no help features. We should be able to associate help text with each selection, as well as, the menu itself. There are no provisions for color, or having a default selection other that the first one.

Implementation

The function select_menu begins by calling the function select_start to create a window for the menu. Next display_select is used to construct the menu. select_loop handles the user input, and moving the selection number up and down. When the user finally chooses an item, we execute the callback routine and return the screen to its original state using the function destroy_window.

```c
int select_menu(struct select_menu *menu, int selection,
            int after)
{
    /* Information about the current window */
    struct window_info cur_win;
    int status;          /* Status information */

    status = select_start(menu, &cur_win);
    if (status != MENU_OK)
        return (status);

    status = display_select(menu, selection);

    if (status == MENU_OK) {
        selection = select_loop(menu, selection);
```

```
    } else {
        selection = status;
    }

    if (selection != MENU_ABORT) {
        /* Set screen size to full for callback routine */
        window(1, 1, 80, 25);

        if (after) {
            destroy_window(&cur_win);
            (*menu->item_list[selection].call_back)();
        } else {
            (*menu->item_list[selection].call_back)();
            destroy_window(&cur_win);
        }
    } else
        destroy_window(&cur_win);

    if (selection == MENU_ABORT)
        return (MENU_ABORT);

    return (MENU_OK);
}
```

Window Creation and Destruction

In our menu system we've defined two functions to handle windows. The create_window function makes a blank area on the screen surrounded by a box. All the data under the window are saved so that when we call destroy_window the screen is returned to the state it was in before the window appeared.

The function create_window is defined as:

```
/************************************************************
 * create_window -- create a window                        *
 *                                                          *
 * Parameters                                               *
 *     x1, y1, x2, y2 -- corners of the window              *
 *     cur_win -- pointer to where to save window           *
 *             data. (Used by destroy window.)              *
 *                                                          *
 * Returns                                                  *
 *     MENU_OK -- no problem                                *
 *     MENU_ERROR -- something went wrong                   *
 ************************************************************/
int create_window(int x1, int y1, int x2, int y2,
    struct window_info *cur_win)
```

It will store all the window data into the structure `cur_win`. This includes all the information needed to restore the screen to the state it was in before the new window was created.

The actual implementation involves a number of library calls to get information about the current screen.

The opposite of `create_window` is `destroy_window`. This function is defined as:

```
/**********************************************************
 * destroy_window -- destroy a window and return the      *
 *                      screen to the state before the     *
 *                      window was created.                *
 *                                                         *
 * Restriction: Windows must be destroyed in reverse       *
 *                 order of creation.                       *
 *                                                         *
 * Parameter                                               *
 *       cur_win -- the window to destroy                   *
 **********************************************************/
void destroy_window(struct window_info *cur_win)
```

This function takes the information stored in the `cur_win` structure and uses it to restore the screen.

Fill-in-the-blank Menus

A fill-in-the-blank type menu displays a series of blanks and allows the user to fill in the blanks. For example, the following menu asks the user for his name and address:

Again, the first thing we do when designing the function to handle these menus is to define the data structures. The basic structure for a fill-in-the-blank menu is:

```
struct fill_in_menu {
    int loc_x, loc_y;   /* Location of the menu */
    int size_x, size_y; /* Size of the menu (including border) */
    char *background;   /* All fixed text  */

    /* Pointer to list of blanks to fill in */
    struct blank *blank_list;
};
```

The fields `loc_x`, `loc_y`, `size_x`, and `size_y` define the location and size of the menu. We have lumped all the fixed text (screen title, blank names, and other stuff) into one big text string, `background`. Finally there is the list of blanks.

A blank is defined by the structure:

```
struct blank {
    int loc_x, loc_y;    /* Where the blank is located */
    char *answer;        /* Place to put answer */
    int len;             /* Max length of the answer */
    int (*verify)(char *);/* Verification routine */
};
```

The fields `loc_x` and `loc_y` are used to place the blank within the window. The result will be put in the string `answer`. Default values can be put in this variable before the `fill_in_menu` function is called. The variable `len` is the length of answer (including the terminating `NULL`). Finally we have a pointer to the `verify` function. This function will be called to make sure that the answer is correct. It returns a value of `VERIFY_OK` if the answer is legal and `VERIFY_ERROR` if not.

The declaration for the `fill_in_menu` function is:

```
/************************************************************
 * fill_in_menu -- handle a fill in the blank menu         *
 *                                                          *
 * Parameters                                               *
 *      menu -- menu to process                             *
 *                                                          *
 * Returns                                                  *
```

```
*          MENU_ABORT -- user typed in ESC to abort       *
*          MENU_ERROR -- some sort of error occurred      *
*          otherwise -- character that finished the menu  *
**********************************************************/
int fill_in_menu(struct fill_in_menu *menu);
```

Implementation Details

The implementation of our `fill_in_menu` function follows a familiar pattern:

```
create the window
display the menu
enter a while loop
    Handle input characters
destroy window
```

The actual code for this function is presented at the end of this chapter.

get_string

Our `fill_in_menu` function makes heavy use of the function `get_string`. This function handles what amounts to a one-line menu. It is responsible for collecting the user input into a string, as well as taking care of the verification of the input data by calling the user-specified verification routine.

Getting a Character

You might think that getting a character from the keyboard is a simple thing. After all, there is a library function `getch` that does it; yet, we've written over a hundred lines to perform this simple task. Why so much?

First of all, our function returns not just a character, but a unique code for each extended key (function keys, editing keys and cursor movement keys). Also we've built in a lot of automatic debugging code. If the user specified the option -R*file* on the command, every keystroke he types will be saved in the "record file." This can be played back by the playback option -P*file*. This is an extremely useful debugging tool because the user can record everything that occurred before the program bombed, change some code, and quickly return to the same place in his program. One more option, the pace option (-A) allows the user to slow down this frantic playback. When pace is enabled, every time the user presses a key, another character is read from the playback file.

The Return Bug

Turbo C Version 2.0 will warn you if you have a function that returns a value and does not end with a **return** statement. Thus, the following function causes a warning:

```
int funct(int ch)
{
    switch (ch) {
        default:
            return (-1);
    }
}
```

A solution is to put a dummy **return** at the end.

```
int funct(int ch)
{
        switch (ch) {
        default:
            return (-1);
        }
    return (0);      /* Make Turbo C happy */
}
```

But newer compilers, like Turbo C++ Version 2.0, have this bug fixed. They notice that the last **return** statement is never executed and issue a warning: Unreachable code. Sometimes you just can't win.

Conditional compilation to the rescue. We've bracketed our extra **return** statements with #if RETURN_BUG directives. So when we use the old compiler, we #define RETURN_BUG and the new one causes us to put in #undef RETURN_BUG.

```
int funct(int ch)
{
    switch (ch) {
        default:
            return (-1);
        }
#ifdef RETURN_BUG
```

```
        return (0);          /* Make Turbo C happy */
#endif RETURN_BUG
}
```

Such compiler dependent code is not that uncommon in portable applications. In the EMACS editor, one of the most widely ported applications, there are a large number of conditionals with names like LONG_DIV_BOTCH so that the program can get around compiler programs.

Now all we have to do is to decide when to set RETURN_BUG. Fortunately Turbo C++ has a pre-defined symbol: __TURBOC__ that can be used to tell which flavor of the compiler we are running on. If the value of the constant is set to more than hex 296, we must define RETURN_BUG. So at the beginning of our program we put the lines:

```
#if __TURBOC__ <= 0x296
#undef RETURN_BUG /* Turbo C++ won't make warnings */
#else
#define RETURN_BUG /* Turbo C version 2.0 generates bad warnings */
#endif /* __TURBOC__ /*
```

You might ask why didn't we just use __TURBOC__ instead of RETURN_BUG. The answer is that we want to limit the compiler dependent part of our code to the beginning of the program. This program might be used with other buggy compilers and this way keeps the compiler version stuff and the bug works around relatively separate.

Summary

We have defined a fairly complete menuing system. It allows the program designer to create complex menus using fairly simple data structures. These data structures are the most important part of this system; they must be as simple as possible, yet allow the user maximum flexibility.

The lack of a help function is a severe limitation. (We'll add it in the next version.) Also, even though the data structures have been tremendously simplified they are still somewhat difficult to define, forcing the programmer to go through many trial and error steps to get a good looking menu.

In the next chapter we'll show you how to create a menu generator to fix that problem.

Listing 10-2. "menu.h"

```c
/************************************************************
 * menu.h -- define data structures for a menu             *
 *                                                          *
 * There are two types of menus.                           *
 *                                                          *
 * Selection menus allow displays of a list of items and*
 * allows the user to select an item in the list.          *
 *                                                          *
 * Fill in the blank menus allow the user to fill in       *
 * a set of data.                                          *
 ************************************************************/
struct select_menu {
    /* Location of upper left corner of menu */
    int loc_x, loc_y;

    /* Title of this menu */
    char *title;

    /* Pointer to the list of items to select */
    struct select_item *item_list;
};


/*
 * One of these is defined for each item in the
 * selection list.
 */
struct select_item {
    char *name;          /* Name of the item */
    void (*call_back)(void);/* Function to call when selected */
};


struct fill_in_menu {
    int loc_x, loc_y;   /* Location of the menu */
    int size_x, size_y; /* Size of the menu (including border) */
    char *background;   /* All fixed text  */

    /* Pointer to a list of blanks to fill in */
    struct blank *blank_list;
};


struct blank {
    int loc_x, loc_y;   /* Where the blank is located */
    char *answer;       /* Place to put answer */
    int len;            /* Max length of the answer */
```

continued

Listing 10-2 continued

```
    int (*verify)(char *);/* Verification routine */
};


/*
 * These numbers must be negative so as not to conflict
 * with values returned by select_one
 */
#define MENU_OK          -1       /* Menu executed normally */
#define MENU_ABORT       -2       /* User aborted command */
#define MENU_ERROR       -3      /* Error occurred in menu system */


#define VERIFY_OK         0       /* Data for blank is OK */
#define VERIFY_ERROR     -1       /* Error in verify */

/***********************************************************
 * select_one -- handle a selection menu return            *
 *               the index of the selection                *
 *                                                         *
 * Parameter                                               *
 *      menu -- menu to process                            *
 *      selection -- default selection                     *
 *                                                         *
 * Returns                                                 *
 *      index -- index of item selection                   *
 *      MENU_ABORT -- user typed in ESC to abort           *
 *      MENU_ERROR -- error occurred                       *
 ***********************************************************/
int select_one(struct select_menu *menu, int selection);


/***********************************************************
 * select_menu -- handle a selection menu                  *
 *                                                         *
 * Parameter                                               *
 *      menu -- menu to process                            *
 *      selection -- default selection                     *
 *      after -- call the callback routine after           *
 *                       destroying the window             *
 *                                                         *
 * Returns                                                 *
 *      MENU_OK -- item selected.  Callback routine         *
 *              executed.                                  *
 *      MENU_ERROR -- error occurred in system             *
 *      MENU_ABORT -- user typed in ESC to abort           *
 ***********************************************************/
```

continued

Listing 10-2 continued

```
int select_menu(struct select_menu *menu, int selection,
                int after);


/*************************************************************
 * fill_in_menu -- handle a fill in the blank menu         *
 *                                                         *
 * Parameters                                              *
 *      menu -- menu to process                            *
 *                                                         *
 * Returns                                                 *
 *      MENU_ABORT -- user typed in ESC to abort           *
 *      MENU_ERROR -- some sort of error occurred          *
 *      otherwise -- character that finished the menu      *
 *************************************************************/
int fill_in_menu(struct fill_in_menu *menu);
```

Listing 10-3. "menu.c"

```
#if __TURBOC__ <= 0X296
#undef RETURN_BUG  /* Turbo C++ won't make warnings */
#else
#define RETURN_BUG /* Turbo C verSION 2.0 generates bad warnings */
#endif   /* __TURBOC__ */
/*************************************************************
 * menu -- menu handler                                    *
 *                                                         *
 * Two types of menus are supported.                       *
 *      Selection menu -- user can select an item.         *
 *      Fill in the blank menus -- fill in the data        *
 *                                                         *
 * Routines supplied                                       *
 *      int select_menu(struct select_menu *menu,          *
 *              int selection, int after)                  *
 *                                                         *
 *      menu -- selection menu to use                      *
 *      selection -- default selection                     *
 *      after -- call the callback routine after           *
 *                      destroying the window              *
 *                                                         *
 *      Return MENU_OK -- item selected.                   *
 *              MENU_ERROR -- internal error in system     *
 *              MENU_ABORT -- user typed ESC to exit       *
 *--------------------------------------------------------*
```

continued

Listing 10-3 continued

```
*        int select_one(struct select_menu *menu,          *
*                int selection)                            *
*                                                          *
*        menu -- selection menu to use                     *
*        selection -- default selection                    *
*                                                          *
*        Return index of item selection                    *
*                MENU_ERROR -- internal error in system    *
*                MENU_ABORT -- user typed ESC to exit       *
*----------------------------------------------------------*
* fill_in_menu -- handle a fill in the blank menu          *
*                                                          *
* Parameters                                               *
*        menu -- menu to process                           *
*                                                          *
* Returns                                                  *
*        MENU_ABORT -- user typed in ESC to abort          *
*        MENU_ERROR -- an error occurred                    *
*        Otherwise character that ended the menu entry     *
************************************************************/
#include <stdio.h>
#include <stdlib.h>
#include <string.h>
#include <conio.h>
#include <ctype.h>
#include "menu.h"
#include "menu-int.h"
#include "keys.h"


/**********************************************************
 * draw_box -- draws a box using double lines             *
 *      from (x1,y1) to (x2,y2)                            *
 **********************************************************/
void draw_box(int x1, int y1, int x2, int y2)
{
    int x, y; /* Current location */


    /* Draw top */
    gotoxy(x1+1, y1);
    for (x = x1; x < (x2-1); x++)
        putch(0xCD);                /* Horizontal line */


    /* Draw bottom */
    gotoxy(x1+1, y2);
```

continued

Keep Pace with Today's Micro-computer Technology with:

Brady Publishing and Software

Brady Publishing books and software are always up-to-the-minute and geared to meet your needs:

- Using major applications
- Beginning, intermediate, and advanced programming
- Covering MS-DOS and Macintosh systems
- Business applications software
- Star Trek™ games
- Typing Tutor

Available at your local book or computer store or order by telephone:
(800) 624-0023

///BradyLine

College Marketing Group
50 Cross Street
Winchester, MA 01890

ATT: **Cheryl Read**

Listing 10-3 continued

```
        for (x = x1; x < (x2-1); x++)
            putch(0xCD);              /* Horizontal line */


        /* Draw Sides */
        for (y = y1+1; y < y2; y++) {
            gotoxy(x1, y);           /* Vertical Line */
            putch(0xBA);


            gotoxy(x2, y);
            putch(0xBA);             /* Vertical Line */
        }
        gotoxy(x1, y1);
        putch(0xC9);                 /* Top left corner */


        gotoxy(x1, y2);
        putch(0xC8);                 /* Bottom left corner */


        gotoxy(x2, y1);              /* Top right corner */
        putch(0xBB);


        gotoxy(x2, y2);              /* Bottom right corner */
        putch(0xBC);
}
/***********************************************************
 * display_select -- Display a select menu                 *
 *                                                         *
 * Parameter                                               *
 *      menu -- menu to process                            *
 *      selection -- the selection to start with           *
 *                                                         *
 * Returns                                                 *
 *      Index of item selected                             *
 *      MENU_ABORT -- user typed in ESC to abort           *
 ***********************************************************/
int display_select(struct select_menu *menu, int selection)
{
    int item;           /* The current item number */
    int cur_y;          /* Current location for output */
    int title_x;        /* Place to put the title */
    int x_size;         /* Size of menu in X direction */


    cur_y = 1;  /* Title starts here */
```

continued

Listing 10-3 continued

```c
    x_size = get_x_size(menu);
    /* Center title */
    title_x = (x_size - strlen(menu->title)+1)/2;
    gotoxy(title_x, cur_y);
    textattr(REVERSE);
    (void)cputs(menu->title);
    textattr(NORMAL);

    cur_y += 2;            /* Text starts here */

    for (item = 0; menu->item_list[item].name != NULL; item++) {
        gotoxy(2, cur_y);
        (void)cputs(menu->item_list[item].name);
        cur_y++;
    }

    /* Underline current selection */
    gotoxy(2, selection + 3);
    textattr(REVERSE);
    cputs(menu->item_list[selection].name);
    textattr(NORMAL);
    return (MENU_OK);
}
/************************************************************
 * select_loop -- handle the selection loop               *
 *                                                        *
 * Parameters                                             *
 *      menu -- the menu to get data                      *
 *      selection -- the current selection                *
 *                                                        *
 * Returns                                                *
 *      MENU_ABORT -- user typed an escape                *
 *      index -- index of selection from user             *
 ************************************************************/
int select_loop(struct select_menu *menu, int selection)
{
    int ch;      /* Character from user input */
    int item;    /* Current item for display */

    /*
     * Main loop -- wait for user to select an entry
     */
    while (1) {
        /* Underline current selection */
        gotoxy(2, selection + 3);
```

continued

Listing 10-3 continued

```
textattr(REVERSE);
cputs(menu->item_list[selection].name);
textattr(NORMAL);

ch = x_getch();

/* Clear old selection */
gotoxy(2, selection + 3);
cputs(menu->item_list[selection].name);

switch (ch) {
    case KEY_ENTER:
        return (selection);
    case KEY_UP:
        if (selection > 0)
            selection--;
        break;
    case KEY_DOWN:
        if (menu->item_list[selection+1].name != NULL)
            selection++;
        break;
    case KEY_ESC:
        return (MENU_ABORT);
    default:
        if (isupper(ch))
            ch = tolower(ch);

        for (item = 0;
             menu->item_list[item].name != NULL;
             item++) {
            int menu_ch; /* First character from menu */

            menu_ch = menu->item_list[item].name[0];
            if (isupper(menu_ch))
                menu_ch = tolower(menu_ch);

            if (menu_ch == ch) {
                selection = item;
                goto found_it;
            }
        }
        (void)putch(BELL);        /* Beep at the user */
found_it:
        break;
```

continued

Listing 10-3 continued

```
        }
    }
#ifdef RETURN_BUG
    return (0); /* Make TC happy */
#endif RETURN_BUG
}
/***********************************************************
 * get_x_size -- compute the size (in x) of a select       *
 *                       menu.                              *
 *                                                          *
 * Parameters                                               *
 *     menu -- menu to get size for                         *
 *                                                          *
 * Returns                                                  *
 *     size in x direction                                  *
 ***********************************************************/
int get_x_size(struct select_menu *menu)
{
    int x_size;          /* Size in X direction */
    int item;            /* Current item number */


    /* Compute x width as well -- start with title */
    x_size = strlen(menu->title);
    for (item = 0; menu->item_list[item].name != NULL; item++) {
        if (strlen(menu->item_list[item].name) > x_size)
            x_size = strlen(menu->item_list[item].name);
    }


    x_size += 4;         /* One for box/One for margin/both sides */
    return (x_size);
}
/***********************************************************
 * get_y_size -- compute the size (in y) of a select       *
 *                       menu.                              *
 *                                                          *
 * Parameters                                               *
 *     menu -- menu to get size for                         *
 *                                                          *
 * Returns                                                  *
 *     size in y direction                                  *
 ***********************************************************/
int get_y_size(struct select_menu *menu)
{
    int item;            /* Current item number */
    int y_size;          /* Size in y direction */
```

continued

Listing 10-3 continued

```
    y_size = 2;              /* Two lines for menu and title */


    for (item = 0; menu->item_list[item].name != NULL; item++) {
        /* Do nothing */
    }


    y_size += item;


    y_size += 2-1;        /* Add in borders/one top/one bottom */
                          /* -1 because previous loop overcounts */
    return (y_size);
}
/***********************************************************
 * select_start -- start a selection menu                  *
 *                                                         *
 * Compute size of a selection menu and create window      *
 * for it.                                                 *
 *                                                         *
 * Parameters                                              *
 *      menu -- menu to display                            *
 *      cur_win -- the window to save stuff                *
 *                                                         *
 * Returns                                                 *
 *      MENU_OK -- no error                                *
 *      MENU_ERROR -- error occurred                       *
 ***********************************************************/
int select_start(struct select_menu *menu,
                 struct window_info *cur_win)
{
    int status;            /* Status to be returned */
    int x_size;            /* Size of menu in x direction */
    int y_size;            /* Size of menu in y direction */

    x_size = get_x_size(menu);
    y_size = get_y_size(menu);


    status = create_window(menu->loc_x, menu->loc_y,
                           menu->loc_x + x_size,
                           menu->loc_y + y_size, cur_win);


    if (status != MENU_OK) {
        destroy_window(cur_win);
    }
    return (status);
```

continued

Listing 10-3 continued

```
}
/***********************************************************
 * select_one -- handle a selection menu return            *
 *               the index of the selection                *
 *                                                         *
 * Parameter                                               *
 *      menu -- menu to process                            *
 *      selection -- default selection                     *
 *                                                         *
 * Returns                                                 *
 *      index -- index of item selection                   *
 *      MENU_ABORT -- user typed in ESC to abort           *
 *      MENU_ERROR -- error occurred                       *
 ***********************************************************/
int select_one(struct select_menu *menu, int selection)
{
    /* Information about the current window */
    struct window_info cur_win;
    int status;          /* Status to be returned */

    status = select_start(menu, &cur_win);

    if (status != MENU_OK)
        return (status);

    status = display_select(menu, selection);

    if (status != MENU_OK) {
        selection = select_loop(menu, selection);
    } else {
        selection = status;
    }

    destroy_window(&cur_win);
    if (selection == MENU_ABORT)
        return (MENU_ABORT);
    return (MENU_OK);
}
/***********************************************************
 * select_menu -- handle a selection menu                  *
 *                                                         *
 * Parameter                                               *
 *      menu -- menu to process                            *
 *      selection -- default selection                     *
 *      after -- call the callback routine after           *
```

continued

Listing 10-3 continued

```
 *                        destroying the window         *
 *                                                      *
 * Returns                                              *
 *      MENU_OK -- item selected.  Callback routine     *
 *              executed.                                *
 *      MENU_ERROR -- error occurred in system          *
 *      MENU_ABORT -- user typed in ESC to abort        *
 ************************************************************/
int select_menu(struct select_menu *menu,
                int selection, int after)
{
    /* Information about the current window */
    struct window_info cur_win;
    int status;          /* Status information */

    status = select_start(menu, &cur_win);
    if (status != MENU_OK)
        return (status);


    status = display_select(menu, selection);

    if (status == MENU_OK) {
        selection = select_loop(menu, selection);
    } else {
        selection = status;
    }


    if (selection != MENU_ABORT) {
        /* Set screen size to full for callback routine */
        window(1, 1, 80, 25);
        if (after) {
            destroy_window(&cur_win);
            (*menu->item_list[selection].call_back)();
        } else {
            (*menu->item_list[selection].call_back)();
            destroy_window(&cur_win);
        }
    } else
        destroy_window(&cur_win);

    if (selection == MENU_ABORT)
        return (MENU_ABORT);


    return (MENU_OK);
}
```

continued

Listing 10-3 continued

```
/****************************************************
 * get_string -- get a string from the screen       *
 *                                                   *
 * Parameter                                         *
 *      blank -- the blank to fill in                *
 *                                                   *
 * Returns                                           *
 *      key that ends the strings                    *
 *      or MENU_ABORT if esc pressed                 *
 ****************************************************/
int get_string(struct blank *blank)
{
    int x_pos = 0;      /* X position within answer */
    int ch;             /* Character we are working on */


    while (1) {
        textattr(REVERSE);
        gotoxy(blank->loc_x, blank->loc_y);
        (void)cprintf("%-*s", blank->len, blank->answer);
        textattr(NORMAL);


        gotoxy(blank->loc_x + x_pos, blank->loc_y);


        ch = x_getch();
        switch (ch) {

            case KEY_BS:
                if (x_pos > 1)
                    (void)strcpy(&blank->answer[x_pos-1],
                             &blank->answer[x_pos]);
                /* Fall through */
            case KEY_LEFT:
                if (x_pos > 0)
                    x_pos--;
                break;
            case KEY_RIGHT:
                if (blank->answer[x_pos] != '\0')
                    x_pos++;
                break;

            case KEY_ESC:
                return (MENU_ABORT);
```

continued

Listing 10-3 continued

```
            case KEY_ENTER:
                if (x_pos != 0)
                    blank->answer[x_pos] = '\0';
                if (blank->verify(blank->answer) == VERIFY_OK)
                    return (ch);
                putch(BELL);
                break;
            default:
                if (isprint(ch)) {
                    /* At start, kill rest of answer */
                    if (x_pos == 0)
                        blank->answer[1] = '\0';

                    if (blank->answer[x_pos] == '\0')
                        blank->answer[x_pos+1] =  '\0';

                    blank->answer[x_pos] = ch;
                    x_pos++;
                } else {
                    /* See if we should get out of here */
                    if (blank->verify(blank->answer) ==
                                                VERIFY_OK)
                        return (ch);
                    putch(BELL);
                }
                break;
        }
    }
    #ifdef RETURN_BUG
    return (0); /* Make TC happy */
    #endif RETURN_BUG
}
/***********************************************************
 * fill_in_menu -- handle a fill in the blank menu         *
 *                                                         *
 * Parameters                                              *
 *      menu -- menu to process                            *
 *                                                         *
 * Returns                                                 *
 *      MENU_ABORT -- user typed in ESC to abort           *
 *      MENU_ERROR -- an error occurred                    *
 *      Otherwise character that ended the menu entry      *
 ***********************************************************/
int fill_in_menu(struct fill_in_menu *menu)
{
```

continued

Listing 10-3 continued

```
struct window_info cur_win; /* Place for window data */
int status;          /* Return status */
int blank_count;     /* Number of blanks to fill in */
int cur_blank;       /* Blank we are filling in now */
int ch;              /* Character returned from last string op */

status = create_window(menu->loc_x, menu->loc_y,
                    menu->loc_x + menu->size_x,
                    menu->loc_y + menu->size_y,
                    &cur_win);

if (status != MENU_OK) {
    destroy_window(&cur_win);
    return (status);
}

/*
 * Put the background in the window
 */
gotoxy(1,1);
cputs(menu->background);
for (blank_count = 0;
     menu->blank_list[blank_count].answer != NULL;
     blank_count++)
    /* Just count the number of blanks */;

for (cur_blank = 0; cur_blank < blank_count; cur_blank++) {
    struct blank *blank;    /* Blank we are displaying */

    blank = &menu->blank_list[cur_blank];
    textattr(REVERSE);
    gotoxy(blank->loc_x, blank->loc_y);
    (void)cprintf("%-*s", blank->len, blank->answer);
}
textattr(NORMAL);
cur_blank = 0;

while (1) {
    ch = get_string(&menu->blank_list[cur_blank]);
    switch (ch) {
        case KEY_BACK_TAB:
        case KEY_UP:
            if (cur_blank > 0)
                cur_blank--;
```

continued

Listing 10-3 continued

```
                    break;
                case KEY_TAB:
                case KEY_DOWN:
                    if (cur_blank < (blank_count-1))
                        cur_blank++;
                    break;
                case KEY_ENTER:
                    cur_blank++;
                    if (cur_blank == blank_count)
                        goto menu_done;
                    break;
                default:
                    goto menu_done;
            }
        }
menu_done:
    destroy_window(&cur_win);
    if (ch == KEY_ESC)
        ch = MENU_ABORT;
    return (ch);
}
/************************************************************
 * create_window -- create a window                        *
 *                                                          *
 * Parameters                                               *
 *      x1, y1, x2, y2 -- corners of the window             *
 *      cur_win -- pointer to where to save window          *
 *              data. (Used by destroy window.)             *
 *                                                          *
 * Returns                                                  *
 *      MENU_OK -- no problem                               *
 *      MENU_ERROR -- something went wrong                  *
 ************************************************************/
int create_window(int x1, int y1, int x2, int y2,
        struct window_info *cur_win)
{
    cur_win->x1 = x1;
    cur_win->y1 = y1;
    cur_win->x2 = x2;
    cur_win->y2 = y2;

    cur_win->text_save = malloc((x2 - x1 + 1) *
                                    (y2 - y1 + 1) * 2);
```

continued

Listing 10-3 continued

```
        if (cur_win->text_save == NULL)
            return (MENU_ERROR);


        /* Save the text info */
        gettextinfo(&cur_win->info);


        if (gettext(x1, y1, x2, y2, cur_win->text_save) == 0) {
            free(cur_win->text_save);
            cur_win->text_save = NULL;
            return (MENU_ERROR);
        }


        /* Limit us to a simple window */
        window(x1, y1, x2, y2);
        clrscr();


        draw_box(1, 1, x2 - x1, y2 - y1+1);
        /* Window - border */
        window(x1+1, y1+1, x2-1, y2-1);


        return (MENU_OK);
}
/************************************************************
 * destroy_window -- destroy a window and return the       *
 *                        screen to the state before the   *
 *                        window was created.              *
 *                                                         *
 * Restriction: Windows must be destroyed in reverse       *
 *              order of creation.                         *
 *                                                         *
 * Parameter                                               *
 *      cur_win -- the window to destroy                   *
 ************************************************************/
void destroy_window(struct window_info *cur_win)
{
    struct text_info *info;     /* Text info for old window */


    info = &cur_win->info;


    window(info->winleft, info->wintop,
            info->winright, info->winbottom);
```

continued

Listing 10-3 continued

```
        textattr(info->attribute);
        gotoxy(info->curx, info->cury);

        puttext(cur_win->x1, cur_win->y1,
                cur_win->x2, cur_win->y2, cur_win->text_save);

        if (cur_win->text_save != NULL)
            free(cur_win->text_save);
}
```

Listing 10-4. "keys.h"

```
#define KEY_ENTER       0x000D   /* Enter or return key */
#define KEY_UP          0x4048   /* Arrow key */
#define KEY_DOWN        0x4050   /* Arrow key */
#define KEY_RIGHT       0x404D   /* Arrow key */
#define KEY_LEFT        0x404B   /* Arrow key */
#define KEY_ESC         0x001B   /* Escape key */
#define KEY_BS          0x0008   /* Backspace key */
#define KEY_TAB         0x0009   /* Tab key */
#define KEY_BACK_TAB    0x400F   /* Shifted tab key */
#define KEY_INSERT      0x4052   /* Insert key */
#define KEY_DELETE      0x4053   /* Delete key */
#define KEY_END         0x404F   /* END key */

#define KEY_F1          0x403B   /* F1 function key */
#define KEY_F2          0x403C   /* F2 function key */
#define KEY_F3          0x403D   /* F3 function key */

int x_getch(void);          /* Get a character (extended version) */

/***********************************************************
 * debug_flags -- handle the debug flags                   *
 *              -R<file> for replay file                   *
 *              -C<file> for capture file                  *
 *              -P turns on pacing                         *
 *                                                         *
 * Note: This should delete its args from the stack        *
 *       but doesn't                                       *
 *                                                         *
 * Parameters                                              *
 *       argv, argc -- from command line                   *
 ***********************************************************/
void debug_flags(int argc, char *argv[]);
```

Listing 10-5. "xget.c"

```
/***********************************************************
 * xgetc -- get a character from the keyboard             *
 *          --- a greatly expanded version.               *
 *                                                        *
 * Functions:                                             *
 *      x_getch -- get a character                        *
 *      debug_flags -- check command line for flag        *
 *                     options and open special files     *
 ***********************************************************/
#include <stdio.h>
#include <conio.h>
#include <dos.h>


/***********************************************************
 * real_getch -- really gets the character                *
 *                                                        *
 * Get a character from the keyboard.  If an extended     *
 * code, make a 16-bit number with the high bit set.      *
 *                                                        *
 * Returns                                                *
 *      extended character from the keyboard              *
 ***********************************************************/
static int real_getch(void)
{
    int ch;      /* Character we are processing */


    ch = getch();        /* Get a single character */
    if (ch != '\0')
        return (ch);     /* Simple character */


    ch = getch();        /* Get real character */


    return ((0x40 << 8) | ch);
}
/* Get playback keys from here */
static FILE *playback_file = NULL;
/* Record data into this file */
static FILE *record_file = NULL;
static int pace = 0;                      /* <SP> paces playback
*/
/***********************************************************
 * x_getch -- extended version of getch                   *
 *                                                        *
 * Get a character from the keyboard.  If an extended     *
 * code, make a 16-bit number with the high bit set.      *
```

continued

Listing 10-5 continued

```
 *                                                        *
 * Returns                                                *
 *      extended character from the keyboard              *
 **********************************************************/
int x_getch(void)
{
    int ch;      /* Character we are processing */

    if (playback_file != NULL) {
        /* If pacing, wait for user */
        if (pace)
            (void)getch();


        if (fread((char *)&ch, 1, sizeof(ch), playback_file)
            == sizeof(ch))
            return (ch);

        /* Eof seen */
        (void)fclose(playback_file);
        playback_file = NULL;
    }

    ch = real_getch();
    if (record_file != NULL) {
        (void)fwrite((char *)&ch, 1, sizeof(ch), record_file);
    }
    return (ch);
}
/**********************************************************
 * debug_flags -- handle the debug flags                  *
 *              -P<file> for playback file                *
 *              -R<file> for record file                  *
 *              -A turns on pacing                        *
 *                                                        *
 * Note: This should delete its args from the stack       *
 *      but doesn't                                       *
 *                                                        *
 * Parameters                                             *
 *      argv, argc -- from command line                   *
 **********************************************************/
void debug_flags(int argc, char *argv[])
{
    char *name;  /* Name of current file */
```

continued

Listing 10-5 continued

```
    while ((argc > 1) && (argv[1][0] == '-')) {
        switch (argv[1][1]) {
            case 'P':
                name = &argv[1][2];
                playback_file = fopen(name, "rb");
                if (playback_file == NULL) {
                    (void)fprintf(stderr,"Unable to open %s\n",
                                            name);
                }
                break;
            case 'R':
                name = &argv[1][2];
                record_file = fopen(name, "wb");
                if (record_file == NULL) {
                    (void)fprintf(stderr,"Unable to open %s\n",
                                            name);
                }
                break;
            case 'A':
                pace = 1;
                break;
            default:
                break;
        }
    argc--;
    argv++;
    }
}
```

Listing 10-6. "menu-int.h"

```
/************************************************************
 * menu-int.h -- define data structures for use            *
 *               by menu internals.  Used by menu          *
 *               handlers and builders                     *
 *                                                         *
 ************************************************************/
/*
 * Useful for general window handling package
 */
struct window_info {
    char *text_save;    /* Pointer to text under this window */
    int x1,y1,x2,y2;    /* Window location */
    /* Information on old window */
    struct text_info info;
```

continued

Listing 10-6 continued

```
};
/************************************************************
 * create_window -- create a window                        *
 *                                                          *
 * Parameters                                               *
 *      x1, y1, x2, y2 -- corners of the window             *
 *      cur_win -- pointer to where to save window          *
 *              data. (Used by destroy window.)             *
 *                                                          *
 * Returns                                                  *
 *      MENU_OK -- no problem                               *
 *      MENU_ERROR -- something went wrong                  *
 ************************************************************/
int create_window(int x1, int y1, int x2, int y2,
    struct window_info *cur_win);


/************************************************************
 * destroy_window -- destroy a window and return the       *
 *                   screen to the state before the        *
 *                   window was created.                   *
 *                                                          *
 * Restriction: Windows must be destroyed in reverse       *
 *              order of creation.                          *
 *                                                          *
 * Parameter                                                *
 *      cur_win -- the window to destroy                    *
 ************************************************************/
void destroy_window(struct window_info *cur_win);


/************************************************************
 * draw_box -- draws a box using double lines               *
 *      from (x1,y1) to (x2,y2)                             *
 ************************************************************/
void draw_box(int x1, int y1, int x2, int y2);


/************************************************************
 * display_select -- Display a select menu                  *
 *                                                          *
 * Parameter                                                *
 *      menu -- menu to process                             *
 *      selection -- the selection to start with            *
 *                                                          *
 * Returns                                                  *
 *      Index of item selected                              *
 *      MENU_ABORT -- user typed in ESC to abort            *
```

continued

Listing 10-6 continued

```
     **********************************************/
int display_select(struct select_menu *menu, int selection);


/************************************************************
 * get_x_size -- compute the size (in x) of a select     *
 *                        menu.                           *
 *                                                        *
 * Parameters                                             *
 *      menu -- menu to get size for                      *
 *                                                        *
 * Returns                                                *
 *      size in x direction                               *
 ************************************************************/
int get_x_size(struct select_menu *menu);


/************************************************************
 * get_y_size -- compute the size (in y) of a select     *
 *                        menu.                           *
 *                                                        *
 * Parameters                                             *
 *      menu -- menu to get size for                      *
 *                                                        *
 * Returns                                                *
 *      size in y direction                               *
 ************************************************************/
int get_y_size(struct select_menu *menu);
/*
 * A few video attributes
 */
#define NORMAL     LIGHTGRAY      /* Color for normal text */
#define REVERSE    ((LIGHTGRAY<<4) + BLACK)

#define BELL    7                 /* Beep character */
```

Some Test Programs

Listing 10-7. "Select.c"

```
/************************************************************
 * mtest -- test menu system                              *
 ************************************************************/
#include <stdio.h>
#include <stdlib.h>
```

continued

Listing 10-7 continued

```c
#include <conio.h>
#include "menu.h"

static void do_replace(void);     /* Replace callback routine */
static void do_backup(void);      /* Backup callback routine */
static void do_cancel(void);      /* Cancel callback routine */

struct select_item list1[] = {
  {"Replace", do_replace},
  {"Overwrite", do_backup},
  {"Cancel", do_cancel},
  {NULL, NULL}
};

struct select_menu select1 = {
    10, 10,                 /* Location */
    "Test Menu",
    list1
};

main()
{
    clrscr();
    select_menu(&select1, 0, 0);
    /*
     * Show result and wait for user to finish
     */
    (void)getch();
    return (0);
}
/**********************************************************
 * do_replace -- callback function for replace selection *
 **********************************************************/
void do_replace(void)
{
    gotoxy(1,1);
    cputs("Replace called");
}
/**********************************************************
 * do_backup -- callback function for backup selection   *
 **********************************************************/
void do_backup(void)
{
    gotoxy(1,1);
    cputs("Overwrite called");
```

continued

Listing 10-7 continued

```
}
/*************************************************
 * do_cancel -- callback function for cancel selection  *
 *************************************************/
void do_cancel(void)
{
    gotoxy(1,1);
    cputs("Cancel called");
}
```

Listing 10-8. "fill.c"

```
/*************************************************
 * mtest3 -- test menu system                    *
 *************************************************/
#include <stdio.h>
#include <stdlib.h>
#include <conio.h>
#include "menu.h"

static int verify_ok(char *answer);
static char name[30] = "Smith, John";        /* Person's name */
static char address[30] = "100 Main Street"; /* Street address */
/* City, State Zip */
static char city_state[30] = "Anytown, AL 12345";

#define X_LOC   16
struct blank blanks[] = {
    {
        X_LOC, 1,        /* Location of blank */
        name,            /* answer */
        sizeof(name),    /* Length */
        verify_ok        /* Verify the answer */
    }, {
        X_LOC, 2,        /* Location of blank */
        address,         /* answer */
        sizeof(address),/* Length */
        verify_ok        /* Verify the answer */
    }, {
        X_LOC, 3,        /* Location of blank */
        city_state,      /* answer */
        sizeof(city_state),/* Length */
```

continued

Listing 10-8 continued

```
         verify_ok          /* Verify the answer */
    }, {
         -1, -1,            /* Location of blank */
         NULL,              /* answer */
         0,                 /* Length */
         NULL               /* Verify the answer */
    }
};


/* Menu's background */
char background[] = "\
     Name:\r\n\
  Address:\r\n\
City/State/Zip:";


struct fill_in_menu menu = {
    5, 5,                   /* Location of the menu */
    50, 4,                  /* Size of menu */
    &background[0],

    blanks
};


main()
{
    clrscr();
    fill_in_menu(&menu);
    return (0);
}
/***********************************************************
 * verify_ok -- verify everything as ok                    *
 ***********************************************************/
#pragma warn -par          /* Next routine does not use parameter */
static int verify_ok(char *answer)
{
    return (VERIFY_OK);
}
#pragma warn .par          /* Restore warning */
```

Menu Creation Utility

Introduction

Our menu package gives us a convenient way of displaying and handling menus — once we've set up the data structures. Although we've tried to design our data structures to be as simple as possible, it's still difficult to get the data right. Menus are visual, and it's difficult to translate a screen layout (I want a box there) into a C structure (`struct box box = {3, 6}`).

What we need is a way of creating menus visually, on the screen where we can see what they look like. Then they can be automatically translated into C data structures. Our "menumaker" tool allows us to skip the tedious trial and error process where we look at a menu, change some number in the source, compile, and look again. It gives us a simple and obvious way of getting what we want on the screen into C code.

Menumaker Design

Our menu package gives us two main types of menus: fill-in-the-blank and selection. Since these two are vastly different things, we've split the `menumaker` program into two modules, one for each type.

The program is somewhat limited. It allows the user to only create menus, it cannot edit existing menus. Also it is a one-at-a-time editor. Multiple menus cannot be edited. But even with these limitations, this is the longest program in the book, totalling some 2,500 lines. More code would make this program more functional, but we're also using it as an example and we've got to fit it into this book.

Our program starts by asking the user what type of menu he wants to create.

```
┌─────────────────────────────────────┐
│ ┌─────────────────────────────────┐ │
│ │                                 │ │
│ │        Choose menu type         │ │
│ │                                 │ │
│ │   Selection Menu (Callback)     │ │
│ │   Selection Menu (Index)        │ │
│ │   Fill-In-The-Blank Menu        │ │
│ │                                 │ │
│ └─────────────────────────────────┘ │
└─────────────────────────────────────┘
```

Creating Selection Menus

If the user wants to create a selection menu, we start by creating a default version. Its title is "title" and it contains no items.

```
┌─────────────────────────────────┐
│ ┌─────────────────────────────┐ │
│ │                             │ │
│ │            title            │ │
│ │                             │ │
│ └─────────────────────────────┘ │
└─────────────────────────────────┘
```

The following commands can be used to edit the menu:

Arrow Keys   If in move mode — move the menu around the screen.

                    If in selection mode — move current selection up or down.

F1   Toggle between move menu mode and move selection item mode.

F2   Edit the title

                    A fill-in-the-blank menu is displayed and the user can change the title value.

F3   Edit item

                           A fill-in-the-blank menu is displayed and the user can edit
                           the item name and (if a callback menu) the name of the
                           callback routine.

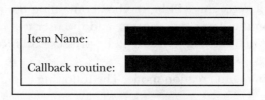

INSERT   Insert an item

                           Adds a new item to the list.

DELETE   Deletes current item

END   End editing and write the menu

These commands are implemented in a large **switch** statement in the function
`gen_select` (see listing at the end of the chapter). Each function by itself is
simple, taking from 5 to 20 lines. Combined, they take up three pages of code,
almost the entire `gen_select` routine.

When the END key is pressed, the program calls `write_select_menu`. This
function does the work of writing out the actual C code. As you examine this
function you will notice that it's about a page of fairly ugly C code. We've got
a series of complex `fprintf` statements that are writing C code. It's easy to
get the real C code confused with the generated C code.

What can we do to make this better? We don't know. There should be some
ways of making this clearer, but we don't know what they are. Perhaps we
could create a template file containing a model of the C code we are generat-
ing and write a program to turn it into `fprintf` statement. We don't have all
the answers and if you figure out a way to make sense out of this mess, use it.
(Then let us know how it turned out.)

Creating a Fill-in-the-blank Menu

Our code for making fill-in-the-blank menus is somewhat longer, since this type of menu is more complex. When the user selects "fill-in-the-blank" from the main menu we start by asking him to pick an upper left corner for the menu. Using the arrow keys he positions the cursor and presses ENTER.

A box is displayed. This will be the box containing the menu. The cursor is positioned on the lower right corner and the user can move it anywhere on the screen. When the box looks right, he presses ENTER again.

Now we are in menu creation mode. The following commands are available:

F1	Move
	If on a blank, move the blank.
	If on the box, resize the box.
F3	Edit
	Edit the current blank.
INSERT	Create a blank
	A menu is displayed and the user is allowed to type in information describing the blank.
DELETE	Delete
	Delete the current blank.
Arrow Keys	Move
	Move the cursor.
Printing Characters	Any printing characters will be put on the screen. These are used to form the background text for the menu.
END	Finished
	Go to the write phase.

Like gen_select, these commands are implemented as **switch** statements in the routine do_fill_in. Unlike gen_select, all our commands are not simple and several times we must call other functions to handle the work. Actually, we could have put all the code in the switch statements, but that would make the function do_fill_in huge, as well as hide the structure of the program.

When the END command is executed, the function write_blank_menu is executed. This one is longer and uglier than write_select_menu. Again, there has to be a better way. We just wish we knew what it was.

"qsort" Problem

Writing this program uncovered another compiler dependent bug. The type of last parameter to the qsort routine changed between Turbo C Version 2.0 and Turbo C++ 2.0. This results in the strange code:

```
#ifdef OLD_STYLE
int  cmp_blanks(struct blank **b1, struct blank **b2)
#define B1 (b1)
#define B2 (b2)
#else OLD_STYLE
int  cmp_blanks(const void *b1, const void *b2)
#define B1 ((struct blank **)(b1))
#define B2 ((struct blank **)(b2))
#endif OLD_STYLE
```

As you can see, the function declaration must change depending on the compiler version used. In order to keep our sanity, we've defined macros for the parameters, so that we have something simple and consistent to work with. The constant OLD_STYLE is set at the beginning of the program, along with our old friend RETURN_BUG.

Program Details

The actual program is fairly simple. No new or advanced concepts are introduced by this program; it is merely a collection of a large number of functions needed to handle the myriad of details needed for the automatic construction of menus.

Expanding the Program

Our menumaker program is extremely simple. It only allows the creation of a single menu (no editing, no multiple menus). But even this stripped down version is fairly long. Despite its limitation, this program is useful in producing good quality menus. But what we really want is a general purpose menu maker that can handle a screen full of menus — all the menus for a program. Also we need an editing capability so that we can change something once it has been written.

Our program has one major limitation; there is no help. A good help system can make or break a program. Still, we've got the beginnings of a very professional programming system.

Listing 11-1. "menumaker.c"

```c
#ifdef __TURBOC__ <= 0x296
#undef RETURN_BUG /* Turbo C++ won't make warnings */
#undef OLD_STYLE        /* Use new style calling sequence */
#else
#define RETURN_BUG/* Turbo C verSION 2.0 generates bad warnings */
#define OLD_STYLE       /* Use old style calling sequence */
#endif /* __TURBOC__ */
/*******************************************************
 * makemenu -- menu maker software                     *
 *                                                     *
 * This program builds menus for use with the menu     *
 * library.  It allows the user to design menus using  *
 * the arrow keys and the mouse.                        *
 *******************************************************/

#include <stdio.h>
#include <conio.h>
#include <dos.h>
#include <math.h>
#include <ctype.h>
#include <stdlib.h>
#include <mem.h>
#include <string.h>
#include "keys.h"
#include "menu.h"
#include "menu-int.h"

#define MAX_X   80 /* Limits of X Movements */
#define MAX_Y   25 /* Limits of Y Movements */
```

continued

Listing 11-1 continued

```
int    cur_x = 1;    /* Current X location of the cursor */
int    cur_y = 1;    /* Current Y location of the cursor */


#define BELL 7
/*
 * Structure to describe a box
 */
struct box {
    /* location of the box */
    int    left, right, top, bottom;


    /* Place to save text under the box */
    unsigned int text_save[(MAX_Y + MAX_X) * 2];
};


/*
 * Operations that can be done on text under a box
 */
enum op_enum {
    OP_SAVE, OP_RESTORE
};


#define VIDEO_INT        0x10    /* Video interrupt */
#define VIDEO_READ       0x8     /* Read character/attribute */
#define VIDEO_WRITE      0x9     /* Write character/attribute */
/************************************************************
 * move_cursor -- move the cursor until a non-movement     *
 *              character is pressed                        *
 *                                                          *
 * Returns                                                  *
 *      character that finished the movement                *
 ************************************************************/
int    move_cursor(void)
{
    int    ch;        /* Current character */

    gotoxy(cur_x, cur_y);

    while (1) {
        ch = x_getch();

        switch (ch) {
        case KEY_UP:
            if (cur_y > 1)
```

continued

Listing 11-1 continued

```
                cur_y--;
            break;
        case KEY_DOWN:
            if (cur_y < MAX_Y)
                cur_y++;
            break;
        case KEY_LEFT:
            if (cur_x > 1)
                cur_x--;
            break;
        case KEY_RIGHT:
            if (cur_x < MAX_X)
                cur_x++;
            break;
        default:
            return (ch);
        }
        gotoxy(cur_x, cur_y);
    }
#ifdef RETURN_BUG
    return (0);              /* Tell TC that we do return a value */
#endif RETURN_BUG
}


/***********************************************************
 * do_video -- handle a single video operation            *
 *                                                         *
 *      x, y -- place to get/save data                     *
 *      save -- place to save the data                     *
 *      operation -- the operation to use                  *
 *                        OP_SAVE or OP_RESTORE            *
 ***********************************************************/
void  do_video(int x, int y, unsigned int *save,
               enum op_enum operation)
{
    gotoxy(x, y);
    if (operation == OP_SAVE) {
        _AH = VIDEO_READ;
        _BH = 0;
        geninterrupt(VIDEO_INT);
        *save = _AX;
    } else {
        _CX = (*save);
        _BH = 0;
        _BL = _CH;
```

continued

Listing 11-1 continued

```
            _AL = _CL;
            _AH = VIDEO_WRITE;
            _CX = 1;
            geninterrupt(VIDEO_INT);
        }
}
/************************************************************
 * process_box_text -- handle the saving/restoring         *
 *                of text and attributes under a box        *
 *                                                          *
 * Parameters                                               *
 *      x1, y1, x2, y2 -- the box location                  *
 *      save -- place to save the data                      *
 *      operation -- the operation to use                   *
 *                       OP_SAVE or OP_RESTORE              *
 ************************************************************/
void  process_text(int x1, int y1, int x2, int y2,
                     unsigned int *save, enum op_enum operation)
{
    int    x, y;     /* Current location */

    /* Handle top/bottom */
    for (x = x1; x <= x2; x++) {
        do_video(x, y1, save, operation);
        save++;

        do_video(x, y2, save, operation);
        save++;
    }

    /* Handle Sides */
    /*   Note: (y2-1) because top/bottom takes care of corners */
    for (y = y1 + 1; y <= (y2 - 1); y++) {
        do_video(x1, y, save, operation);
        save++;

        do_video(x2, y, save, operation);
        save++;
    }
}
/************************************************************
 * resize_box -- change a box                               *
 *                                                          *
 * Parameters                                               *
 *      box_ptr -- pointer to the box created               *
```

continued

Listing 11-1 continued

```
 *        flag -- if 0, don't do a text save 1st time      *
 *                through.                                  *
 *                                                          *
 * Returns                                                  *
 *        character that ends the box.                      *
 ************************************************************/
int   resize_box(struct box * box_ptr, int flag)
{
    int    x1, x2, y1, y2;        /* Box location */
    int    fixed_x, fixed_y;      /* Fixed point location */
    int    ch;          /* Current character */

    /*
     * Find the fixed point as well as moving point
     */
    if (abs(box_ptr->left - cur_x) <
        abs(box_ptr->right - cur_x)) {
        cur_x = box_ptr->left;
        fixed_x = box_ptr->right;
    } else {
        fixed_x = box_ptr->left;
        cur_x = box_ptr->right;
    }

    if (abs(box_ptr->top - cur_y) <
        abs(box_ptr->bottom - cur_y)) {
        cur_y = box_ptr->top;
        fixed_y = box_ptr->bottom;
    } else {
        fixed_y = box_ptr->top;
        cur_y = box_ptr->bottom;
    }

    /*
     * Enter box loop
     */
    while (1) {
        gotoxy(1, MAX_Y);
        cputs("Use arrows to size the box");
        clreol();

        if (fixed_x < cur_x) {
            x1 = fixed_x;
            x2 = cur_x;
```

continued

Listing 11-1 continued

```
    } else {
        x1 = cur_x;
        x2 = fixed_x;
    }

    if (fixed_y < cur_y) {
        y1 = fixed_y;
        y2 = cur_y;
    } else {
        y1 = cur_y;
        y2 = fixed_y;
    }

    /*
     * Save area under the box
     */
    if (flag)
        process_text(x1, y1, x2, y2,
                    box_ptr->text_save, OP_SAVE);
    flag = 1;

    draw_box(x1, y1, x2, y2);

    gotoxy(cur_x, cur_y);
    ch = x_getch();

    switch (ch) {
    case KEY_UP:
        if (cur_y > 1)
            cur_y--;
        break;
    case KEY_DOWN:
        if (cur_y < MAX_Y)
            cur_y++;
        break;
    case KEY_LEFT:
        if (cur_x > 1)
            cur_x--;
        break;
    case KEY_RIGHT:
        if (cur_x < MAX_X)
            cur_x++;
        break;
    default:
        box_ptr->top = y1;
```

continued

Listing 11-1 continued

```
                box_ptr->bottom = y2;
                box_ptr->left = x1;
                box_ptr->right = x2;
                return (ch);
        }
        /*
         * Restore area under the box
         */
        process_text(x1, y1, x2, y2,
                    box_ptr->text_save, OP_RESTORE);
    }
#ifdef RETURN_BUG
    return (0);            /* Tell TC that we do return a value */
#endif RETURN_BUG
}
/************************************************************
 * make_box -- create a box                                *
 *                                                          *
 * Place a double-lined box on the screen.                 *
 * Invoked by the create_menu function                     *
 *                                                          *
 * Places a 1x1 box on the screen.  Cursor moves the       *
 * lower right corner.                                      *
 *                                                          *
 * Parameters                                               *
 *      box_ptr -- pointer to the box created               *
 *                                                          *
 * Returns                                                  *
 *      character that ends the box.                        *
 ************************************************************/
int   make_box(struct box * box_ptr)
{
    int   fixed_x, fixed_y;     /* Fixed point location */

    /*
     * If at limits, move to place where we can create a box.
     */
    if (cur_x == MAX_X)
        cur_x--;

    if (cur_y == MAX_Y)
        cur_y--;

    /*
     * Create 1x1 Box
```

continued

Listing 11-1 continued

```
        */
        fixed_x = cur_x;
        fixed_y = cur_y;
        /*
         * Move cursor down/right one
         */
        cur_x++;
        cur_y++;

        box_ptr->top = fixed_y;
        box_ptr->bottom = cur_y;
        box_ptr->left = fixed_x;
        box_ptr->right = cur_x;
        return (resize_box(box_ptr, 1));
}
/***********************************************************
 * background_text -- fill in the background text          *
 *                                                         *
 * Returns                                                 *
 *      1st non-printing character typed                   *
 ***********************************************************/
int     background_text(void)
{
        int   ch;       /* Character from input */

        while (1) {
            ch = move_cursor();
            if (isprint(ch) && ((ch & 0xFF00) == 0)) {
                putch(ch);
                cur_x++;
                if (cur_x == MAX_X) {
                    cur_x = 1;
                    cur_y++;
                    if (cur_y == MAX_Y)
                        cur_y = 1;
                }
            } else
                break;
        }
        return (ch);
}


#define MAX_BLANKS 30
struct blank new_blanks[MAX_BLANKS];
char *new_verify_funct[MAX_BLANKS]; /* Name of verify routines */
```

continued

Listing 11-1 continued

```
char blank_name[20];    /* The name of the blank */
char default_str[30];   /* Default value */
char len_str[3];        /* Length */
char verify_str[20];    /* Verification routine */

extern int verify_ok(char *);
extern int verify_callback(char *);
int verify_len(char *);

struct blank blank_list[] = {
    {24, 3, blank_name, sizeof(blank_name), verify_callback},
    {24, 4, default_str, sizeof(default_str), verify_ok},
    {24, 5, len_str, sizeof(len_str), verify_len},
    {24, 6, verify_str, sizeof(verify_str), verify_callback},
    {0, 0, NULL, 0, NULL}
};

struct fill_in_menu blank_menu = {
    5, 5,
    55, 8,
" Enter description of blank\r\n\
\r\n\
 Name of answer:\r\n\
 Default Value:\r\n\
 Length of Answer:\r\n\
 Verification routine:",
    blank_list};
/************************************************************
 * verify_len -- verify a length number                    *
 *                                                          *
 * Parameters                                               *
 *      len_ans -- length in string form to verify         *
 *                                                          *
 * Returns                                                  *
 *      VERIFY_OK -- length ok                              *
 *      VERIFY_ERROR -- a problem                           *
 ************************************************************/
int verify_len(char *len_ans)
{
    int len = atoi(len_ans);    /* Integer version of same */

    if ((len > 0) && (len <= sizeof(default_str)))
        return (VERIFY_OK);
    return (VERIFY_ERROR);
}
```

continued

Listing 11-1 continued

```c
/***********************************************************
 * create_blank -- add a blank to the menu                 *
 ***********************************************************/
void create_blank(void)
{
    int ch;             /* Character from string input */
    int cur_blank;      /* Current blank number */

    (void)strcpy(default_str, "");
    (void)strcpy(len_str, "30");
    (void)strcpy(verify_str, "verify_ok");
    ch = fill_in_menu(&blank_menu);
    if (ch < 0)
        return;
    for (cur_blank = 0; new_blanks[cur_blank].answer != NULL;
         cur_blank++) {
        /* Do nothing */
    }
    new_blanks[cur_blank].loc_x = cur_x;
    new_blanks[cur_blank].loc_y = cur_y;
    new_blanks[cur_blank].answer = strdup(default_str);
    new_blanks[cur_blank].len = atoi(len_str);
    new_verify_funct[cur_blank] = strdup(verify_str);
}
/***********************************************************
 * edit_blank -- edit an already defined blank             *
 *                                                         *
 * Parameters                                              *
 *      cur_blank -- the blank to edit                     *
 ***********************************************************/
void edit_blank(int cur_blank)
{
    int ch;              /* Character from string input */

    (void)strcpy(default_str, new_blanks[cur_blank].answer);
    (void)sprintf(len_str, "%d", new_blanks[cur_blank].len);
    (void)strcpy(verify_str, new_verify_funct[cur_blank]);
    ch = fill_in_menu(&blank_menu);
    if (ch < 0)
        return;
    free(new_blanks[cur_blank].answer);
    new_blanks[cur_blank].answer = strdup(default_str);
    new_blanks[cur_blank].len = atoi(len_str);
    free(new_verify_funct[cur_blank]);
    new_verify_funct[cur_blank] = strdup(verify_str);
```

continued

Listing 11-1 continued

```
}
/*************************************************************
 * display_blanks -- display the current blanks              *
 *************************************************************/
void display_blanks(void)
{
    int cur_blank;        /* The blank we are outputting now */

    for (cur_blank = 0; /* Taken care below */; cur_blank++) {
        struct blank *blank;    /* Blank we are displaying */

        blank = &new_blanks[cur_blank];
        if (blank->answer == NULL)
            break;
        textattr(REVERSE);
        gotoxy(blank->loc_x, blank->loc_y);
        (void)cprintf("%-*s", blank->len, blank->answer);
    }
    textattr(NORMAL);
}
/*************************************************************
 * move_blank -- move a blank across the screen              *
 *                                                           *
 * Parameters                                                *
 *      cur_blank -- the blank to move                       *
 *                                                           *
 * Returns                                                   *
 *      char that ended the move                             *
 *************************************************************/
int move_blank(int cur_blank)
{
    /* Shorthand for the blank we are moving */
    struct blank *blank_ptr = &new_blanks[cur_blank];
    /* Save the location in case of abort */
    int old_x = blank_ptr->loc_x;
    int old_y = blank_ptr->loc_y;
    int ch;       /* Current character */

    cur_x = blank_ptr->loc_x;
    /* cur_y already at blank location */

    while (1) {
        gotoxy(1, MAX_Y);
        cputs("Arrow keys move blank");
        clreol();
```

continued

Listing 11-1 continued

```
            display_blanks();

            gotoxy(cur_x, cur_y);
            ch = x_getch();

            gotoxy(cur_x, cur_y);
            /* Clear old blank */
            cprintf("%*s", blank_ptr->len, " ");
            switch (ch) {
                case KEY_UP:
                    if (cur_y > 1)
                        cur_y--;
                    break;
                case KEY_DOWN:
                    if (cur_y < (MAX_Y-1))
                        cur_y++;
                    break;
                case KEY_LEFT:
                    if (cur_x > 1)
                        cur_x--;
                    break;
                case KEY_RIGHT:
                    if ((cur_x + blank_ptr->len) < MAX_X)
                        cur_x++;
                    break;
                case KEY_ESC:
                    blank_ptr->loc_x = old_x;
                    blank_ptr->loc_y = old_y;
                    return (MENU_ABORT);
                default:
                    blank_ptr->loc_x = cur_x;
                    blank_ptr->loc_y = cur_y;
                    return (ch);
            }
            blank_ptr->loc_x = cur_x;
            blank_ptr->loc_y = cur_y;
    }
#ifdef RETURN_BUG
    return (0);            /* Tell TC that we do return a value */
#endif RETURN_BUG
}
/********************************************************
 * in_box -- returns true if cursor on a box line       *
 *                                                       *
 * Parameters                                            *
```

continued

Listing 11-1 continued

```
 *       box -- box to check                                 *
 *                                                           *
 * Returns                                                   *
 *       1 -- on the box                                     *
 *       0 -- not on the box                                 *
 ************************************************************/
int in_box(struct box *box)
{
    if ((cur_y == box->top) || (cur_y == box->bottom)) {
        return ((box->left <= cur_x) && (cur_x <= box->right));
    }
    if ((cur_x == box->left) || (cur_x == box->right)) {
        return ((box->top <= cur_y) && (cur_y <= box->bottom));
    }
    return (0);
}
/************************************************************
 * find_blank -- find which blank contains the              *
 *               current cursor                             *
 *                                                          *
 * Returns                                                  *
 *       blank number or -1 for no blank anywhere near      *
 ************************************************************/
int find_blank(void)
{
    int cur_blank;

    for (cur_blank = 0; new_blanks[cur_blank].answer != NULL;
            cur_blank++) {
        if ((new_blanks[cur_blank].loc_y == cur_y) &&
            (new_blanks[cur_blank].loc_x <= cur_x) &&
            (cur_x < new_blanks[cur_blank].loc_x +
                                new_blanks[cur_blank].len))
                return (cur_blank);
    }
    return (-1);
}
extern struct fill_in_menu file_menu;   /* File information */
extern FILE *out_file;          /* File to write to */
extern char name_of_menu[];     /* Name for this menu */


/************************************************************
 * cmp_blanks -- qsort cmp routine for blank answers        *
 *                                                          *
 * Parameters                                               *
```

continued

Listing 11-1 continued

```
 *       b1, b2 -- pointers to the two blanks            *
 *                                                       *
 * Returns                                               *
 *       r < 0    b1 < b2                                *
 *       r > 0    b1 > b2                                *
 *       r = 0    b1 = b2                                *
 ***********************************************************/
#ifdef OLD_STYLE
int cmp_blanks(struct blank **b1, struct blank **b2)
#define B1 (b1)
#define B2 (b2)
#else OLD_STYLE
int cmp_blanks(const void *b1, const void *b2)
#define B1 ((struct blank **)(b1))
#define B2 ((struct blank **)(b2))
#endif OLD_STYLE
{

    if ((*B1)->answer == NULL) {
        if ((*B2)->answer == NULL)
            return (0);
        return (1);
    }


    if ((*B2)->answer == NULL)
        return (-1);


    return (strcmp((*B1)->answer, (*B2)->answer));
}


/***********************************************************
 * cmp_verify -- qsort cmp routine for verify function   *
 *                      names                            *
 *                                                       *
 * Parameters                                            *
 *      v1, v2 -- pointers (indirect) to names           *
 *                                                       *
 * Returns                                               *
 *      r < 0    v1 < v2                                 *
 *      r > 0    v1 > v2                                 *
 *      r = 0    v1 = v2                                 *
 ***********************************************************/
#ifdef OLD_STYLE
int cmp_verify(char **v1, char **v2)
#define V1 (v1)
```

continued

Listing 11-1 continued

```
#define V2 (v2)
#else OLD_STYLE
int cmp_verify(const void *v1, const void *v2)
#define V1 ((char **)(v1))
#define V2 ((char **)(v2))
#endif OLD_STYLE
{
    if ((*V1) == NULL) {
        if ((*V2) == NULL)
            return (0);
        return (1);
    }

    if ((*V2) == NULL)
        return (-1);

    return (strcmp(*V1, *V2));
}
/***********************************************************
 * write_blank_menu -- write out data for a blank         *
 *                       menu                              *
 ***********************************************************/
void  write_blank_menu(struct box *box_ptr)
{
    int    status;  /* Status of menu call */
    int    cur_blank;   /* Current item we are dealing with */
    /* A place to sort names */
    char *sort_names[MAX_BLANKS];
    /* A place to sort blanks */
    struct blank *sort_blanks[MAX_BLANKS];

    status = fill_in_menu(&file_menu);
    if (status < 0)
        return;

    (void) fprintf(out_file, "/*\n");
    (void) fprintf(out_file, " *  Generated by menumaker\n");
    (void) fprintf(out_file, " */\n");
    (void) fprintf(out_file, "#include <stdlib.h>\n");
    (void) fprintf(out_file, "#include <stdio.h>\n");
    (void) fprintf(out_file, "#include \"menu.h\"\n");
    (void) fprintf(out_file, "\n");

    (void) memset(sort_blanks, '\0', sizeof(sort_blanks));
    for (cur_blank = 0; cur_blank < MAX_BLANKS; cur_blank++) {
```

continued

Listing 11-1 continued

```
        sort_blanks[cur_blank] = &new_blanks[cur_blank];
}
qsort(sort_blanks, MAX_BLANKS, sizeof(char *), cmp_blanks);


(void)fprintf(out_file,"/*\n");
(void)fprintf(out_file," * Answer blanks\n");
(void)fprintf(out_file," */\n");
for (cur_blank = 0; cur_blank < MAX_BLANKS; cur_blank++) {
    if (sort_blanks[cur_blank]->answer == NULL)
        break;


    if (sort_blanks[cur_blank+1]->answer != NULL) {
        if (strcmp(sort_blanks[cur_blank]->answer,
                sort_blanks[cur_blank+1]->answer) == 0)
            /* Skip duplicates */
            continue;
    }
    (void)fprintf(out_file,"char %s[%d];\n",
            sort_blanks[cur_blank]->answer,
            sort_blanks[cur_blank]->len);
}
(void) fprintf(out_file,"\n");


(void) memset(sort_names, '\0', sizeof(sort_names));
for (cur_blank = 0; cur_blank < MAX_BLANKS; cur_blank++) {
    sort_names[cur_blank] = new_verify_funct[cur_blank];
}
qsort(sort_names, MAX_BLANKS, sizeof(char *), cmp_verify);


(void)fprintf(out_file,"/*\n");
(void)fprintf(out_file," * Verification routines\n");
(void)fprintf(out_file," */\n");
for (cur_blank = 0; cur_blank < MAX_BLANKS; cur_blank++) {
    if (sort_names[cur_blank] == NULL)
        break;


    if (sort_names[cur_blank+1] != NULL) {
        if (strcmp(sort_names[cur_blank],
                sort_names[cur_blank+1]) == 0)
            /* Skip duplicates */
            continue;
    }
    (void)fprintf(out_file,"extern int %s(char *answer);\n",
            sort_names[cur_blank]);
```

continued

Listing 11-1 continued

```
    }
    (void) fprintf(out_file,"\n");


    (void) fprintf(out_file, "/*\n");
    (void) fprintf(out_file,
            " * %s_blanks -- blanks list for the %s menu\n",
            name_of_menu, name_of_menu);
    (void) fprintf(out_file, " */\n");
    (void) fprintf(out_file, "struct blank %s_blanks[] = {\n",
        name_of_menu);


    for (cur_blank = 0; new_blanks[cur_blank].answer != NULL;
         cur_blank++) {
        /* Blank we are working on */
        struct blank *blank_ptr = &new_blanks[cur_blank];
        (void) fprintf(out_file, "\t{\n");
        (void) fprintf(out_file, "\t\t%d, %d, /* Loc X, Y */\n",
                blank_ptr->loc_x - box_ptr->left,
                blank_ptr->loc_y - box_ptr->top);
        (void) fprintf(out_file,"\t\t%s,\t/* Answer */\n",
                blank_ptr->answer);
        (void) fprintf(out_file,"\t\t%d,\t/* Length */\n",
                blank_ptr->len);
        (void) fprintf(out_file,
                "\t\t%s\t/* Verification routine */\n",
                new_verify_funct[cur_blank]);
        (void) fprintf(out_file,"\t},\n");
    }
    (void) fprintf(out_file, "\t/* End of list */\n");
    (void) fprintf(out_file, "\t{ 0, 0, NULL, 0, NULL }\n");
    (void) fprintf(out_file, "};\n");
    (void) fprintf(out_file, "/*\n");
    (void) fprintf(out_file, " * The menu: %s\n", name_of_menu);
    (void) fprintf(out_file, " */\n");
    (void) fprintf(out_file,
            "struct fill_in_menu %s_menu = {\n", name_of_menu);
    (void) fprintf(out_file,
            "    %d, %d,        /* Location of menu (x,y) */\n",
                box_ptr->left, box_ptr->top);
    (void) fprintf(out_file,
                "    %d, %d,        /* Size of menu (x,y) */\n",
                box_ptr->right - box_ptr->left,
                box_ptr->bottom, box_ptr->top);
    (void) fprintf(out_file, "  /* Background text */\n");
    (void) fprintf(out_file, "  \"\\\n");
```

continued

Listing 11-1 continued

```
            for (cur_y = box_ptr->top+1;
                 cur_y < box_ptr->bottom; cur_y++) {
                for (cur_x = box_ptr->left+1;
                     cur_x < box_ptr->right; cur_x++) {
                    int ch;

                    if (find_blank() >= 0)
                        ch = ' ';
                    else {
                        gotoxy(cur_x, cur_y);
                        _AH = VIDEO_READ;
                        _BH = 0;
                        geninterrupt(VIDEO_INT);
                        ch = _AL;
                    }
                    switch (ch) {
                        case '\"':
                        case '\'':
                        case '\\':
                            (void)fprintf(out_file,"\\%c", ch);
                            break;
                        default:
                            (void)fprintf(out_file,"%c", ch);
                            break;
                    }
                }
                if (cur_y < (box_ptr->bottom - 1))
                    (void)fprintf(out_file, "\\r\\n\\n");
                else
                    (void)fprintf(out_file, "\",\n");
            }
        (void)fprintf(out_file, "\t%s_blanks\n", name_of_menu);
        (void)fprintf(out_file, "};\n");
        (void)fclose(out_file);
}
/*******************************************************
 * do_fill_in -- create a fill in menu                 *
 *******************************************************/
void  do_fill_in(void)
{
    int ch;             /* Current character */
    struct box box;     /* The box that holds our menu */
    int cur_blank;      /* Current blank to display */
    int first;          /* First time through */
```

continued

Listing 11-1 continued

```
memset((char *)new_blanks, '\0', sizeof(new_blanks));

gotoxy(1, MAX_Y);
cputs("Choose starting location and hit enter");
clreol();

(void)move_cursor();

ch = make_box(&box);
first = 1;

while (1) {
    gotoxy(1, MAX_Y);
    cputs("END - finished  F3 - EDIT");
    clreol();
    gotoxy(cur_x, cur_y);

    if (! first) {
        ch = background_text();
    }
    first = 0;

    if (ch == KEY_END)
        break;

    switch (ch) {
        /*
         * F1 -- move blank or box
         */
        case KEY_F1:
            cur_blank = find_blank();
            if (cur_blank >= 0) {
                move_blank(cur_blank);
            } else {
                if (in_box(&box))
                    resize_box(&box, 0);
            }
            break;
        case KEY_F3:
            cur_blank = find_blank();
            if (cur_blank >= 0)
                edit_blank(cur_blank);
        case KEY_DELETE:
            cur_blank = find_blank();
```

continued

Listing 11-1 continued

```
                 if (cur_blank >= 0) {
                     free(new_blanks[cur_blank].answer);
                     free(new_verify_funct[cur_blank]);

                     gotoxy(new_blanks[cur_blank].loc_x,
                             new_blanks[cur_blank].loc_y);
                     cprintf("%*s",
                             new_blanks[cur_blank].len, " ");

                     while (new_blanks[cur_blank].answer != NULL) {
                         new_blanks[cur_blank] =
                                     new_blanks[cur_blank +1];
                         new_verify_funct[cur_blank] =
                                     new_verify_funct[cur_blank +1];

                         cur_blank++;
                     }
                 } else
                     putch(BELL);
                 break;
             case KEY_INSERT:
                 create_blank();
                 break;
             /*
              * ENTER -- ignore this key
              */
             case KEY_ENTER:
                 break;
             default:
                 putch(BELL);
                 break;
         }

         display_blanks();
     }
     write_blank_menu(&box);
}
extern void do_select();       /* Handle creation of select menu */
extern void do_select_one();/* Handle create select one menu */
/*
 * Items in the initial menu
 */
struct select_item init_items[] = {
     {"Selection Menu (Callback)", do_select},
     {"Selection Menu (Index)", do_select_one},
```

continued

Listing 11-1 continued

```
    {"Fill In the Blank Menu", do_fill_in},
    {NULL, NULL}
};

/*
 * The initial menu
 */
struct select_menu init_menu = {
    25, 9,          /* Location of the menu */
    "Choose menu type",
    init_items
};

main(int argc, char *argv[])
{
    int    status;

    debug_flags(argc, argv);
    clrscr();
    status = select_menu(&init_menu, 0, 1);
    if (status != MENU_OK)
        exit(1);

    clrscr();
    return (0);
}
```

Listing 11-2. "menusel.c"

```
/**********************************************************
 * makesel -- menu maker software                        *
 *                                                       *
 * Routines for building a selection menu.               *
 **********************************************************/

#include <stdio.h>
#include <conio.h>
#include <dos.h>
#include <math.h>
#include <ctype.h>
#include <stdlib.h>
#include <mem.h>
#include <string.h>
#include "keys.h"
```

continued

Listing 11-2 continued

```c
#include "menu.h"
#include "menu-int.h"


#define MAX_X   80 /* Limits of X Movements */
#define MAX_Y   25 /* Limits of Y Movements */


#define BELL 7
/***********************************************************
 * verify_ok -- verify routine that thinks everything      *
 *              is ok.                                      *
 *                                                         *
 * Parameter                                               *
 *      answer -- answer to check (if we were checking)    *
 *                                                         *
 * Returns                                                 *
 *      VERIFY_OK of course                                *
 ***********************************************************/
#pragma warn -par   /* We don't use answer in next function */
int    verify_ok(char *answer)
{
    return (VERIFY_OK);
}
#pragma warn .par   /* Turn back on warning */
/***********************************************************
 * verify_callback -- verify the callback blank            *
 *                                                         *
 * Parameters                                              *
 *      answer -- the name of the callback routine         *
 *                                                         *
 * Returns                                                 *
 *      VERIFY_OK -- if answer is a legal C name           *
 *      VERIFY_ERROR -- if not                             *
 ***********************************************************/
int    verify_callback(char *answer)
{
    if (!isalpha(*answer) && (*answer != '_'))
        return (VERIFY_ERROR);

    while (*answer) {
        if (!isalnum(*answer) && (*answer != '_'))
            return (VERIFY_ERROR);
        answer++;
    }
    return (VERIFY_OK);
}
```

continued

Listing 11-2 continued

```
FILE *out_file;    /* File to write data on */
int   verify_file(char *name)
{
    out_file = fopen(name, "w");
    if (out_file == NULL)
        return (VERIFY_ERROR);
    return (VERIFY_OK);
}
/*
 * Title of the menu
 */
#define MAX_TITLE 50
char  build_title[MAX_TITLE] = "Title";

char  file_name[20];    /* Name of file to write to */
char  name_of_menu[20]; /* Name of the new menu */
/*
 * Blanks for filling in the name of the menu
 */
struct blank file_blanks[] = {
    {11, 1, file_name, sizeof(file_name), verify_file},
    {11, 2, name_of_menu, sizeof(name_of_menu), verify_callback},
    {-1, -1, NULL, 0, NULL}
};


/*
 * The menu to change titles of a select menu
 */
struct fill_in_menu file_menu = {
    5, 5,             /* Location x, y */
    MAX_TITLE + 12, 4,   /* Size X, Y */
    "File name:\r\n\
Menu name:",
    file_blanks
};


char  new_name[30];/* New entry on the menu */
char  new_callback[30]; /* New callback routine */


/*
 * Blanks used to handle edit/insert of callback entry in menu
 */
struct blank callback_blanks[] = {
    {20, 2, new_name, sizeof(new_name), verify_ok},
    {20, 3, new_callback, sizeof(new_callback), verify_callback},
```

continued

Listing 11-2 continued

```
        {-1, -1, NULL, 0, NULL}
};
/*
 * Menu used to handle edit/insert of callback entry in menu
 */
struct fill_in_menu callback_menu = {
    5, 5,            /* Loc X, Y */
    60, 4,           /* Size X, Y */
    "                      Item Parameters\r\n\
Item Name:\n\r\
Callback routine:",
    callback_blanks
};


/*
 * Blanks used to handle edit/insert of no callback entry in menu
 */
struct blank no_callback_blanks[] = {
    {20, 2, new_name, sizeof(new_name), verify_ok},
    {-1, -1, NULL, 0, NULL}
};


/*
 * Menu used to handle edit/insert of no callback entry in menu
 */
struct fill_in_menu no_callback_menu = {
    5, 5,            /* Loc X, Y */
    40, 10,          /* Size X, Y */
    "       Item Parameters\r\n\
Item Name:\n\r",
    no_callback_blanks
};


#define MAX_ITEMS 20    /* Max items in a menu */
/*
 * The item list for the menu we are making
 */
struct select_item build_items[MAX_ITEMS];
/*
 * List of callback procedures for the new menu
 */
char *callback_name[MAX_ITEMS];


/*
 * The menu
```

continued

Listing 11-2 continued

```
 */
struct select_menu build_menu = {
    30, 15,
    build_title,
    build_items
};


/*
 * Blanks for filling in the title menu
 */
struct blank title_blanks[] = {
    {8, 1, build_title, sizeof(build_title), verify_ok},
    {-1, -1, NULL, 0, NULL}
};
/*
 * The menu to change titles of a select menu
 */
struct fill_in_menu title_menu = {
    5, 5,             /* Location x, y */
    MAX_TITLE + 12, 2,   /* Size X, Y */
    "Title:",
    title_blanks
};

/* Window for the menu being built */
struct window_info build_window;
/*********************************************************
 * write_select_menu -- write out data for a select     *
 *                       menu                            *
 *                                                       *
 * Parameters                                            *
 *     callback -- true if callback type menu            *
 *********************************************************/
void  write_select_menu(int callback)
{
    int    status;  /* Status of menu call */
    int    item;    /* Current item we are dealing with */

    status = fill_in_menu(&file_menu);
    if (status < 0)
        return;

    (void) fprintf(out_file, "/*\n");
    (void) fprintf(out_file, " *  Generated by menumaker\n");
    (void) fprintf(out_file, " */\n");
```

continued

Listing 11-2 continued

```c
    (void) fprintf(out_file, "#include <stdlib.h>\n");
    (void) fprintf(out_file, "#include <stdio.h>\n");
    (void) fprintf(out_file, "#include \"menu.h\"\n");
    (void) fprintf(out_file, "\n");
    if (callback) {
        (void) fprintf(out_file, "/*\n");
        (void) fprintf(out_file, " * Dummy callback routines\n");
        (void) fprintf(out_file, " */\n");

        for (item = 0; build_items[item].name != NULL; item++) {
            /* Shorthand for name */
            char *name = callback_name[item];


            (void) fprintf(out_file,
                        "/* Dummy %s callback routine */\n",
                        name);
            (void) fprintf(out_file, "/*\n");
            (void) fprintf(out_file,
                        " * %s -- callback routine \n", name);
            (void) fprintf(out_file, " */\n");
            (void) fprintf(out_file, "void %s(void)\n", name);
            (void) fprintf(out_file, "{\n");
            (void) fprintf(out_file,
                        "    (void)printf(\"%s called\\n\");\n",
                        name);
            (void) fprintf(out_file, "}\n");
        }
    }
    (void) fprintf(out_file, "/*\n");
    (void) fprintf(out_file,
                " * %s_items -- item list for the %s menu\n",
                name_of_menu, name_of_menu);
    (void) fprintf(out_file, " */\n");
    (void) fprintf(out_file,
                "struct select_item %s_items[] = {\n",
                name_of_menu);
    for (item = 0; build_items[item].name != NULL; item++) {
        (void) fprintf(out_file, "    {\"%s\", %s},\n",
                    build_items[item].name,
                    callback ? callback_name[item] : "NULL");
    }
    (void) fprintf(out_file,
            "    {NULL, NULL}              /* End of list */\n");
    (void) fprintf(out_file, "};\n");
    (void) fprintf(out_file, "/*\n");
```

continued

Listing 11-2 continued

```
      (void) fprintf(out_file, " * The menu: %s\n", name_of_menu);
      (void) fprintf(out_file, " */\n");
      (void) fprintf(out_file,
                 "struct select_menu %s_menu = {\n", name_of_menu);
      (void) fprintf(out_file,
                 "   %d, %d,          /* Location of menu (x,y) */\n",
                 build_menu.loc_x, build_menu.loc_y);
      (void) fprintf(out_file, "   \"%s\", /* Title */\n",
                 build_menu.title);
      (void) fprintf(out_file,
                 "   %s_items        /* Item list */\n",
                 name_of_menu);
      (void) fprintf(out_file, "};\n");
      (void) fclose(out_file);
}
/*********************************************************
 * gen_select -- generic select builder                 *
 *                                                       *
 * Parameters                                            *
 *      callback -- true if callback menu being created  *
 *               -- false -- no callbacks                *
 *********************************************************/
void  gen_select(int callback)
{
    int    item;    /* Current item number */
    int    selection;    /* Current selection */
    int    ch;      /* User character input */
    int    x_size, y_size;      /* Size of the menu */
    enum {
        M_MOVE, M_SELECT
    }    mode = M_MOVE;          /* Move or edit menu */
    int    quit = 0;/* We're done flag */
    int    status;  /* Status of current menu */

    clrscr();
    memset((char *) build_items, '\0', sizeof(build_items));

    selection = 0;                  /* Start out at beginning */

    while (!quit) {
        gotoxy(1, MAX_Y);
        if (mode == M_MOVE)
            (void) cputs(
                    "Arrows - move  F1 - change to select mode");
        else
```

continued

Listing 11-2 continued

```
        (void) cputs(
                "Arrows - select   F1 - change to move mode");

    (void) cputs("  F2 - Title  F3 - Edit item");
    clreol();

    x_size = get_x_size(&build_menu);
    y_size = get_y_size(&build_menu);

    create_window(build_menu.loc_x, build_menu.loc_y,
            build_menu.loc_x + x_size,
            build_menu.loc_y + y_size,
                    &build_window);

    display_select(&build_menu, selection);
    ch = x_getch();

    destroy_window(&build_window);

    switch (ch) {
        /*
         * F1 -- toggle MOVE/SELECT
         */
    case KEY_F1:
        if (mode == M_MOVE)
            mode = M_SELECT;
        else
            mode = M_MOVE;
        break;


        /*
         * F2 -- Edit title
         */
    case KEY_F2:
        {
            char  title_save[sizeof(build_title)];

            strcpy(title_save, build_title);
            status = fill_in_menu(&title_menu);

            /* Check for abort or other user funny */
            if (status < 0)
                strcpy(build_title, title_save);
        }
```

continued

Listing 11-2 continued

```
                break;
        case KEY_F3:
            if (build_items[selection].name != NULL) {
                strcpy(new_name, build_items[selection].name);
                if (callback)
                    strcpy(new_callback,
                            callback_name[selection]);

                if (callback)
                    status = fill_in_menu(&callback_menu);
                else
                    status = fill_in_menu(&no_callback_menu);

                if (status > 0) {
                    free(build_items[selection].name);
                    build_items[selection].name =
                                            strdup(new_name);
                    if (callback) {
                        free(callback_name[selection]);
                        callback_name[selection] =
                                            strdup(new_callback);
                    }
                }
            }
            break;
            /*
             * Insert -- create new entry
             */
        case KEY_INSERT:
            if (callback)
                status = fill_in_menu(&callback_menu);
            else
                status = fill_in_menu(&no_callback_menu);

            if (status > 0) {
                for (item = MAX_ITEMS - 2; item >= selection;
                    item--) {
                    build_items[item + 1] = build_items[item];
                    callback_name[item + 1] =
                                        callback_name[item];
                }
                build_items[selection].name = strdup(new_name);
                if (callback)
                    callback_name[selection] =
                                        strdup(new_callback);
```

continued

Listing 11-2 continued

```
        }
        break;
    case KEY_DELETE:
        if (build_items[selection].name != NULL) {
            free(build_items[selection].name);
            if (callback)
                free(callback_name[selection]);

            for (item = selection;
                  build_items[item].name != NULL;
                  item++) {

                build_items[item] = build_items[item + 1];
                if (callback)
                    callback_name[item] =
                                    callback_name[item + 1];
            }
        }
        break;

        /*
         * UP -- move menu or selection up one
         */
    case KEY_UP:
        if (mode == M_MOVE) {
            if (build_menu.loc_y > 1)
                build_menu.loc_y--;
        } else {
            if (selection > 0)
                selection--;
        }
        break;
        /*
         * DOWN -- move menu or selection down one
         */
    case KEY_DOWN:
        if (mode == M_MOVE) {
            if (build_menu.loc_y + y_size < MAX_Y)
                build_menu.loc_y++;
        } else {
            selection++;
            if (build_items[selection].name == NULL)
                selection--;
        }
        break;
```

continued

Listing 11-2 continued

```
                    /*
                     * Left -- move menu left
                     */
            case KEY_LEFT:
                if (build_menu.loc_x > 1)
                    build_menu.loc_x--;
                break;
                    /*
                     * Right -- move menu to the right
                     */
            case KEY_RIGHT:
                if (build_menu.loc_x + x_size < MAX_X)
                    build_menu.loc_x++;
                break;
                    /*
                     * END -- quit and exit this routine
                     */
            case KEY_END:
                quit = 1;
                break;
            default:
                putch(BELL);          /* Beep at user */
                break;
            }
        }
    write_select_menu(callback);
}
/********************************************************
 * do_select -- handle a selection menu                *
 ********************************************************/
void  do_select(void)
{
    gen_select(1); /* Select with callbacks */
}
/********************************************************
 * do_select_one -- handle a select_one type menu      *
 ********************************************************/
void  do_select_one(void)
{
    gen_select(0); /* Select, but don't allow callbacks */
}
```

## Chapter 12

Recursion

Introduction

When used right, recursion can be a very powerful tool. Unfortunately, it can be somewhat tricky to use. This chapter introduces you to recursive thinking, as well as providing you with some practical uses.

A recursive function is one that calls itself. In other words, if a function `do_it` directly or indirectly calls `do_it` then it is a recursive function. The classic example of a recursive function is the factorial. This function is defined as

```
fact(n)
    (n > 0)     n * f(n-1)
    (n = 0)     1
```

To compute `fact(3)` we must perform the steps

```
fact(3)
    = 3 * fact(2)
        = 2 * fact(1)
            = 1 * fact(0)
                = 1
            = 1         (1 * 1)
        = 2             (2 * 1)
    = 6                 (3 * 2)
```

Recursion is not complex, as long as we keep two simple rules in mind. A function may call itself if at each stage it makes the problem simpler and there is a definite ending point.   Our factorial function follows these rules. The problem is made simpler at each step since `fact(n-1)` is simpler than `fact(n)`. The ending point is reached at `fact(0)`.

We use recursion in everyday life. The syntax of English is recursive. We can define a sentence as:

sentence :== simple sentence

sentence :== simple sentence "and" sentence.

Thus, we can break down any sentence, no matter how complex, into a series of simple sentences strung together by the word "and."

The DOS directory structure is also recursively defined. A directory can contain any number of entries. Each entry can be either a file or a directory. This is an example of treewise recursion. Graphically, the directory structure looks like an inverted tree. The root is the top and the leaves (files) are on the bottom.

The Dupfile Program

Steve works as a volunteer at the local railroad museum. Like most people the museum staff are not very computer literate. They quickly loaded up their hard disk with a number of utilities from various sources.

Unfortunately there is a great deal of duplication. For example, there appears to be a complete set of the DOS utilities in the directory `\BIN`, as well as in `\DOS`. Finding and eradicating these duplicates is a time-consuming task. It would be nice if we had a program that would scan the entire disk looking for duplicates and let us delete them.

We are going to create a program that searches the disk for duplicate files and allows the user to interactively delete them.

The first step in this process is to define our data structures. The two main objects we are dealing with are directories and files. For each file, we will need to know the file name and the directory that contains it. Our structure for the file entries is:

```
struct file_entry {
    char *name;             /* Name of this file */
    unsigned short crc;     /* CRC for this file */
    struct dir_entry *dir; /* Directory where this file resides */
};
```

The field name holds the name of the file (file name only, no path information). The directory information is pointed to by the field dir. The CRC field is used to hold "checksum" information (this will be discussed later).

The structure holding the directory information is very similar to the one for files.

```
struct dir_entry {
    char *name;                      /* Name of this entry */
    struct dir_entry *parent;     /* Pointer to parent directory */
};
```

The parent field points to the directory containing this entry. The top level directory or root has no parent so the value of its parent is NULL.

Note that we can find the full path for a file by following the linked list of directory entries (using the parent field) up to the root.

For example, suppose our disk contains the following files:

In directory \

```
AUTOEXEC.BAT
DOS
UTIL
```

In directory \DOS

```
FORMAT.COM
DATE.COM
```

In directory \UTIL

```
TOUCH.EXE
VI.EXE
PROG
```

In directory \UTIL\PROG

```
MAKE.EXE
TC.EXE
```

Then our data tree for this disk would look like.

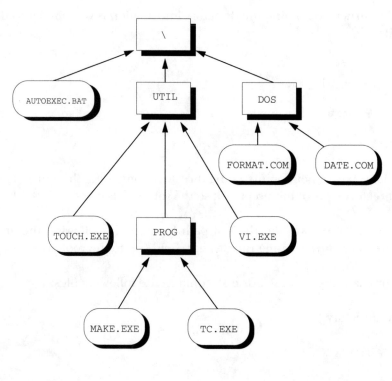

struct dir_entry

struct file_entry

Scanning the File System Recursively.

The actual code to scan the file system is rather simple. We start at the root directory scanning each entry in the current directory. If we encounter a file, we add it to our list of files. If we encounter a directory, we add it to our list of directories and call scan with our new directory.

The pseudo code for this function is:

```
scan(name)
{
    while (more_files) {
        next_file(name);
        if (directory) {
            create_new_directory_node;
            scan(name);
        } else {
            create_new_file_entry;
        }
    }
}
```

The real code is presented at the end of the chapter. Although the task of scanning a multi-level directory is complex, our code is rather simple. The implementation takes up a little over a page and most of that is concerned with the bookkeeping details needed in creating new file and directory entries.

Our function `scandir` takes two arguments `parent` and `path`. The parameter `path` is the full path name of the directory we are going to scan. The parameter `parent` points to the `dir_entry` structure for this directory. It is called `parent` because this directory is the parent directory for any subdirectories found at this level.

Turbo C provides two directory scanning functions: `findfirst` and `findnext`. The function `findfirst` is used to initiate a directory scan. It is called once, to find the first entry in the directory that matches the file specification indicated by the `path` and `attrib` parameters. Its definition is:

```
int findfirst(char *path, struct file_block *file_block;
        int attrib)
```

where

path   is the full path name of the directory and files to be
                scanned.

file_block   is a DOS structure where file information is stored. This
                structure is passed to findnext to continue the scan.

attrib   is a set of file attributes. The function will look for files with
                matching attributes. For this program, we are looking for
                all files so our attribute list is:

```
#define FA_LIST (FA_RDONLY|FA_HIDDEN|FA_SYSTEM|FA_DIREC|FA_ARCH)
```

This will cause all files to match. For a complete list of attributes and what they
mean see your DOS manual.

The function findfirst finds only the first matching entry in a directory.
To find later entries we must use the function findnext. This function is
defined as:

```
int findnext(struct file_block *file_block)
```

where

file_block is the file block parameter from the previous call to
findfirst or findnext.

Note that findnext does not need a path or attributes to find a file. All
search information has been stored in the file_block. This is updated on
each call to findnext.

Both findfirst and findnext return a status of zero when a file is found
and non-zero for an error.

When findfirst and findnext locate a file, the name is stored in the
variable file_block.ff_name. The attributes are stored in
file_block.ff_attrib.

If we encounter a directory, we construct a new path (called new_path) and
a directory entry structure (called new_dir_entry). Finally, we make a recursive call to scandir to scan this new directory.

A file is somewhat easier to handle. All we have to do is create a new file entry. At this time we do not compute a CRC for the file. CRCs take time and we don't want to produce one unless we absolutely have to.

Checking the Results of the Scan

After creating the function scandir, it's a good idea to check it out before producing the rest of the program. We do this two ways, first by putting in some progress messages in the scandir function and secondly by printing the results after scanning.

Our diagnostic messages are enabled using the "-d" option on the command line. These messages help us uncover a problem we overlooked in the first version of the function. We didn't have any special code to handle the files "." and "..".

The special file "." is created by DOS and is an alias for the current directory. Because our first version of the function treated this file as a normal directory, we quickly got into an infinite recursion. Our algorithm went something like this:

```
scandir(\)
    first entry "."
    scandir (\.)
        first entry "."

        scandir (\.\.)

            first entry "."

            scandir (\.\.\.)
```

The diagnostic messages at the beginning of scandir quickly showed us the problem and we added code to correct it.

With our diagnostic messages, we are able to track the progress of scandir. In order to check the results we need to print the file list. This should be easy since all the files are stored in the array file_list. But the problem is that only the names are stored and we want to print the full path.

The function `full_name` is designed to convert a `file_list` entry into a full file name. First it calls `fill_dir_name` to get the directory and then adds the name of the file onto the end.

The function `full_dir_name` illustrates another use of recursion. Our full path consists of many components each with their own `dir_entry` structure. A set of pointers run from the lowest subdirectories to the root. Unfortunately, for printing we need to start at the root and work our way down. We could do this iteratively, working our way up along the tree. But we would need an array to store the intermediate results, as well as some fancy control statements to make sure we did everything in the proper order.

Recursion simplifies this process greatly. Our recursive algorithm for converting the `dir_entry` into a name is:

```
full_dir_name()
    convert our parent dir_entry to a string
    add on our name
```

This algorithm satisfies one of our two rules of recursion: It makes the problem simpler at each level. We need to satisfy the other rule: The algorithm must stop someplace.

In this case, the easiest place to stop is at the very top level (one level before the root). This occurs when our `dir_entry pointer` is null. Since this is actually one level on top of the highest level, the directory name for this entry is `NULL` (empty string).

The actual algorithm for this function is:

```
static void full_dir_name(char *name,struct dir_entry *dir)
{
    if (dir == NULL) {
        name[0] = '\0';          /* No entry -- no name */
        return;
    }
    full_dir_name(name, dir->parent);     /* Do the first part */
    (void)strcat(name, dir->name);  /* Add this path component */
    (void)strcat(name, "\\");       /* Add directory separator */
}
```

Although only seven lines long, this function performs some very complex functions. It follows a linked list to its head, saving intermediate values and constructs a path from the list in reverse order. Because recursion is used, these very complex tasks can be written in a few simple lines of code.

Sorting the List

Sorting the list is done using the library function `qsort` (quick sort). The function `cmp_files` is used by `qsort` to compare two file names. Sorting can easily take 10-30 seconds. Users are very impatient people and don't like sitting around 30 seconds while their computer does nothing. They want to see something that tells them that the program isn't hung up.

In addition to its regular duties, the function `cmp_files` outputs an illusion of progress. In this case, it is a spinning line at the bottom of the screen. This gives the appearance that the computer is working at high speed sorting the files.

Handling the Duplicates

After the files are sorted the function `process_dups` goes through the list looking for duplicate names. When it finds a duplication it computes a CRC for each file and prints the results or turns control over to the function `interactive`.

CRC Function

CRC stands for Cycle Redundancy Check. It was originally used in digital communications. Transmission lines are not perfect and many times errors will be introduced into a packet of data. Communication engineers needed some way of checking the integrity of the data. One solution was to add a CRC on the end of each packet. The algorithm for computing a CRC was designed to detect a wide array of errors and to be easy to implement in hardware.

CRC checking is currently implemented in most popular PC communication protocols, including `MODEM7`, `XMODEM`, and `KERMIT`.

Because of its popularity and ready availability, the use of the CRC has grown from communications to become a general purpose file check number. In our program, we use it for checking to see if two files not only have the same name, but also have identical contents.

The actual code for the function `compute_crc` was adapted from a public domain program. It uses a table of pre-computed values (`crc_table`). A program to generate this table is included at the end of this chapter. Our `Makefile` will automatically use this program to generate the table if needed.

User Interface

A user interface should be as simple as possible. In this case, we display a list of files and allow the users to select the files he wants deleted. Each file is identified by letter. For example, our screen might look like:

```
A            \ANSI.SYS                      5CE2
B            \DOS\ANSI.SYS                  5CE2
```

Typing the letter "A" will cause the word "`Deleted`" to appear beside the first entry.

```
A Deleted \ANSI.SYS                         5CE2
B            \DOS\ANSI.SYS                  5CE2
```

In order to given the user a chance to recover, typing "A" a second time will remove the message. Finally, when the user types a space, the program will delete any marked files and go on to the next set of duplications.

Summary

Recursion is a very powerful programming tool. Our program would be much more complicated without it.

We have seen how treewise recursion can be used to scan an entire disk for files. We also used simple recursion to walk down a liked list with a minimal amount of code.

Recursion can be tricky. Two simple rules must be followed: The problem must be simplified at each stage and there must be some end point.

Once mastered, recursion can greatly simplify your programs and increase your programming power.

Listing 12-1. "dupfile.c"

```c
#undef DEBUG      /* Real program */
#if __TURBOC__  <= 296
#undef RETURN_BUG   /* Turbo C++ won't make warnings */
#undef OLD_STYLE    /* Use new style calling sequence */
#else               /* older Turbo C */
#define RETURN_BUG  /* Turbo C generates extra warnings */
#define OLD_STYLE   /* Use old style calling sequence */
#endif /* __TURBOC__ */
/************************************************************
 * dupfile -- check the file system for duplicates         *
 *                                                         *
 * Usage:                                                  *
 *      dupfile [options] [root]                           *
 *                                                         *
 *      Root is the top level directory to check.          *
 *      This program will descend through the directory    *
 *      tree finding file with a duplicate name and CRC.   *
 *      When found, the user is asked if he wants to       *
 *      delete any of the files.                           *
 *                                                         *
 * Options                                                 *
 *      -d -- debug (print information as program works)   *
 *      -r -- print the raw list (before sorting)          *
 *      -s -- print the list after sorting                 *
 *      -p -- print list of duplicates (only)              *
 ************************************************************/
#include <stdlib.h>
#include <stdio.h>
#include <dir.h>
#include <dos.h>
#include <string.h>
#include <fcntl.h>
#include <io.h>
#include <ctype.h>


#define TRUE 1
#define FALSE 0


#define BACKSPACE 8
#define CONTROL_C 3


#define NAME_SIZE 60     /* Length of longest name */


int debug = FALSE;       /* Print debug information */
```

continued

Listing 12.1 continued.

```
#define MAX_FILES (10 * 1024)

/*
 * Structure of a directory entry
 */
struct dir_entry {
    char *name;                 /* Name of this entry */
    struct dir_entry *parent;   /* Pointer to parent directory */
};


/*
 * Regular file entry
 */
struct file_entry {
    char *name;                 /* Name of this file */
    unsigned short crc;         /* CRC for this file */
    struct dir_entry *dir;/* Directory where this file resides */
};

struct file_entry **file_list;/* Pointers to the list of files */
int num_files = 0;              /* Number of files in the list */
int print_only = FALSE;         /* Print the list of duplicates */

main(int argc, char *argv[])
{
    char *root;                 /* Where to start scanning */
    struct dir_entry root_dir;/* The root directory for search */
    int print_raw = FALSE;  /* Print file last AFTER scanning */
    int print_sort = FALSE; /* Print file list after sorting */

    /* Scan a directory */
    void scandir(struct dir_entry *, char *);
    void usage(void);   /* Tell how to use us */
    void print_files(void);/* Print the entire file list */
    /* Compare two file entries */
#ifdef OLD_STYLE
    int cmp_files(struct file_entry **, struct file_entry **);
#else OLD_STYLE
    int cmp_files(const void *, const void *);
#endif OLD_STYLE
    void process_dups(void);/* Handle duplicate files */

    while ((argc > 1) && (argv[1][0] == '-')) {
        switch (argv[1][1]) {
```

continued

Listing 12.1 continued.

```
                    case 'd':
                        debug = TRUE;
                        break;
                    case 'r':      /* Print raw list */
                        print_raw = TRUE;
                        break;
                    case 's':      /* Print sorted list */
                        print_sort = TRUE;
                        break;
                    case 'p':
                        print_only = TRUE;
                        break;
                    default:
                        usage();
                        /*NOTREACHED*/
                }
            argc--;
            argv++;
        }

        switch (argc) {
            case 1:
                root = "\\";
                break;
            case 2:
                root = argv[1];
                break;
            default:
                usage();
                /*NOTREACHED*/
        }

        file_list = malloc(MAX_FILES * sizeof(struct file_entry *));

        if (file_list == NULL) {
            (void)fprintf(stderr,
                "Error: Not enough memory for file list\n");
            exit (1);
        }

        if (root[strlen(root) -1] == '\\')
            root[strlen(root) -1] = '\0';

        root_dir.parent = NULL;      /* No parent for the root */
        root_dir.name = strdup(root);
```

continued

Listing 12.1 continued.

```
        scandir(&root_dir, root);
        if (print_raw)
            print_files();

        (void)cprintf("Sorting %d files\r\n", num_files);
        qsort(file_list, num_files, sizeof(struct file_entry *),
                cmp_files);
        cputs(" \r\n");          /* Move past progress spinner */

        if (print_sort)
            print_files();

        process_dups();
        return (0);
}
/************************************************************
 * scandir -- scan a directory and add all its files to    *
 *                the file list.                            *
 *                                                          *
 * Parameters                                               *
 *       parent -- directory entry for this path            *
 *       path -- full name of directory to scan.            *
 *                (Must **NOT** end with \)                 *
 ************************************************************/
static void scandir(struct dir_entry *parent,char *path)
{
/* Attributes of the files we want to look at */
#define FA_LIST   (FA_RDONLY|FA_HIDDEN|FA_SYSTEM|FA_DIREC|FA_ARCH)

    char cur_path[300]; /* Current path with file name */
    char new_path[300]; /* Path name for sub-directories */
    int first = TRUE;   /* First time through */
    int status;         /* Status of last find directive */
    struct ffblk file_block;/* Attributes of the file block */

    if (debug)
        (void)printf("Scanning %s\n", path);

    (void)strcpy(cur_path, path);
    (void)strcat(cur_path, "\\");
    (void)strcat(cur_path, "*.*");

    while (1) {
        if (first) {
```

continued

Listing 12.1 continued.

```
            status = findfirst(cur_path, &file_block, FA_LIST);
            first = FALSE;
    } else
            status = findnext(&file_block);

    if (status != 0)
        return;

    if (strcmp(file_block.ff_name, ".") == 0)
        continue;

    if (strcmp(file_block.ff_name, "..") == 0)
        continue;

    if (debug)
        (void)printf("File name: %s\n", file_block.ff_name);

    if ((file_block.ff_attrib & FA_DIREC) != 0) {
        /* Directory */
        struct dir_entry *new_dir_entry;/* New dir entry */

        /* Create a new path */
        (void)strcpy(new_path, path);
        (void)strcat(new_path, "\\");
        (void)strcat(new_path, file_block.ff_name);

        /* Create new directory entry */
        new_dir_entry = malloc(sizeof(struct dir_entry));
        new_dir_entry->parent = parent;
        new_dir_entry->name = strdup(file_block.ff_name);

        scandir(new_dir_entry, new_path);
    } else {
        /* Enter normal file */
        struct file_entry *new_file_entry;/* New file */

        if (num_files >= (MAX_FILES-1)) {
            static error_msg_sent = FALSE;

            if (!error_msg_sent) {
                (void)fprintf(stderr,
                            "Error:Too many files\n");
                error_msg_sent = TRUE;
            }
```

316   *Advanced C*

Listing 12.1 continued.

```
            }
            new_file_entry = malloc(sizeof(struct file_entry));
            new_file_entry->name = strdup(file_block.ff_name);
            new_file_entry->crc = 0;
            new_file_entry->dir = parent;


            file_list[num_files] = new_file_entry;
            num_files++;
        }
    }
}
/***********************************************************
 * full_dir_name -- full compute directory name from      *
 *                    current component                    *
 *                                                         *
 * Parameter                                               *
 *      name -- place to put the resulting name            *
 *      dir -- directory to print                          *
 *                                                         *
 * This routine uses recursion to work its way up to       *
 * the root of this tree.  Once there, it starts           *
 * storing path components and works its way down the      *
 * tree.                                                   *
 ***********************************************************/
static void full_dir_name(char *name,struct dir_entry *dir)
{
    if (dir == NULL) {
        name[0] = '\0';                 /* No entry -- no name */
        return;
    }
    full_dir_name(name, dir->parent);    /* Do the first part */
    (void)strcat(name, dir->name);  /* Add this path component */
    (void)strcat(name, "\\");        /* Add directory separator */
}
/***********************************************************
 * full_name -- compute the full name of a file           *
 *              (Including all directory components)       *
 *                                                         *
 * Parameter                                               *
 *      name -- full name of the file                      *
 *      file -- the file to print                          *
 ***********************************************************/
static void full_name(char *name,struct file_entry *file)
{
    full_dir_name(name, file->dir);
```

continued

Listing 12.1 continued.

```
        (void)strcat(name, file->name);
}
/************************************************************
 * print_files -- print all the files in the list          *
 ***********************************************************/
static void print_files(void)
{
    int current;            /* Current file number */
    char current_name[NAME_SIZE];/*Name of current file */


    for (current = 0; current < num_files; current++)
        full_name(current_name, file_list[current]);
        (void)printf("%s\n", current_name);
}
/************************************************************
 * cmp_files -- check two files for <, > or =              *
 *              (Used by qsort)                             *
 *                                                          *
 * Parameters                                               *
 *      f1, f2 -- two file entries                          *
 ***********************************************************/
#ifdef OLD_STYLE
int cmp_files(struct file_entry **f1, struct file_entry **f2)
#define F1 (f1)
#define F2 (f2)
#else OLD_STYLE
int cmp_files(const void *f1, const void *f2)
#define F1 ((struct file_entry **)(f1))
#define F2 ((struct file_entry **)(f2))
#endif OLD_STYLE
{
    static int progress = 0;
    static char *spin_chars = "|/-\\";
    static int spin_index = 0;


    progress++;
    if ((progress % 256) == 0) {
        (void)putch(spin_chars[spin_index]);
        (void)putch(BACKSPACE);
        spin_index++;
        if (spin_index == (sizeof(spin_chars)-1))
            spin_index = 0;
    }
    return (strcmp((*F1)->name, (*F2)->name));
}
```

continued

Listing 12.1 continued.

```
#define DUP(index) ((strcmp(file_list[(index)]->name, \
                     file_list[(index)+1]->name)) == 0)
/*************************************************************
 * process_dups -- process files looking for duplicates *
 *************************************************************/
static void process_dups(void)
{
    int current;          /* Current file number */
    int last;             /* Last entry in a duplicated series */

    void interactive(int, int); /* Handle interactive mode */
    void print_dups(int, int);  /* Print duplicate files */
    void crc_list(int, int); /* Compute CRC values for a range */

    for (current = 0; current < (num_files-1); current++) {

        if (DUP(current)) {
            for (last = current+1;
                     last < (num_files-1); last++) {
                if (!DUP(last)) {
                    break;
                }
            }
            crc_list(current, last);

            if (print_only)
                print_dups(current, last);
            else
                interactive(current, last);

            current = last;
        }
    }
}
/*************************************************************
 * full_cmp_files -- check two files for <, > or =        *
 *               (Used by qsort for sorting by crc/path)  *
 *                                                         *
 * Parameters                                              *
 *      f1, f2 -- two file entries                         *
 *************************************************************/
#ifdef OLD_STYLE
int full_cmp_files(struct file_entry **f1,
                   struct file_entry **f2)
#define F1 (f1)
```

continued

Listing 12.1 continued.

```
#define F2 (f2)
#else OLD_STYLE
int full_cmp_files(const void *f1, const void *f2)
#define F1 ((struct file_entry **)(f1))
#define F2 ((struct file_entry **)(f2))
#endif OLD_STYLE
{
    /* Two CRC values */
    unsigned short crc1 = (*F1)->crc;
    unsigned short crc2 = (*F2)->crc;
    char full1[NAME_SIZE];      /* First name (with dir parts) */
    char full2[NAME_SIZE];      /* Second name (with dir parts) */

    if (crc1 != crc2) {
        if (crc1 > crc2)
            return (1);
        else
            return (-1);
    }

    full_name(full1, *F1);
    full_name(full2, *F2);
    return (strcmp(full1, full2));
}
/************************************************************
 * crc_list -- compute crc values for all files            *
 *             and sort by crc.                             *
 *                                                          *
 * Parameters                                               *
 *      first, last -- index of first/last duplicate        *
 *                     entry                                *
 ************************************************************/
void crc_list(int first, int last)
{
    int   current; /* Current entry for computing */

    /* Compute the CRC for a single file */
    unsigned short compute_crc(char *);

#ifdef OLD_STYLE
    int   cmp_files(struct file_entry **, struct file_entry **);
#else OLD_STYLE
    int   cmp_files(const void *, const void *);
#endif OLD_STYLE
```

continued

Listing 12.1 continued.

```
        for (current = first; current <= last; current++) {
            char  current_name[NAME_SIZE];

            full_name(current_name, file_list[current]);
            file_list[current]->crc = compute_crc(current_name);

        }
        qsort(&file_list[first], last - first + 1,
            sizeof(struct file_entry *), full_cmp_files);
}


/***********************************************************
 * print_dups -- print list of duplicate files            *
 *                                                         *
 * Parameters                                              *
 *      first, last -- index of first/last duplicate       *
 *                        entry                            *
 ***********************************************************/
void print_dups(int first, int last)
{
    char current_name[NAME_SIZE]; /* Full name of current file */

    (void)printf("%s Duplicated\n", file_list[first]->name);
    for (/*First already set*/; first <= last; first++) {
        full_name(current_name, file_list[first]);
        (void)printf("    %-40s %04X\n",
                    current_name, file_list[first]->crc);
    }
}
/***********************************************************
 * interactive -- handle interactive mode                  *
 *      Display file list and ask user which to            *
 *      get rid of                                         *
 *                                                         *
 * Parameters                                              *
 *      first, last -- index of first/last duplicate       *
 *                        entry                            *
 *                                                         *
 * Warning: Does not handle more than 24 files.            *
 ***********************************************************/
#define MAX_INTERACTIVE 24
void interactive(int first, int last)
{
    char current_name[NAME_SIZE]; /* Full name of current file */
    char deleted[MAX_INTERACTIVE];  /* True if file is deleted */
```

continued

Listing 12.1 continued.

```
/* Number of entries we are handling */
int  num_entries = last - first + 1;
int current;                          /* Current entry */


clrscr();
(void)memset(deleted, '\0', sizeof(deleted));
if (num_entries > MAX_INTERACTIVE)
    num_entries = MAX_INTERACTIVE;


for (current = 0; current < num_entries; current++) {
    full_name(current_name, file_list[first+current]);
    gotoxy(1, current+1);
    (void)cprintf("%c         %-40s %04X", 'A'+current,
        current_name,
        file_list[first+current]->crc);
}
gotoxy(1, 25);
#define CMD_STR \
    "Type letter of file to delete or <space> to continue."
(void)cputs(CMD_STR);
while (1) {
   char ch; /* Character from input */


    for (current = 0; current < num_entries; current++) {
        gotoxy(3, current+1);
        if (deleted[current])
            (void)cputs("Deleted");
        else
            (void)cputs("       ");
    }


    gotoxy(sizeof(CMD_STR), 25);
    ch = getch();
    if (ch == ' ')
        break;


    if (ch == CONTROL_C) {
        clrscr();
        exit (0);
    }


    if (islower(ch))
        ch = toupper(ch);
    ch -= 'A';
```

continued

Listing 12.1 continued.

```
            if (ch < num_entries)
                deleted[ch] = !deleted[ch];
        }
        clrscr();
        for (current = 0; current < num_entries; current++) {
            if (deleted[current]) {
                full_name(current_name, file_list[first+current]);
#ifdef DEBUG
                (void)printf("erase %s\n", current_name);
#else DEBUG
                (void)unlink(current_name);
#endif DEBUG
            }
        }
}


#include "crc-tab.h"
/***********************************************************
 * compute_crc -- compute the CRC for a given file       *
 *                                                       *
 * Parameters                                            *
 *      name -- the name of the file (full path)         *
 *                                                       *
 * Returns                                               *
 *      CRC for the file                                 *
 *      0 -- for errors (msg sent)                       *
 ***********************************************************/
unsigned short compute_crc(char *name)
{
    int in_fd;                  /* File descriptor of the file */
    static char buffer[1024*20];/* Buf for the chars in file */
    int read_size;              /* Size of last read */
    unsigned short crc_code;    /* CRC computed so far */


    /* Compute next section of the CRC */
    void crc_buffer(char *buffer,int count,
                unsigned short *crc_code);


    in_fd = open(name, O_BINARY|O_RDONLY);
    if (in_fd < 0) {
        (void)fprintf(stderr,"Unable to open %s\n", name);
        return (0);
    }
```

continued

Listing 12.1 continued.

```
        crc_code = 0;
        while (1) {
            read_size = read(in_fd, buffer, sizeof(buffer));
            if (read_size <= 0)
                break;

            crc_buffer(buffer, read_size, &crc_code);
        }
        (void)close(in_fd);
        return (crc_code);
}
/************************************************************
 * crc_buffer -- build the CRC for a buffer                 *
 *                                                          *
 * Parameters                                               *
 *      buffer -- buffer containing data                    *
 *      count -- number of bytes in buffer                  *
 *      crc_code -- CRC code so far (updated)               *
 ************************************************************/
void crc_buffer(register char *buffer,int count,
                    unsigned short *crc_code)
{
    register unsigned int local_crc; /* Local, reg ver of CRC */

    local_crc = *crc_code;

    for (/*count already set */; count > 0; count--) {
        /* Compute next byte in CRC */
        local_crc = (local_crc>>8) ^
                    crc_table[(local_crc ^ (*buffer)) & 0x00ff];
        buffer++;
    }

    /* Store result */
    *crc_code = local_crc;
}
/************************************************************
 * usage -- tell the user what to do                        *
 ************************************************************/
static void usage(void)
{
    (void)printf("Usage is:\n");
    (void)printf("dupfile [options] [directory]\n");
    (void)printf(
            "    Directory is the top directory to search\n");
```

continued

Listing 12.1 continued.

```
        (void)printf("        (default = root of current disk)\n");
        (void)printf("Options\n");
        (void)printf(
           "        d -- debug (print information as program works)\n");
        (void)printf(
                  "        r -- print the raw list (before sorting)\n");
        (void)printf("        s -- print the list after sorting\n");
        (void)printf("        p -- print list of duplicates (only)\n");
        exit (1);
}
```

Listing 12-2. "table.c"

```
#include <stdio.h>
#include <stdlib.h>

#define CRC_POLY    0xA001         /* Polynomial for this CRC */


#define u_short unsigned short   /* Shorthand */

/************************************************************
 * crc_entry -- compute an entry into the crc table      *
 *                                                        *
 * Parameters                                             *
 *      element -- element number of this entry           *
 *      genpoly -- polynomial for our funny division      *
 *                                                        *
 * Returns                                                *
 *      value for the table entry                         *
 ************************************************************/
u_short crc_entry(u_short data, u_short genpoly)
{
    static int i;
    u_short accum = 0;


    data <<= 1;
    for (i = 8; i > 0; i--)
    {
        data >>= 1;
        if ((data ^ accum) & 0x0001)
            accum = (accum >> 1) ^ genpoly;
```

continued

Listing 12.2 continued.

```
        else
            accum >>= 1;
    }
    return (accum);
}
main(void)
{
    int i;          /* Element index */

    (void)printf("unsigned short crc_table[256] = {");
    for (i = 0; i < 256; i++ ) {
        if ((i % 8) == 0)
            (void)printf("\n     ");

        (void)printf(" 0x%04X", crc_entry(i, CRC_POLY));
        if (i != 255)
            (void)printf(",");
    }
    (void)printf("\n};\n");

    return (0);
}
```

Listing 12-3. "Makefile"

```
#
# Make the program DUPFILE.
#
# Note: We may need to create a CRC table, in which
# case we generate using the program "table".
#
# Of course, we may have to compile the program first.
#
# All handled automatically by the makefile.
#
all: dupfile.exe

table.exe: table.c
    tcc -wall -mt -etable table.c

crc-tab.h: table.exe
    table.exe >crc-tab.h

dupfile.exe: dupfile.c crc-tab.h
    tcc -N -v -wall -ml -edupfile dupfile.c
```

Recursive Descent Parser

Introduction

Parsing is the process in which text input, such as English, is turned into something the computer can understand. Parsing is used extensively in compilers, but other programs such as spreadsheets and database also use some parsing. In this chapter, we will construct a simple parser that takes equations as input and produces answers for output.

There are many different parsing methods such as LR and LL(1). We will use a method of parsing called *recursive descent*. This method lends itself well to hand coding. Its drawbacks are that it's not very efficient and does not handle errors well.

More advanced parsing methods lend themselves easily to machine generation. Indeed there are many parser generators such as the UNIX yacc command and the Free Software Foundations program "bision." These tools are very useful for large projects.

The Grammar

In this chapter we will handle a small project, a simple calculator. First, we must define our grammar. This defines the language that we are going to use. A generally accepted way of writing grammar is to use BNF format:

expression	:= term + expression
	:= term - expression
	:= term
	:= - expression
term	:= factor * term
	:= factor / term
	:= factor
factor	:= integer
	:= (expression)

For example, the expression "(1 + 2) * 3" would break down as follows:

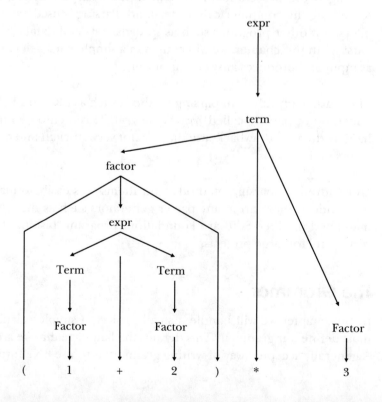

In this grammar the words `expression`, `term` and `factor` are non-terminals. This is because during our parsing, when we encounter a nonterminal we must parse further. The operators, "+", "-", "*", "/", and "()", as well as the integers, are terminals. When we encounter them, we're done; they cannot be broken down further.

We must be careful when constructing our grammar. The same nonterminal cannot be on the left side of the equation and the first item on the right side. For example, the following would cause an infinite recursion:

expression :== expression + term

Our grammar is made so that the operators "*" and "/" are part of the factor while "+" and "-" are part of the expression. This means that "*" and "/" will be processed before "+" and "-" and have precedence over them.

Error Handling

When an error is encountered in a recursive descent parser, it's difficult to recover. In our calculator we take the easy way out: we abort the entire parser and print an error message. No attempt is made to figure out what went wrong and continue parsing.

Tokenizing

Our equation starts out as a series of characters. The tokenizer converts these into a series of words. If we put the string "(1 + 2) * 3" in we would get `T_L_PAREN`, `T_INT(1)`, `T_PLUS`, `T_INT(2)`, `T_R_PAREN`, `T_TIMES`, `T_INT(3)`, `T_EOF` out. Fortunately for us, there are only eight words (terminals) in the entire grammar. Data definitions for tokens are:

```
enum token_type {
    T_L_PAREN,      /* ( character */
    T_R_PAREN,      /* ) character */
    T_PLUS,         /* + operator */
    T_MINUS,        /* - operator (unary or binary) */
    T_TIMES,        /* * operator */
    T_DIV,          /* / operator */
    T_INT,          /* Integer number */
    T_EOF,          /* End of file */
    };
```

```
struct token {
    enum token_type token_type;   /* Type of token */
    int   position;   /* Position within the line */
    int value;        /* Value of number if type is T_INT */
};
```

Note the `position` field is used for printing the error message.

Constructing the Parser

Our parser will be built from the grammar. Each nonterminal in the language has its own routine. These will be constructed from the grammar itself.

Parsing the Factor

The factor is the lowest level of our grammar. It is defined as:

factor :== integer

     :== (expression)

We need to define a function that parses this element in our grammar. When we enter this function the variable `cur_token` has been set to the first token of our factor. Looking at our grammar we see that a factor can begin with an integer or a left parenthesis. So we construct a simple switch to handle each case. There is one more case we want take care of. If something other than an integer or parenthesis shows up, we bail out. So far the function looks like:

```
switch (cur_token.token_type) {
    case T_INT:
        /* handle integer */
    case T_L_PAREN:
        /* handle ( */
    default:
        /* bail out */
}
```

The integer case is easy. We save the value, call `next_token` to move past the integer and return.

If we see a parenthesis, we move past it and call `expr` to process the expression. At the end of the expression we expect to see a closing parenthesis. If we don't get one, we report an error. The full code for our `factor` routine is:

```
int factor(void)
{
    int value;              /* Value to be returned */

    switch (cur_token.token_type) {
        case T_INT:
            value = cur_token.value;
            next_token();
            return (value);
        case T_L_PAREN:
            next_token();                   /* Move past L paren */

             value = expr();

            if (cur_token.token_type == T_R_PAREN) {
                next_token();
                return (value);
            } else {
                error("Expected Closing paren");
            }
            break;
        default:
            error("Syntax error:Expect integer or open paren");
            /*NOTREACHED*/
    }
    return (0);     /* Make Turbo C happy */
}
```

Term

To code term, we start with the grammar:

term   :== factor * term

                    :== factor / term

                    :== factor

From this, we see that every term starts with a factor, so we call `factor`. Next we can get a "*", "/" or something else. Again, a switch statement is called for to handle each of these cases. As you can see, our implementation of term just follows the grammar.

```
int term(void)
{
    int factor_value;        /* Value of the first factor */
    int term_value;          /* Value of term on right side */

    factor_value = factor();

    switch (cur_token.token_type) {
        case T_EOF:
            return (factor_value);
        case T_TIMES:
            next_token();
            term_value = term();
            return (factor_value * term_value);
        case T_DIV:
            next_token();
            term_value = term();
            if (term_value == 0)
                error("Divide by zero");
            return (factor_value / term_value);
        default:
            return (factor_value);
    }
}
```

Expression

The implementation of expression is similar to term, except for one joker — the unary minus. Our grammar for expression is:

expression   :== term + expression

                   :== term - expression

                   :== term

                   :== - expression

In our implementation we first check for a minus and handle it. The rest of the function follows the same rules we used to create term. A full implementation of our parser is presented at the end of this chapter.

Handling User Input

This program works in two modes. The user can type an expression on the command line or if the program is run without arguments, the program will enter interactive mode. In interactive mode, it repeatedly asks the user for an expression and computes the result.

If there are command line arguments, the program puts them together in a single line, then calls the line at time parser.

Errors

Errors are handled by aborting and printing a message. One of the problems with recursive descent parsers is that it is difficult to unwind the parser when an error occurs. Rather than set an error flag and pass it up through each function level, we decided to use the C routine `longjmp` to short circuit the whole process.

The standard function `setjmp` can be used to mark a place for the code to return to, `from` any level. The function normally returns a 0. Our error function uses the companion function `longjmp` to return to `setjmp` point. When we execute the function `longjmp(error_jump, 1)`, we return to the `setjmp` call in the function `do_line`, discarding the call stack produced after the initial `setjmp`.

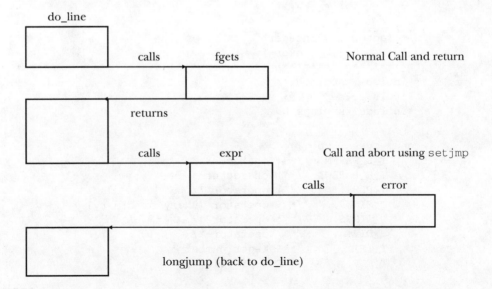

It is not considered good form to make extensive use of set jmp since it confuses the C calling structure; however, this routine does provide the programmer with a mechanism for handling exception conditions like error aborts.

Listing 13-1. "calc.c"

```
/**********************************************************
 * calc -- a calculator program                          *
 *                                                        *
 * Usage:                                                 *
 *       calc <expression>                                *
 * or                                                     *
 *       calc                                             *
 *       Expr? <expression>          (interactive mode)   *
 *                                                        *
 * Legal operators                                        *
 *       * / + - ()                                       *
 *                                                        *
 * Language Definition                                    *
 *                                                        *
 * expr :== term + expr                                   *
 *      :== term - expr                                   *
 *      :== - expr                                        *
 *      :== term                                          *
 *                                                        *
 * term :== factor * term                                 *
 *      :== factor / term                                 *
 *      :== factor                                        *
 *                                                        *
 * factor :== integer                                     *
 *        :== ( expr )                                    *
 **********************************************************/
#include <stdio.h>
#include <setjmp.h>
#include <strings.h>

enum token_type {
    T_L_PAREN,   /* ( character */
    T_R_PAREN,   /* ) character */
    T_PLUS,      /* + operator */
    T_MINUS,     /* - operator (unary or binary) */
    T_TIMES,     /* * operator */
    T_DIV,       /* / operator */
    T_INT,       /* Integer number */
    T_EOF,       /* End of file */
};
```

continued

Listing 13-1 continued

```c
struct token {
    enum token_type token_type; /* Type of token */
    int position;         /* Position within the line */
    int value;            /* Value of number if type is T_INT */
};


char line[250]; /* Input line */
int cur_char;   /* Index of current character within the line
*/


struct token cur_token; /* Token parsed from the line */


jmp_buf error_jump; /* Holds information to get out of trouble
*/


void error(char *message);
int expr(void);
/*********************************************************
 * next_token -- advance to the next token and          *
 *               set cur_token to it's value            *
 *********************************************************/
void next_token(void)
{
    /* Move past whitespace */

    while (isspace(line[cur_char]))
        cur_char++;

    cur_token.position = cur_char;
    switch (line[cur_char]) {
        case '(':
            cur_token.token_type = T_L_PAREN;
            break;
        case ')':
            cur_token.token_type = T_R_PAREN;
            break;
        case '*':
            cur_token.token_type = T_TIMES;
            break;
        case '/':
            cur_token.token_type = T_DIV;
            break;
        case '+':
            cur_token.token_type = T_PLUS;
            break;
```

continued

Listing 13-1 continued

```
            case '-':
                cur_token.token_type = T_MINUS;
                break;
            case '\0':
                cur_token.token_type = T_EOF;
                break;
            case '0':
            case '1':
            case '2':
            case '3':
            case '4':
            case '5':
            case '6':
            case '7':
            case '8':
            case '9':
                cur_token.token_type = T_INT;
                cur_token.value = 0;
                while (isdigit(line[cur_char])) {
                    cur_token.value = cur_token.value * 10 +
                            line[cur_char] - '0';
                    cur_char++;
                }
                cur_char--; /* Move to last char in number */
                break;
            default:
                error("Can't understand token");
                /*NOTREACHED*/
        }
    cur_char++; /* Move to character after token */
}
/************************************************************
 * factor -- parse a factor                                 *
 *                                                          *
 * Definition                                               *
 *                                                          *
 * factor :== integer                                       *
 *        :== ( expr )                                      *
 *                                                          *
 * Returns                                                  *
 *      value of the factor                                 *
 ************************************************************/
int factor(void)
{
    int value;  /* Value to be returned */
```

continued

Listing 13-1 continued

```
    switch (cur_token.token_type) {
        case T_INT:
            value = cur_token.value;
            next_token();
            return (value);
        case T_L_PAREN:
            next_token();         /* Move past L paren */

            value = expr();

            if (cur_token.token_type == T_R_PAREN) {
                next_token();
                return (value);
            } else {
                error("Expected Closing paren");
            }
            break;
        default:
            error("Syntax error:Expect integer or open paren");
            /*NOTREACHED*/
    }
    return (0); /* Make Turbo C happy */
}

/***********************************************************
 * term -- parse a term                                    *
 *                                                         *
 * Definition                                              *
 *                                                         *
 * term :== factor * term                                  *
 *      :== factor / term                                  *
 *      :== factor                                         *
 *                                                         *
 * Returns                                                 *
 *      value of the term                                  *
 ***********************************************************/
int term(void)
{
    int factor_value;   /* Value of the first factor */
    int term_value;     /* Value of term on right side */

    factor_value = factor();

    switch (cur_token.token_type) {
        case T_EOF:
```

continued

Listing 13-1 continued

```
              return (factor_value);
          case T_TIMES:
              next_token();
              term_value = term();
              return (factor_value * term_value);
          case T_DIV:
              next_token();
              term_value = term();
              if (term_value == 0)
                  error("Divide by zero");
              return (factor_value / term_value);
          default:
              return (factor_value);
      }
}
/************************************************************
 * Expr -- return the value of an expression               *
 *                                                          *
 * Definition                                               *
 *                                                          *
 * expr :== term + expr                                     *
 *      :== term - expr                                     *
 *      :== - expr                                          *
 *      :== term                                            *
 *                                                          *
 * Returns                                                  *
 *      value of the expression                             *
 ************************************************************/
int expr(void)
{
    int term_value;    /* Value of term part */
    int expr_value;    /* Value of expression part */

    if (cur_token.token_type == T_MINUS) {
        next_token();
        return (- expr());
    }

    term_value = term();

    switch (cur_token.token_type) {
        case T_EOF:
            return (term_value);
        case T_PLUS:
            next_token();
```

continued

Listing 13-1 continued

```
                    expr_value = expr();
                    return (term_value + expr_value);
              case T_MINUS:
                    next_token();
                    expr_value = expr();
                    return (term_value - expr_value);
              default:
                    return (term_value);
        }
}
/***********************************************************
 * do_line -- compute value of single line expression    *
 ***********************************************************/
void do_line(void)
{
     int value;  /* Value of the expression */


     /*
      * Set jump buffer in case of error
      */
     if (setjmp(error_jump) == 0) {
         /*
          * Start tokenizer
          */
         cur_char = 0;
         next_token();

         value = expr();
         if (cur_token.token_type != T_EOF)
             error("Extra data on line");

         (void)printf("Result:%d\n", value);
     }
}
/***********************************************************
 * error -- print an error message and bail out          *
 *                                                        *
 * Parameters                                             *
 *      message -- message to print                       *
 *                                                        *
 * Note: This function returns to do_line through the     *
 *      use of longjmp                                    *
 ***********************************************************/
void error(message)
char *message;
```

continued

Listing 13-1 continued

```
{
    (void)fprintf(stderr,"Error:%s\n", message);
    (void)fprintf(stderr,"%s\n", line);
    (void)fprintf(stderr,"%*s\n", cur_token.position+1, "^");
    longjmp(error_jump, 1);
    /*NOTREACHED*/
}
/**********************************************************
 * Interactive -- handle interactive mode                 *
 **********************************************************/
void interactive(void)
{
    while (1) {
        (void)printf("Expr? ");
        if (fgets(line, sizeof(line), stdin) == NULL) {
            break;        /* EOF Seen -- user type ^D */
        }

        /* Remove extra newline */
        line[strlen(line)-1] = '\0';


        /*
         * Check for blank line
         */
        if (strlen(line) == 0)
            break;


        do_line();
    }
}
/**********************************************************
 * main --  main program                                  *
 **********************************************************/
main(argc, argv)
int argc;
char *argv[];
{
    if (argc == 1) {
        interactive();
    } else {
        line[0] = '\0';
        while (argc > 1) {
            (void)strcat(line, argv[1]);
            (void)strcat(line," ");
```

continued

Listing 13-1 continued

```
            argc--;
            argv++;
        }
        do_line();
    }
    return (0);
}
```

Chapter 14

Screen Mimic Program

Introduction

Steve is the Director of Management Information Services at the San Diego Railway Museum. That's a fancy title meaning that he comes down and repairs their computers when they're having trouble. Although these people know all about trains, they don't know about computers. When they have a problem with a program, the conversation goes something like this:

SDRM: I've got a problem with the computer. The address labels don't print right.

Steve: Where are you?

SDRM: I'm in the San Diego office.

Steve: What part of the program are you in?

SDRM: The part that prints the address labels.

Steve: Are you in the "Print" or "Report" menu?

343

SDRM: I don't know. What's the difference? The menu I've got has a box around it, if that helps.

Steve: Not really, almost all the mailing list menus have boxes around them.

The result is that Steve has to make a trip to the office to see what their screen looks like. This scenario is an example of a problem that plagues the computer literate. The person on the other end of the phone doesn't know how to describe what is going on with his computer.

What we need is a way of looking at his screen without having to go to a remote site. We can do this by having our client connect his computer to a modem and running a mimic program to send the contents of the screen to our machine.

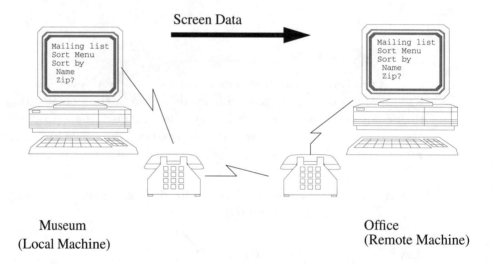

Museum
(Local Machine)

Office
(Remote Machine)

Our mimic program must be a TSR since it is unreasonable to ask the user to exit his application in order to run Mimic. Also exiting the program changes the screen.

Serial Protocols

We need to design a protocol for the data going between our two machines. Any serial protocol must be designed with the following factors in mind:

Simplicity   The protocol should be as simple as possible to minimize programming, errors, and transmission time.

Compactness   The protocol should transmit the maximum amount of data with the minimum amount of overhead.

Reliability   Serial lines are not 100% reliable. Sometimes the data get garbled (especially if you have call waiting on your phone line). The protocol should have some mechanism to make sure that the data arrived correctly.

Speed   The protocol should facilitate the fast transmission of the data.

It is impossible to design a protocol that maximizes all the criteria. There will always be trade-offs. For example, compactness can be gained by using compressions, but that makes the protocol more complex.

XMODEM Protocol

One of the most popular protocols is the XMODEM or MODEM7 protocol designed by Ward Christiansen. A typical packet looks like:

Start Frame	Frame Numb.	Inv. Frame#	Data (128)	Checksum (1 Byte)

Start Frame is the start packet character (Control-A or SOH).

Frame Number is the packet number (0-255).

Inverse Frame Number is the complement of the packet number.

Data is 128 bytes of data.

Checksum is an 8-bit checksum of the data.

In a typical XMODEM transfer, the sender transmits a packet and then waits for a response from the receiver who sends an ACK character if the packet was good (checksum correct) or a NAK if there was a problem.

This protocol is very simple. That's one of the reasons it is so popular. It is somewhat compact, since the overhead consists of only four protocol bytes per 128 data bytes. There is no data compression however.

Reliability is barely adequate. Checksums are not very good at catching multi-bit errors. Studies have shown that transmission noise comes in bursts, which can easily be missed by checksums.

Speed is also only adequate. Although we have a two-way connection between the sender and the receiver, we only use one side at a time. The sender sends a packet, then waits for the receiver to respond. The receiver waits for a packet before responding. That's a lot of waiting.

XMODEM CRC

XMODEM has been enhanced to make it more reliable by changing the checksum into a CRC.:

Start Frame	Frame Numb.	Inv. Frame#	Data (128)	CRC (2 Bytes)

CRC stands for Cycle Redundancy Check and is a complex polynomial computed from the data portion of the packet. It is designed so that it can catch all errors up to 16 bits in length and almost all 17-bit errors.

The XMODEM/CRC protocol is a good example of how a protocol can evolve. The designers of this protocol wanted to keep almost all of the old XMODEM features, but improve the reliability.

An additional feature of almost all programs that use XMODEM/CRC is that they are compatible with the old XMODEM protocol. During the initialization process, the programs check to see if XMODEM/Checksum or XMODEM/CRC is being used and configure themselves accordingly.

Sliding Windows

One of the problems with the various flavors of XMODEM protocols is that they are slow. After transmitting a packet, the sender must wait until the receiver acknowledges the packet before proceeding. Why waste that time? Why not just keep sending?

That's the idea behind sliding windows. With a window size of five, the sender can transmit up to five packet without getting an acknowledgment from the receiver. This makes full use of a two way transmission line since the receiver can acknowledge a packet while data are being sent.

For example:

Sender sends Packet 1

Sender can now send up to packet 5

Sender sends Packet 2

Sender sends Packet 3   Receiver acknowledges packet 1

                          Sender can now send up to packet 6

Sender sends Packet 4   Receiver acknowledges packet 3

                          Sender can now send up to packet 7

This method is much faster, but also is more complex. Both sender and receiver have to be able to handle two tasks at the same time. This is extremely tricky on a single task machine like a PC.

Various tricks can be played using this type of protocol. Acknowledge packets can be skipped, their presence can be implied. For example, if the receiver has gotten packets 1, 2, and 3, he can acknowledge just 3. The transmitter figures that if he got 3 okay, that 1 and 2 must have arrived safely.

Screen Transmission Protocol

We need a protocol for transmitting a screen image from one computer to another. First let's decide what we are transmitting:

Characters (8-bit data)
Attributes (Color, Reverse, Blink, etc.)
Cursor Position

Now lets take a look at our four protocol criteria and see which ones are most valuable to us:

Simplicity

Very valuable. We've got to write both sides of this program (the transmitter and the receiver) and we want to do as little work as possible.

Compactness

Not very valuable. A screen contains 25 * 80 or 4000 characters. That's not very much data, so compressing it will not cause a tremendous decrease in transmission time.

Reliability

We'd like the program to work, but we're not worried about transmission errors. An error will merely result in something strange showing up on our screen. The bad data can easily be ignored or we can ask the user to retransmit the screen.

Speed

At 2400 baud (common modem speed), it takes about 20 seconds to transmit a full screen of data. Even if the attribute of every character is different, that's only 40 seconds worth of data. In most cases, there are far less changes on screen, so the transmission time will be shorter. We can live with that. If we can't we can always improve our program.

Since we don't care about reliability and care greatly about simplicity, our protocol is a one-way transmission. Actually, there is an acknowledgment mechanism; if we don't get the data, we yell at the user.

To keep things simple we decided to use single characters to signal special operations. These characters were chosen because they are at the high end of the character set and not frequently used. They are:

0x80<x>   Position cursor to X location

0x81<y>   Position cursor to Y location

0x82<att>   Set attribute to <att>

0x83<code>   Display code on screen (used to display codes 0x80-0x84)

0x84   Clear screen

We chose single character codes because they are both compact and simple.

After defining this protocol we showed it to a friend and after explaining it to him for some time, he remarked, "Oh, I see. It's something like the ESC codes in ANSI.SYS."

Suddenly, we realized that we didn't have to write another protocol. We could take advantage of the one already available in DOS. Since no special receiving program is needed, we can use a simple terminal program, like the one we wrote for Chapter 7. Thus, we have defined one-half of our programming task out of existence.

Send Screen Program

Our mimic program is designed as a TSR that uses interrupt level programming to send data out the serial port. Thus we're combining two of the hardest types of programs: TSRs and interrupt level programs into one package. That's too much to debug at one batch, so we've decided to break it up into two stages.

The first step will be to write a program that sends the contents of the screen to a remote computer. After we get this debugged we can go on to combine it with our TSR code (see Chapter 6).

The program "sendscr" is designed to transmit the contents of the screen to a remote computer. It consists of three major sections: `make_line`, `start_trans`, and a serial interrupt handler.

The function `make_line` compares a single line of data from a copy of what's on the remote machine against what's on the local screen, It then produces a string to be sent to the remote machine. This involves using escape sequences to position the cursor to the proper spot, setting attributes and sending new characters from the local screen.

`make_line` does not actually send the data, it merely readies it. When we have finished scanning a line, we call `start_trans` to start sending. This turns on the serial port interrupts and sends the first character. When the character has been sent, the serial chip will interrupt, throwing us into the `serial_interrupt` routine. This function grabs the next character from the output string and gives it to the serial chip.

The variable `sending` is set while transmission is occurring. When the last character is sent, the variable is set to 0. After the transmission is started, we must wait until this variable is cleared before starting the next line.

Our code was designed for line-by-line transmissions, so we could minimize the impact that "mimic" would have on the performance of the local system. We have to share the CPU with the current application. If we did 25 lines at once, we might lock up the system for some time and annoy the user. By doing it in 25 small chucks, we minimize our impact.

The Mimic Program

The "mimic" program itself was produced by combining the "tsr hello" program from Chapter 6 with the "sendscr" program. Since this program runs continuously, there is no hot key to invoke it so all the hot key related functions have been **#ifdef**ed out.

Another change we made was to add a pacing variable. We don't want to compare screens every clock tick. That would eat up too much CPU time. Instead we pace ourselves. Every time we do some work, the variable `count-down` is set to `PACE_VALUE`. Each clock tick the counter is decremented by one. When it reaches zero, we start work.

Summary

The "mimic" program combines two of the most difficult types of programs: interrupt programs and TSR programs into one. We used a debug program "sendscr" to debug the interrupt part and a debug TSR program "hello world" to handle the TSR part. Understanding both these programs separately allowed us to combine them with a minimum of trouble.

Our "mimic" program performs the main job well, but it could use some bells and whistles. For example, a modem handler, so that we could dial the remote system, would be nice. Also we could use a "chat" mode. But you've been given the source and you've got the tools to make these changes and customize it.

The techniques presented here should allow you to create, debug, and maintain a set of useful and user friendly programs.

Listing 14-1. "sendscr.c"

```c
#define LOG_FILE
#define DISPLAY
#define REAL_SEND
/***********************************************************
 * sendscr -- send a copy of the screen out through        *
 *            the serial port                              *
 *                                                         *
 * Usage:                                                  *
 *      sendscr                                            *
 *                                                         *
 * Note: Some of the code may look a little strange.       *
 * We are designing this for use with the TSR program      *
 * mimic.                                                  *
 ***********************************************************/

#include <dos.h>
#include <stdlib.h>
#include <conio.h>
#include <stdio.h>
#include <mem.h>
#include "serial.h"
#ifndef TRUE
#define TRUE 1
#define FALSE 0
#endif TRUE
#ifdef LOG_FILE
FILE *log_file;
#endif LOG_FILE


#define ESC '\033'


#define MAX_X 80        /* Size of screen in X */
#define MAX_Y 25        /* Size of screen in Y */
/*
 * Worst case
 *      Cursor movement                       <ESC>[xx;xxH (8 Chars)
 *      Each char has foreground  color change <ESC>[xxm (5 C)
 *      Each char has background color change <ESC>[xxm (5 chars)
 *      Each char has blink       change <ESC>[xxm (5 chars)
 *      The character                                1
 *      Fudge                                        1
 *                                           _____
 *                                           Total      25
 *
 * Add in 30 for a fudge and positioning.
```

continued

Listing 14-1 continued

```
 */
#define OUT_BUF_SIZE (MAX_X*25 + 30)
static char out_buf[OUT_BUF_SIZE];
static char *out_ptr;              /* Pointer to next char out */
static char *last_ptr;   /* Pointer to last character in buffer */
static int sending = 0;            /* We're sending now */

/* Screen we've got now */
static char local_screen[MAX_Y*MAX_X*2];
static char *local_ptr;            /* Local version of the screen */

static char remote_screen[MAX_Y*MAX_X*2];
static char *remote_ptr;          /* Remove version of the screen */

int remote_x, remote_y;           /* Where we are remotely */
unsigned int out_att;             /* Current output attributes */
void interrupt (*old_vect_C)(void);

main()
{
    /* input character handler */
    void    interrupt serial_interrupt();
    void init(void);

    /* routine to send the data */
    void    send_it(void);

    /* set up the input buffer */
    void    init_buf(void);

#ifdef DISPLAY
#define EVEN(i) (((i) & 1) == 0)
    clrscr();
    {
        int i,j;

        for (i = 0; i < 24; i++) {
            (void)printf("%2d ", i);
            if (EVEN(i))
                (void)printf("\033[7m");   /* Reverse */

            if (i == 5)
                (void)printf("\033[5m");   /* Blink */
```

continued

Listing 14-1 continued

```
            for (j = 4; j <= 80; j++)
                (void)printf("%d", j % 10);

            if (EVEN(i))
                (void)printf("\033[0m");   /* Reverse */
        }
        (void)printf("Last line");(void)fflush(stdout);
    }
#endif DISPLAY
#ifdef LOG_FILE
    log_file = fopen("send.log", "w");
    if (log_file == NULL) {
        (void)fprintf(stderr,"Unable to open log file\n");
        exit (1);
    }
#endif LOG_FILE

    disable();
    old_vect_C = getvect(0xC);
    setvect(0xC, serial_interrupt);
    enable();

    init();

#ifdef REAL_SEND
    /* enable interrupts */
    outportb(0x21, inportb(0x21) & 0xE7);
    outportb(0x20, 0x20);
#endif REAL_SEND

    /* Clear the remote screen */
    (void)memset(remote_screen, '\0', sizeof(remote_screen));

    send_it();
    disable();
    setvect(0xC, old_vect_C);
    enable();
#ifdef LOG_FILE
    (void)fclose(log_file);
#endif LOG_FILE
#ifdef DISPLAY
    getch();
#endif DISPLAY
    return (0);
}
```

continued

Listing 14-1 continued

```
/************************************************************
 * init -- initialize the port                             *
 ************************************************************/
void init(void)
{
#ifdef REAL_SEND
        _AH = 0;
        _AL = 0xE3;        /* 9600 baud/no parity/one stop/8 data */
        _DX = 0;
        geninterrupt(0x14);

        /* don't allow interrupts while we do this */
        disable();
        /* disable all interrupt interrupts */
        outportb((int)&COM->interrupt_enable,   0);

        outportb((int)&COM->format,
          F_BAUD_LATCH|F_NO_BREAK|F_PARITY_NONE|F_STOP1|F_DATA8);

        outportb((int)&COM->format,
              F_NORMAL|F_NO_BREAK|F_PARITY_NONE|F_STOP1|F_DATA8);

        outportb((int)&COM->out_control,
               O_OUT1|O_OUT2|O_RTS|O_DTR);

        /* read the input registers to
         * clear their i-have-data flags */
        (void)inportb((int)&COM->data);
        (void)inportb((int)&COM->interrupt_enable);
        (void)inportb((int)&COM->interrupt_id);
        (void)inportb((int)&COM->status);

        outportb(0x20, 0x20);                    /* clear interrupts */
        enable();
    #endif REAL_SEND
}


/************************************************************
 * trans_1 -- transmit a single character to the output *
 *            Turn off interrupts if done               *
 ************************************************************/
void trans_1(void)
{
```

continued

Listing 14-1 continued

```
        outportb((int)&COM->data, *out_ptr);
        out_ptr++;

        if (out_ptr >= last_ptr) {
            /* Turn off interrupts */
            outportb((int)&COM->interrupt_enable,   0);
            sending = 0;
        }
}
/***********************************************************
 * serial_interrupt -- interrupt handler for serial     *
 *      input                                            *
 *                                                       *
 * Called in interrupt mode by the hardware when         *
 * a character is received on the serial input           *
 ***********************************************************/
void interrupt serial_interrupt()
{
    disable();

    (void)inportb((int)&COM->status);

    /* tell device we have read interrupt */
    (void)inportb((int)&COM->interrupt_enable);
    (void)inportb((int)&COM->interrupt_id);

    trans_1();
    outportb(0x20, 0x20);
    enable();
}
/***********************************************************
 * start_trans -- start transmission                    *
 ***********************************************************/
static void start_trans(void)
{
#ifdef REAL_SEND
    disable();
    out_ptr = out_buf;
    sending = 1;
    outportb((int)&COM->interrupt_enable,   I_TRANS_EMPTY);
    trans_1();
    enable();
#endif REAL_SEND
}
```

continued

Listing 14-1 continued

```
/************************************************************
 * send_ch -- put a character in the buffer                 *
 *                                                          *
 * Parameters                                               *
 *      ch -- character to send                             *
 ************************************************************/
#ifdef LOG_FILE
void send_ch(char ch) {
    (*last_ptr) = (ch);
    last_ptr++;
    (void)fputc(ch, log_file);
    (void)fflush(log_file);
}
#else LOG_FILE
#define send_ch(ch) {(*last_ptr) = (ch); last_ptr++;}
#endif LOG_FILE
/************************************************************
 * send_esc -- send an escape code of the form             *
 *             ESC [ <str> m                                *
 *                                                          *
 * Parameters                                               *
 *      str -- string to send                               *
 ************************************************************/
void send_esc(char *str)
{
    send_ch(ESC);
    send_ch('[');
    while (*str) {
        send_ch(*str);
        str++;
    }
    send_ch('m');
}
#define BLINKING(attr)   ((attr) & 0x80)
#define FOREGROUND(attr) ((attr) & 0xF)
#define BACKGROUND(attr) ((attr) & 0x70)
/************************************************************
 * make_line -- take a line from the screen and            *
 *              dump it into the output buffer             *
 ************************************************************/
static void make_line(int line)
{
    int x;        /* General purpose index */
    /* We do not output the last character of the last line
     * as this would cause a scroll
```

continued

Listing 14-1 continued

```
     */
    int x_limit = (line == (MAX_Y)) ? MAX_X-1 : MAX_X;
    char local_ch, remote_ch;    /* Local and remote characters */
    /* Local and remote attributes */
    unsigned char local_att, remote_att;


    /*
     * Loop for each attribute on the screen
     */
    for (x = 1; x <= x_limit; x++) {
        local_ch = *local_ptr;
        remote_ch = *remote_ptr;
        local_att = (unsigned char) *(local_ptr+1);
        remote_att = (unsigned char) *(remote_ptr+1);


        if ((local_ch != remote_ch) ||
            (remote_att != local_att)) {
            if ((remote_x != x) || (remote_y != line)) {
                static char goto_str[10] = {
                /* 0    1    2    3    4    5    6    7     */
                   ESC, '[', 'y', 'y', ';', 'x', 'x', 'H', '\0'
                };
                char *goto_ptr = goto_str;

#ifdef LOG_FILE
                (void)fprintf(log_file,"\ngoto(%d,%d)\n",
                                    x, line);
#endif LOG_FILE
                goto_str[2] = (line/10) + '0';
                goto_str[3] = (line%10) + '0';


                goto_str[5] = (x/10) + '0';
                goto_str[6] = (x%10) + '0';


                for (goto_ptr = goto_str; *goto_ptr != '\0';
                     goto_ptr++) {
                    send_ch(*goto_ptr);
                }
                remote_x = x;
                remote_y = line;
            }
```

continued

Listing 14-1 continued

```
                if (local_att != out_att) {
#ifdef LOG_FILE
                    (void)fprintf(log_file,"\nAttributes %x->%x\n",
                                    out_att, local_att);
#endif LOG_FILE
                    if (BLINKING(local_att) != BLINKING(out_att)) {
                        if (BLINKING(local_att))
                            send_esc("5");
                        else {
                            send_esc("0");
                            local_att = 0x07;        /* Normal color */
                        }
                    }
                    if (FOREGROUND(local_att) !=
                        FOREGROUND(out_att)) {
                        static char for_esc[3] = "3?";

                        for_esc[1] = FOREGROUND(local_att) +'0';
                        send_esc(for_esc);
                    }
                    if (BACKGROUND(local_att) !=
                        BACKGROUND(out_att)) {
                        static char back_esc[3] = "4?";

                        back_esc[1] =
                                    (BACKGROUND(local_att) >> 4) +'0';
                        send_esc(back_esc);
                    }
                    out_att = local_att;
                }
                send_ch(local_ch);
                remote_x++;
            }

        *remote_ptr = local_ch;
        *(remote_ptr+1) = local_att;
        remote_ptr += 2;
        local_ptr += 2;
    }
}


/**********************************************************
 * send_it -- send the screen to the remote              *
 **********************************************************/
static void send_it(void)
```

continued

Listing 14-1 continued

```
{
    int line;
    int i;

    remote_ptr = remote_screen;
    local_ptr = local_screen;
    gettext(1, 1, MAX_X, MAX_Y, local_screen);

    last_ptr = out_buf;

    send_ch(ESC);          /* Erase the screen */
    send_ch('[');
    send_ch('2');
    send_ch('J');
    remote_x = 1;
    remote_y = 1;

    remote_ptr = remote_screen;
    for (i = 0; i < (MAX_X * MAX_Y); i++) {
        *remote_ptr = ' ';
        remote_ptr++;
        *remote_ptr = 0x07;      /* White on black */
        remote_ptr++;
    }
    out_att = 0x07;                  /* White on black */

    start_trans();
    while (sending) {
        /* Wait till not sending */;
    }

    local_ptr = local_screen;
    remote_ptr = remote_screen;

    for (line = 1; line <= MAX_Y; line++) {
        last_ptr = out_buf;

        make_line(line);

        start_trans();
        while (sending)
            /* Wait till not sending */;
    }
}
```

Listing 14-2. "serial.h"

```
/**********************************************************
 * serial.h -- define the structures and bits for the    *
 *       serial i/o hardware                              *
 **********************************************************/
/*
 * define the register structure for the serial i/o
 */
struct sio {
    char    data;             /* data register */
    char    interrupt_enable;/* interrupt enable register */
    char    interrupt_id;/* what kind of interrupt is going on */
    char    format;           /* communications format */
    char    out_control;     /* modem control lines */
    char    status;           /* status byte */
    char    i_status;         /* input status */
    char    scratch;          /* extra pad */
};
#define baud_l data               /* alias for sending baud rate */
#define baud_h interrupt_enable /* alias part 2 */


/*
 * Defines for Interrupt Enable Register (interrupt_enable)
 */
#define I_STATUS (1 << 3) /* interrupt on modem status changed */
/* interrupt on rec. status changed */
#define I_REC_STATUS (1 << 2)
#define I_TRANS_EMPTY (1 << 1)    /* interrupt on trans. empty */
#define I_CHAR_IN (1 << 0)      /* interrupt on character input */


/*
 * Defines for Line control register  (format)
 */
#define F_BAUD_LATCH     (1 << 7) /* enable baud rate registers */
#define F_NORMAL         (0 << 7) /* normal registers enabled */


#define F_BREAK          (1 << 6) /* set a break condition */
#define F_NO_BREAK       (0 << 6) /* no break condition */


#define F_PARITY_NONE    (0 << 3) /* no parity on output */
#define F_PARITY_ODD     (1 << 3) /* odd parity on output */
#define F_PARITY_EVEN    (3 << 3) /* even parity on output*/
#define F_PARITY_MARK    (5 << 3) /* parity bit is always 1 */
#define F_PARITY_SPACE   (7 << 3) /* parity bit is always 0 */
```

continued

Listing 14-2 continued

```
#define F_STOP1          (0 << 2)          /* Use one stop bit */
#define F_STOP2          (1 << 2)          /* Use two stop bits */


#define F_DATA5          (0)     /* 5 data bits on output */
#define F_DATA6          (1)     /* 6 data bits on output */
#define F_DATA7          (2)     /* 7 data bits on output */
#define F_DATA8          (3)     /* 8 data bits on output */


/*
 * Defines for the MODEM control register (out_control)
 */
#define O_LOOP           (1<<4)            /* loopback test */
#define O_OUT1           (1<<3)            /* Extra signal #1 */
#define O_OUT2           (1<<2)            /* Extra signal #2 */
#define O_RTS            (1<<1)            /* Request to send */
#define O_DTR            (1<<0)            /* Data terminal ready */


/*
 * Line Status register (Status)
 */
#define S_TXE            (1 << 6)
#define S_TBE            (1 << 5) /* Transmitter buffer empty */
#define S_BREAK          (1 << 4) /* Break detected on input */
#define S_FR_ERROR       (1 << 3) /* Framing error on input */
#define S_PARITY_ERROR   (1 << 2) /* Input parity error */
#define S_OVERRUN        (1 << 1) /* Input overrun */
#define S_RxRDY          (1 << 0) /* Receiver has character ready */
/*
 * Modem Status Register (i_status)
 */
#define I_DCD            (1 << 7) /* DCD control line is on */
#define I_RI             (1 << 6) /* RI control line is on */
#define I_DSR            (1 << 5) /* DSR control line is on */
#define I_CTS            (1 << 4) /* CTS control line is on */
#define I_DEL_DCD        (1 << 3) /* DCD line changed */
#define I_DEL_RI         (1 << 2) /* RI line changed */
#define I_DEL_DSR        (1 << 1) /* DSR line changed */
#define I_DEL_CTS        (1 << 0) /* CTS line changed */


/*
 * constants are used to define the
 * baud rate for the serial i/o chip
 * (Selected entries from Table-III of the National 8250
 *  data sheet)
 */
```

continued

Listing 14-2 continued

```
#define B1200    96
#define B2400    48
#define B9600    12

/*
 * The location of the i/o registers on the IBM PC
 */
#define COM1     ((struct sio near *)0x3f8)
#define COM2     ((struct sio near *)0x2f8)

/*
 * Use COM1 for this program
 */
#define COM      COM1
#define SPEED    B9600
```

Listing 14-3. "mimic.c"

```
/*********************************************************
 * mimic -- send out the serial port a description      *
 *      of what's on the screen.  In other words mimic it*
 *                                                       *
 * Note: This a tsr program that stays resident and      *
 *       keeps sending while other programs are run      *
 *********************************************************/
#undef DEBUG
#include <dos.h>
#include <bios.h>
#include <stdlib.h>
#include <stdio.h>
#include <conio.h>
#include <mem.h>
#include "serial.h"
#define PACE_VALUE 10            /* Pacing value */;


static int countdown = PACE_VALUE;      /* Pacing timer */
static int sending = 0;              /* We're sending now */


typedef char boolean;
#define TRUE 1
#define FALSE 0
/*********************************************************
```

continued

Listing 14-3 continued

```
 * Define Various Interrupt Vectors                         *
 ***********************************************************/
#define INT_TIMER        0x8     /* Timer interrupt */
#define INT_KEY          0x9     /* Keyboard character pressed */
#define INT_VIDEO        0x10    /* Video information interrupt */
#define INT_DISK         0x13    /* Raw disk I/O interrupt */
#define INT_BREAK        0x1B    /* Control-Break Handler */
#define INT_CONTROL_C    0x23    /* ^C error handler */
#define INT_CRITICAL     0x24    /* Critical Error Handler */
#define INT_IDLE         0x28    /* DOS Idle interrupt */
#define INT_DOS          0x21    /* DOS Calls */


/*
 * Function codes for video interrupt
 */
#define VIDEO_SET_CURSOR_SIZE       0x1  /* Setup cursor size */
#define VIDEO_SET_CURSOR_POSITION   0x2  /* Set cursor location */
#define VIDEO_GET_INFO              0x3  /* Get cursor size/loc */
/*
 * Where the video mode is stored
 */
#define MODE_SEG 0x40
#define MODE_OFFSET 0x49


/*
 * Dos interrupt (INT_DOS) function codes
 */
#define DOS_GET_DOS_BUSY 0x34    /* Get addr of DOS busy flag */
#define DOS_SET_PSP      0x50    /* Set current PSP address */
#define DOS_GET_PSP      0x51    /* Get current PSP address */
#define DOS_LIST_ADDRESS 0x52    /* Get address of DOS lists */


/*
 * Hardware ports we may need
 */
#define KEYBOARD_DATA    0x60    /* Keyboard data port */
#define KEYBOARD_STATUS 0x61     /* Keyboard status port */
/*
 * Place where bios stores shift values
 */
#define KEY_FLAGS        0x417
#define K_RIGHT          (1<<0)  /* Right shift pressed */
#define K_LEFT           (1<<1)  /* Left shift pressed */
#define K_CONTROL        (1<<2)  /* Control pressed */
#define K_ALT            (1<<3)  /* Alt pressed */
```

continued

Listing 14-3 continued

```
#define K_SLOCK         (1<<4)  /* Scroll lock on */
#define K_NLOCK         (1<<5)  /* Num lock on */
#define K_CAPS          (1<<6)  /* Caps lock on */
#define K_INSER         (1<<7)  /* Insert on */
/*
 * Register structure passed to an interrupt routine
 */
#define INTERRUPT_REGS int bp,int di,int si,int ds,int es,\
        int dx,int cx,int bx,int ax,int ip,int cs,int flags

#ifdef UNDEF /* Not used */
static unsigned scancode = 0x58;        /* Numeric pad minus */
static unsigned keymask = 0;            /* No shifts */
#endif UNDEF /* Not used */
unsigned _heaplen = 2;                  /* we don't use the heap */


unsigned int _stklen = (16 *1024);      /* Increase stack size */


/* The following is used to see if we are currently loaded */
static unsigned long int magic_number = 0x54535258L;


#ifdef UNDEF    /* We don't use these features */
/* True if we are in the process of unloading the routine */
static boolean unloading = FALSE;
#endif UNDEF    /* We don't use these features */
 /* Where video mode stored */
static unsigned char far *video_mode;
/***********************************************************
 * The following three interrupts are grabbed only        *
 * when the pop up portion of the TSR is executing so      *
 * that the program won't exit.                            *
 ***********************************************************/
static void interrupt tsr_critical(INTERRUPT_REGS);
static void interrupt tsr_break(void);
#define tsr_control_c tsr_break


void interrupt (*norm_break)(void);
void interrupt (*norm_control_c)(void);
void interrupt (*norm_critical)(void);


static char far *dosbusy;       /* DOS's I'm busy flag */
static int diskflag = 0;        /* Non-zero means disk active */
```

continued

Listing 14-3 continued

```
struct mcb {
    char flag;          /* 'M' -- normal block, 'Z' -- last block */
    unsigned int owner; /* Psp of the owner of this block */
    unsigned int size;      /* Size of the block in paragraphs */
    unsigned char not_used[3];  /* Padding */
    char name[8];                   /* Name of who is using us */
};
static struct mcb far *mcb_start;

#ifdef UNDEF    /* We don't use these features */
static boolean hotkey_found = FALSE;
#endif UNDEF    /* We don't use these features */


/* True if we are currently executing the TSR */
static boolean running = FALSE;


/***********************************************************
 * This is a list of the interrupt vectors permanently  *
 * hooked by the TSR to control when it pops up.        *
 ***********************************************************/
void interrupt tsr_timer(void);         /* Timer interrupt */
void interrupt tsr_idle(void);          /* Dos idle interrupt */
#ifdef UNDEF    /* We don't use these features */
void interrupt tsr_keyboard(void);    /* Key pressed interrupt */
#endif UNDEF    /* We don't use these features */
void interrupt tsr_disk(INTERRUPT_REGS);/* Disk I/O request */


/* Places to save the old versions of the interrupts */
void interrupt (*norm_timer)(void);
#ifdef UNDEF    /* We don't use these features */
void interrupt (*norm_keyboard)(void);
#endif UNDEF    /* We don't use these features */
void interrupt (*norm_idle)(void);
void interrupt (*norm_disk)(void);
/***********************************************************
 * Table containing a list of all interrupt vectors     *
 *      that are always hooked so that we can pop up     *
 ***********************************************************/
struct hook_vect {
    int vect;       /* Vector number of interrupt to intercept */
/* Pointer to new int routine */
    void interrupt (*tsr_vect)(void);
/* Where to put the old routine */
    void interrupt (**old_vect)(void);
} hooks[] = {
```

continued

Listing 14-3 continued

```
        /*Vect        Tsr             Old */
        {INT_TIMER, tsr_timer,       &norm_timer},
        {INT_IDLE,  tsr_idle,        &norm_idle},
#ifdef UNDEF        /* We don't use these features */
        {INT_KEY,   tsr_keyboard,    &norm_keyboard},
#endif UNDEF        /* We don't use these features */
#pragma warn -sus   /* Turn off pointer warning */
/* Turbo C thinks that interrupt routine with
 * registers is different */
/* From a normal interrupt routine */
        {INT_DISK,  tsr_disk,        &norm_disk},
#pragma warn .sus   /* Restore warning for the rest of the pgm */
        /* End of list indicator */
{-1,          NULL,             NULL}
};


/*********************************************************
 * context -- structure to hold almost all the          *
 *      information needed for a context switch.         *
 *                                                       *
 * Information stored                                    *
 *      stack segment: stack_register                    *
 *      psp, dta                                         *
 *      Interrupt handlers (break, control_c,            *
 *                          critical error handler)      *
 *                                                       *
 * Information not stored:                               *
 *      registers -- these are stored on the             *
 *                          interrupt stack              *
 *      floating point registers -- not saved.  It is    *
 *              assumed that the program will not use     *
 *              them.                                     *
 *      screen data -- it is assumed that any window     *
 *                          will save what's under it     *
 *                          before appearing             *
 *********************************************************/
struct context {
    /* Stack location, segment and register (SS, SP) */
    unsigned int stack_segment, stack_register;


#ifdef UNDEF
    /* psp (Program Segment Prefix) */
    unsigned int psp;
#endif UNDEF
```

continued

Listing 14-3 continued

```
        /* dta (Data transfer address)
         * Where DOS does its read/writes */
        char far *dta;


        /* Control Break interrupt handler */
        void interrupt (*int_break)(void);
        void interrupt (*int_control_c)();   /* ^C handler */
        /* Critical error handler */
        void interrupt (*int_crit)(INTERRUPT_REGS);
        /* Information about the screen */
        struct text_info text_info;
        boolean control_break;        /* The control break flag */
};
/*
 * Context for this program (the TSR)
 */
static struct context tsr_context = {
    0, 0,                  /* Stack segment, register */
#ifdef UNDEF
    0,                     /* Psp */
#endif UNDEF
    0,                     /* Dta */
    tsr_break,             /* int_break */
    tsr_control_c,         /* int_control_c */
    tsr_critical,          /* int_crit */
    {1, 1, 80, 25,         /* Window size */
     0x07,                 /* Current text attribute */
     0,                    /* Text mode */
     0, 0,                 /* Screen height/width */
     1,1                   /* Cursor location */
    },
    0,                     /* Control break flag */
};


/* Context of the program that calls us */
static struct context normal_context;


#ifdef UNDEF    /* We don't use these features */
/************************************************************
 * do_unload -- unload the TSR.                            *
 *      Assumes that we unload_ok has been called          *
 *      before this.                                       *
 ************************************************************/
static void do_unload(void)
```

continued

Listing 14-3 continued

```
{
    struct hook_vect *hook;      /* Current interrupt hook */

    /* Current memory segment */
    struct mcb far *current_mcb = mcb_start;

    for (hook = hooks; hook->vect != -1; hook++) {
        setvect(hook->vect, *hook->old_vect);
    }

    while (1) {
        if (current_mcb->owner == _psp)
            freemem(FP_SEG(current_mcb)+1);

        if (current_mcb->flag != 'M')
            break;

        current_mcb =
            MK_FP(FP_SEG(current_mcb) + current_mcb->size + 1, 0);
    }

magic_number = 0;   /* Kill the number */
}


/***********************************************************
 * unload_ok -- true if we are allowed to unload          *
 *                                                        *
 * Returns                                                *
 *      True -- we can unload.                            *
 *      False -- forget about unloading                   *
 *                                                        *
 * This checks to see if the interrupt vectors we         *
 * overwrote have been stomped on by someone else.        *
 * If so, then we can't restore them, so we can't unload* *
 ***********************************************************/
static boolean unload_ok(void)
{
    struct hook_vect *cur_hook; /* Current interrupt hook */

    for (cur_hook = hooks; cur_hook->vect != -1; cur_hook++) {

        if (getvect(cur_hook->vect) !=  cur_hook->tsr_vect)
            return (FALSE);
    }
```

Listing 14-3 continued

```
        return (TRUE);
}
#endif UNDEF     /* We don't use these features */


/************************************************************
 * Get_Context -- get the context of the current           *
 *             process                                     *
 *                                                         *
 * Parameter                                               *
 *      context -- the context to get                      *
 *                                                         *
 * Note: This does *NOT* handle the getting of the         *
 *       stack segment:register.  Stacks are difficult     *
 *       to work with and must be saved at the highest     *
 *       level.                                            *
 ************************************************************/
void get_context(struct context *context)
{
#ifdef UNDEF
    /* Get the PSP address */
    _AH = DOS_GET_PSP;
    geninterrupt(INT_DOS);
    context->psp = _BX;
#endif UNDEF

    context->dta = getdta();
    context->control_break = getcbrk();

    context->int_crit = getvect(INT_CRITICAL);
    context->int_control_c = getvect(INT_CONTROL_C);
    context->int_break = getvect(INT_BREAK);

    gettextinfo(&context->text_info);
}


/************************************************************
 * set_context -- Set the context to the given values      *
 *                                                         *
 * Parameters                                              *
 *      context -- context to save                         *
 *                                                         *
 * Note: We don't save the stack pointer because it's      *
 * tricky to handle and must be done carefully             *
 * elsewhere.                                              *
 ************************************************************/
```

continued

Listing 14-3 continued

```c
void set_context(struct context *context)
{
    struct text_info *text_info = &context->text_info;

#ifdef UNDEF
    /* Set the PSP address */
    _AH = DOS_SET_PSP;
    _BX = context->psp;
    geninterrupt(INT_DOS);
#endif UNDEF

    setdta(context->dta);
    setcbrk(context->control_break);

    setvect(INT_CRITICAL, context->int_crit);
    setvect(INT_CONTROL_C, context->int_control_c);
    setvect(INT_BREAK, context->int_break);

    gotoxy(text_info->curx, text_info->cury);
}

/***********************************************************
 * do_it -- save context and execute the TSR program      *
 ***********************************************************/
static void do_it(void)
{
    static int mode;
    void tsr_main(void);

    disable();

    normal_context.stack_segment = _SS;
    normal_context.stack_register = _SP;

    get_context(&normal_context);
    tsr_context.text_info.curx = normal_context.text_info.curx;
    tsr_context.text_info.cury = normal_context.text_info.cury;
    set_context(&tsr_context);

    _SS = tsr_context.stack_segment;
    _SP = tsr_context.stack_register;

    running = TRUE;
#ifdef UNDEF     /* We don't use these features */
```

continued

Listing 14-3 continued

```
        hotkey_found = FALSE;
#endif UNDEF     /* We don't use these features */

    enable();

    /*
     * Only show yourself in text modes
     */
    mode = *video_mode;

    if (((mode >= 0) && (mode <= 3)) ||
        (mode == 7))
        tsr_main();

    running = FALSE;

    disable();

#ifdef UNDEF     /* We don't use these features */
    if (unloading)
        do_unload();
#endif UNDEF     /* We don't use these features */

    set_context(&normal_context);

    _SP = normal_context.stack_register;
    _SS = normal_context.stack_segment;
    enable();
}


#define PSP_MAGIC      0x20CD  /* This begins each PSP segment */
/***********************************************************
 * is_loaded -- returns true if we are already loaded    *
 *                                                        *
 * This routine walks the memory chain looking for        *
 * any segment that is a PSP.                             *
 *                                                        *
 * When it finds another program, it checks to see        *
 * if that program has the same magic number              *
 * in the same place as we do.                            *
 ***********************************************************/
static boolean is_loaded(void)
{
```

continued

372 *Advanced C*

Listing 14-3 continued

```c
        /* Current item in the mcb chain */
        struct mcb far *current_mcb = mcb_start;

        /* Pointer to current memory block */
        int far *block_ptr; /*

        /* Segment and offset of a possible magic number */
        unsigned int magic_seg, magic_off;

        /* Pointer to the magic number */
        long unsigned int far *magic_ptr;

        while (1) {
            if ((current_mcb->owner != NULL) &&
                (current_mcb->owner != _psp)) {
                block_ptr = MK_FP(current_mcb->owner, 0);

                if (*block_ptr == PSP_MAGIC) {
                    magic_seg = FP_SEG(block_ptr) + _DS - _psp;
                    magic_off = (int)&magic_number;
                    magic_ptr = MK_FP(magic_seg, magic_off);
                    if (*magic_ptr == magic_number)
                        return (TRUE);
                }
            }

            if (current_mcb->flag != 'M')
                break;

            current_mcb =
                MK_FP(FP_SEG(current_mcb) + current_mcb->size + 1, 0);
        }
        return (FALSE);
}

/************************************************************
 * tsr_break -- break interrupt handler                    *
 *                                                          *
 * Since we are a TSR program, we cannot stop for          *
 * any reason, so ignore all breaks.                       *
 ************************************************************/
static void interrupt tsr_break(void)
{
    return;
```

continued

Listing 14-3 continued

```
}
/*************************************************************
 * tsr_critical -- critical error handler              *
 *                                                     *
 * Returns                                             *
 *      AX = 0  -- tell DOS to ignore the error        *
 *************************************************************/
#pragma warn -par  /* We know that we don't use all the parameters */
static void interrupt tsr_critical(INTERRUPT_REGS)
{
    ax = 0;
}
#pragma warn .par        /* Restore warning */
/*************************************************************
 * tsr_disk -- called for each disk interrupt.         *
 *                                                     *
 * This routine keeps track of all the disk interrupts *
 * so that we don't pop up during a disk operation.    *
 *************************************************************/
#pragma warn -par/* We know that we don't use all the params */
static void interrupt tsr_disk(INTERRUPT_REGS)
{
    diskflag++;
    (*norm_disk)();
    ax = _AX;    /* Now pass back all the registers */
    bx = _BX;
    cx = _CX;
    dx = _DX;
    si = _SI;
    di = _DI;
    es = _ES;
    flags = _FLAGS;
    diskflag--;
}
#pragma warn .par        /* Restore warning */


#ifdef UNDEF    /* We don't use these features */
/*************************************************************
 * tsr_keyboard -- keyboard interrupt                  *
 *                                                     *
 * Check to see if the hotkey was pressed and          *
 *   set the flags accordingly.                        *
 *************************************************************/
static void interrupt tsr_keyboard(void)
{
```

continued

Listing 14-3 continued

```
        /* Status information from the keyboard port */
        static int keyboard_status;
        static unsigned char far *key_flags = MK_FP(0, KEY_FLAGS);


        if (running == FALSE) {
            if ((inportb(KEYBOARD_DATA) == scancode) &&
                ((*key_flags & keymask) == keymask)) {

                hotkey_found = TRUE;

                /* Strobe the top bit of the keyboard status reg */
                keyboard_status = inportb(KEYBOARD_STATUS);
                outportb(KEYBOARD_STATUS, keyboard_status |  0x80);
                outportb(KEYBOARD_STATUS, keyboard_status);
                /* Clear the interrupt */
                outportb(0x20, 0x20);
                return;
            }
        }
        /* It's not our key, let the system have it */
        (*norm_keyboard)();
}
#endif UNDEF    /* We don't use these features */
/************************************************************
 * tsr_timer -- timer interrupt routine.                    *
 *                                                          *
 * If it's a good time to pop up and we want to pop up      *
 * this routine will cause us to appear.                    *
 ************************************************************/
static void interrupt tsr_timer(void)
{
    (*norm_timer)();
    if (running == FALSE) {
        if (sending == FALSE) {
            countdown--;
            if ((countdown <= 0) && (*dosbusy == 0)) {
                if (diskflag == 0) {
                    do_it();
                }
            }
        }
    }
}
/************************************************************
 * tsr_idle -- idle interrupt handler                       *
```

continued

Listing 14-3 continued

```
 *                                                          *
 * This is called when DOS is not doing anything much       *
 * to allow TSR programs a chance to execute.               *
 ************************************************************/
static void interrupt tsr_idle(void)
{
    (*norm_idle)();
    if (running == FALSE) {
        if (sending == FALSE) {
            if (diskflag == 0) {
                do_it();
            }
        }
    }
}


int main(void)
{
    struct hook_vect *hook;      /* Current vector for hookup */
    unsigned int far *table_ptr;/* Pointer to DOS tables */

    void init_serial(void);      /* Start the serial I/O */

    init_serial();
    _AH = DOS_GET_DOS_BUSY;
    geninterrupt(INT_DOS);
    dosbusy = MK_FP(_ES, _BX);

    _AH = DOS_LIST_ADDRESS;
    geninterrupt(INT_DOS);
    table_ptr = MK_FP(_ES, _BX);


    /* Entry -1 = start of memory chain */
    mcb_start = MK_FP(*(table_ptr - 1), 0);


#pragma warn -rch /* The following code should be unreachable
if compiled */
/* Correctly, however if word aligned
 * structures are used, it will */
/* kick in and warn the programmer. */
    if (sizeof(struct mcb) != 16) {
        (void)cputs(
          "Compile error: Don't compile with word alignment\n\r");
        exit (1);
```

continued

Listing 14-3 continued

```
        }
#pragma warn .rch          /* Restore warning */

    video_mode = MK_FP(MODE_SEG, MODE_OFFSET);

#ifdef DEBUG
    tsr_main();

#else DEBUG
    if (is_loaded() == FALSE) {
        tsr_context.stack_segment = _SS;
        tsr_context.stack_register = _SP;
#ifdef UNDEF
        tsr_context.psp = _psp;
#endif UNDEF
        tsr_context.dta = getdta();

        for (hook = hooks; hook->vect != -1; hook++) {
            *hook->old_vect = getvect(hook->vect);
            setvect(hook->vect, hook->tsr_vect);
        }

        {
            /* Size of program in paragraphs */
            static unsigned keep_size;

            keep_size = _SS - _psp + (_SP / 16) + 50;
            keep(0, keep_size);
        }
    }
    (void)cputs("Program already loaded\n\r");
#endif DEBUG
    return (0);
}

#define ESC '\033'

#define MAX_X 80        /* Size of screen in X */
#define MAX_Y 25        /* Size of screen in Y */
/*
 * Worst case
 *      Cursor movement                         <ESC>[xx;xxH (8 Chars)
 *      Each char has foreground color change   <ESC>[xxm (5 C)
 *      Each char has background color change   <ESC>[xxm (5 chars)
```

continued

Listing 14-3 continued

```
 *          Each character has blink      change <ESC>[xxm (5 chars)
 *          The character                                 1
 *          Fudge                                         1
 *                                                _____
 *                                                     Total      25
 *
 * Add in 30 for a fudge and positioning.
 */
#define OUT_BUF_SIZE (MAX_X*25 + 30)
static char out_buf[OUT_BUF_SIZE];
static char *out_ptr;            /* Pointer to next char out */
static char *last_ptr;   /* Pointer to last character in buffer */

/* Screen we've got now */
static char local_screen[MAX_Y*MAX_X*2];
static char *local_ptr;          /* Local version of the screen */

static char remote_screen[MAX_Y*MAX_X*2];
static char *remote_ptr;         /* Remove version of the screen */

int remote_x, remote_y;          /* Where we are remotely */
unsigned int out_att;            /* Current output attributes */
void interrupt (*old_vect_C)(void);

/************************************************************
 * init_serial -- initialize the serial interface          *
 *                and send the initial screen               *
 ************************************************************/
void init_serial(void)
{
    /* input character handler */
    void    interrupt serial_interrupt();
    void init(void);

    /* routine to send the data */
    void    send_it(void);

    /* set up the input buffer */
    void    init_buf(void);

    disable();
    old_vect_C = getvect(0xC);
    setvect(0xC, serial_interrupt);
    enable();
```

continued

Listing 14-3 continued

```
      init();


      /* enable interrupts */
      outportb(0x21, inportb(0x21) & 0xE7);
      outportb(0x20, 0x20);


      /* Clear the remote screen */
      (void)memset(remote_screen, '\0', sizeof(remote_screen));


      send_it();
}
/*********************************************************
 * init -- initialize the port                          *
 *********************************************************/
void init(void)
{
      _AH = 0;
      _AL = 0xE3;      /* 9600 baud/no parity/one stop/8 data */
      _DX = 0;
      geninterrupt(0x14);


      /* don't allow interrupts while we do this */
      disable();
      /* disable all interrupt interrupts */
      outportb((int)&COM->interrupt_enable,   0);


      outportb((int)&COM->format,
        F_BAUD_LATCH|F_NO_BREAK|F_PARITY_NONE|F_STOP1|F_DATA8);


      outportb((int)&COM->format,
            F_NORMAL|F_NO_BREAK|F_PARITY_NONE|F_STOP1|F_DATA8);


      outportb((int)&COM->out_control,
            O_OUT1|O_OUT2|O_RTS|O_DTR);


      /* read the input regs to clear their
       * i-have-data flags */
      (void)inportb((int)&COM->data);
      (void)inportb((int)&COM->interrupt_enable);
      (void)inportb((int)&COM->interrupt_id);
      (void)inportb((int)&COM->status);
```

continued

Listing 14-3 continued

```
        outportb(0x20, 0x20);                  /* clear interrupts */
        enable();
}


/***********************************************************
 * trans_1 -- transmit a single character to the output *
 *              Turn off interrupts if done              *
 ***********************************************************/
void trans_1(void)
{

    if (out_ptr >= last_ptr) {
        /* Turn off interrupts */
        outportb((int)&COM->interrupt_enable,   0);
        sending = 0;
        return;
    }
    outportb((int)&COM->data, *out_ptr);
    out_ptr++;
}
/***********************************************************
 * serial_interrupt -- interrupt handler for serial     *
 *      input                                            *
 *                                                       *
 * Called in interrupt mode by the hardware when         *
 * a character is received on the serial input           *
 ***********************************************************/
void interrupt serial_interrupt()
{
        disable();

        (void)inportb((int)&COM->status);

        /* tell device we have read interrupt */
        (void)inportb((int)&COM->interrupt_enable);
        (void)inportb((int)&COM->interrupt_id);

        trans_1();
        outportb(0x20, 0x20);
        enable();
}
/***********************************************************
 * start_trans -- start transmission                    *
 ***********************************************************/
static void start_trans(void)
```

continued

Listing 14-3 continued

```
{
    disable();
    out_ptr = out_buf;
    sending = 1;
    outportb((int)&COM->interrupt_enable,   I_TRANS_EMPTY);
    trans_1();
    outportb(0x20, 0x20);
    enable();
}
/**********************************************************
 * send_ch -- put a character in the buffer              *
 *                                                       *
 * Parameters                                            *
 *      ch -- character to send                          *
 **********************************************************/
#define send_ch(ch) {(*last_ptr) = (ch); last_ptr++;}
/**********************************************************
 * send_esc -- send an escape code of the form           *
 *                ESC [ <str> m                          *
 *                                                       *
 * Parameters                                            *
 *      str -- string to send                            *
 **********************************************************/
void send_esc(char *str)
{
    send_ch(ESC);
    send_ch('[');
    while (*str) {
        send_ch(*str);
        str++;
    }
    send_ch('m');
}
/**********************************************************
 * remove_to -- move remote cursor to a given location   *
 *                                                       *
 * Parameters                                            *
 *      x, y -- where to put the cursor                   *
 **********************************************************/
static void remote_to(int x, int y)
{
    if ((remote_x != x) || (remote_y != y)) {
        static char goto_str[10] = {
        /* 0   1    2    3    4    5    6    7    */
            ESC, '[', 'y', 'y', ';', 'x', 'x', 'H', '\0'
```

continued

Listing 14-3 continued

```
        };
        char *goto_ptr = goto_str;

        goto_str[2] = (y/10) + '0';
        goto_str[3] = (y%10) + '0';

        goto_str[5] = (x/10) + '0';
        goto_str[6] = (x%10) + '0';

        for (goto_ptr = goto_str; *goto_ptr != '\0';
            goto_ptr++) {
            send_ch(*goto_ptr);
        }
        remote_x = x;
        remote_y = y;
    }
}
#define BLINKING(attr) ((attr) & 0x80)
#define FOREGROUND(attr) ((attr) & 0xF)
#define BACKGROUND(attr) ((attr) & 0x70)
/***********************************************************
 * make_line -- take a line from the screen and           *
 *              dump it into the output buffer             *
 ***********************************************************/
static void make_line(int line)
{
    int x;        /* General purpose index */
    /* We do not output the last character of the last line
     * as this would cause a scroll
     */
    int x_limit = (line == (MAX_Y)) ? MAX_X-1 : MAX_X;
    char local_ch, remote_ch;   /* Local and remote characters */
    /* Local and remote attributes */
    unsigned char local_att, remote_att;
    /*
     * Loop for each attribute on the screen
     */
    for (x = 1; x <= x_limit; x++) {
        local_ch = *local_ptr;
        remote_ch = *remote_ptr;
        local_att = (unsigned char) *(local_ptr+1);
        remote_att = (unsigned char) *(remote_ptr+1);

        if ((local_ch != remote_ch) ||
            (remote_att != local_att)) {
```

continued

Listing 14-3 continued

```
                    remote_to(x, line);


            if (local_att != out_att) {
                if (BLINKING(local_att) != BLINKING(out_att)) {
                    if (BLINKING(local_att))
                        send_esc("5");
                    else {
                        send_esc("0");
                        local_att = 0x07;      /* Normal color */
                    }
                }
                if (FOREGROUND(local_att) !=
                    FOREGROUND(out_att)) {
                    static char for_esc[3] = "3?";

                    for_esc[1] = FOREGROUND(local_att) +'0';
                    send_esc(for_esc);
                }
                if (BACKGROUND(local_att) !=
                    BACKGROUND(out_att)) {
                    static char back_esc[3] = "4?";

                    back_esc[1] =
                                (BACKGROUND(local_att) >> 4) +'0';
                    send_esc(back_esc);
                }
                out_att = local_att;
            }
            send_ch(local_ch);
            remote_x++;
        }

        *remote_ptr = local_ch;
        *(remote_ptr+1) = local_att;
        remote_ptr += 2;
        local_ptr += 2;
    }
}


/************************************************************
 * send_it -- send the screen to the remote               *
 ************************************************************/
static void send_it(void)
{
```

continued

Listing 14-3 continued

```
int line;
int i;
/* ESC sequence is clear modes /clear screen */
static char init_str[] = "\033[0m\033[2J";
char *send_ptr;

remote_ptr = remote_screen;
local_ptr = local_screen;
gettext(1, 1, MAX_X, MAX_Y, local_screen);

last_ptr = out_buf;

for (send_ptr = init_str; (*send_ptr) != '\0'; send_ptr++)
    send_ch(*send_ptr);

remote_x = 1;
remote_y = 1;

remote_ptr = remote_screen;
for (i = 0; i < (MAX_X * MAX_Y); i++) {
    *remote_ptr = ' ';
    remote_ptr++;
    *remote_ptr = 0x07;      /* White on black */
    remote_ptr++;
}
out_att = 0x07;              /* White on black */

start_trans();
while (sending) {
    /* Wait till not sending */;
}

local_ptr = local_screen;
remote_ptr = remote_screen;

for (line = 1; line <= MAX_Y; line++) {
    last_ptr = out_buf;

    make_line(line);

    start_trans();
    while (sending)
        /* Wait till not sending */;
}
```

continued

Listing 14-3 continued

```
}
static int cur_line = 0;          /* Line number we are sending
*/
/* 0 == code to tell us to grab screen again */
/**********************************************************
 * tsr_main -- send the next line                         *
 *                                                        *
 * This starts sending the next line of the screen        *
 **********************************************************/
static void tsr_main(void)
{
    countdown = PACE_VALUE;

    if (sending)
        return;

    last_ptr = out_buf;

    if (cur_line == 0) {
        gettext(1, 1, MAX_X, MAX_Y, local_screen);
        remote_ptr = remote_screen;
        local_ptr = local_screen;
    } else {
        make_line(cur_line);
    }

    cur_line++;
    if (cur_line > MAX_Y)
        cur_line = 0;

    remote_to(normal_context.text_info.curx,
            normal_context.text_info.cury);
    start_trans();
}
```

Afterwords

The programs we have presented here are designed to give you a good, practical base for writing advanced C programs. You are invited to use them as seed for writing your own high quality programs.

When writing professional programs, you should keep the following guidelines in mind:

- Listen to the user; write what he wants. Always remember that you are writing for a user or customer. He's the one you have to please. Don't write a very complex, flexible program if the user wants something simple (and less flexible).

- Write user friendly programs. Remember the users may not be computer literate. Make things simple and obvious. Be consistent. Include lots of help. Even with a very verbose and complete help system, many people find computers intimidating.

- Design big, write small. When designing your program, allow for expansion. If your program is any good, it will be modified, expanded, and enhanced. Plan for it.

- Start out small. A small program is easier to get working than a large one. Then add on small improvements to your working base. For example, if you're writing an editor, write one with just an insert command. Clearly a one command editor is not very useful, but once you get it working you can add more commands onto a working base.

- Put in lots of comments, they tell you what you did. Always explain everything with comments. If you needed notes to construct the program, don't leave them on paper, write them in the program. Your comments will be a big help to you and others.

- Remember those who come after you. After the program is written, it has to be maintained and enhanced. Have pity on the maintenance programmer who has to learn and fix your code. Put in lots of comments so that he has a chance.

- Always leave the code better than you found it. Sooner or later you will have to maintain someone else's code. If you're lucky, you will be presented with a well written, clearly commented piece of code. If you're typical, you'll get an uncommented, terse, complex headache. As you go through decoding this mess, add comments, and improve the code. Leave it better than you found it.

- Coding is an art. Style and craftsmanship play a big part in programming. Computer programming is far from being an exact science. Good programs are 90% style and 10% science. Well designed, copiously commented, clearly written programs are highly valued.

We hope that the programs and design methods used in this book can give you a good start. You have what you need to write high quality professional programs. The rest is up to you.

Index

P

Q

R

S

Z

Advanced C Programming
Disk Offer

A companion disk is available for this book. The companion disk contains:

- Memory resident program
- How to setup menu interface
- Cat and Mouse and Breakout games
- Hardware interrupt handlers
- Screen transmission via modem
- File deletion utility
- Sample windowing and graphic functions

To order your disk, simply fill out coupon below and mail it to Prentice Hall Computer Publishing, 11711 N. College Avenue, Carmel, IN 46032, ATTN: Customer Service Department.

Advanced C Programming

I am ordering the companion disk for this book and have enclosed my check for $15.00 payable to Simon & Schuster, Inc.

Please send a ☐ 3.5-inch disk   ISBN: 0-13-663170-3

☐ 5.25-inch disk   ISBN: 0-13-016338-4

Name _____

Address _____

City _____ State _____ Zip _____

Phone Number (   ) _____

Please mail this request to Prentice Hall Computer Publishing, 11711 N. College Avenue, Carmel, IN 46032, ATTN: Customer Service Department. For more information call 1-800-428-5331.

The New Peter Norton Microcomputer Libraries from Brady Publishing

All of the volumes in the Peter Norton Libraries, written in collaboration with The Peter Norton Computing Group, provide clear, in-depth discussions of the latest developments in computer hardware, operating systems, and programming. Fully tested and rigorously reviewed, these libraries deserve a special place on your bookshelf. These libraries are comprised of two series:

The Peter Norton Hardware Library gives you an insider's grasp of your computer and the way it works. Included are such bestselling classics as *Inside the IBM PC, Inside the Apple Macintosh*, and *The Hard Disk Companion*.

The Peter Norton Programming Library offers books and book/disk utilities for readers at all levels of expertise—beginning to intermediate to advanced. They focuses on creating programs that work right away and offers the best tips and techniques in the industry. This library includes *Advanced BASIC, Advanced Assembly Language, QBasic Programing*, and more.

For a direct, no-nonsense approach to performance computing, look to Brady Publishing's Peter Norton Libraries.